Lazarus, Mary and Martha

A Social-Scientific and Theological Reading of John

Philip F. Esler
and
Ronald A. Piper

scm press

To Jerome H. Neyrey SJ

British Library Cataloguing in Publication data

A catalogue record for this book is available from the British Library

0 334 04016 7/978 0 334 04016 3

First published in 2006 by SCM Press
9–17 St Alban's Place,
London N1 0NX

www.scm-canterburypress.co.uk

SCM Press is a division of
SCM-Canterbury Press Ltd

Printed and bound in Great Britain by
William Clowes Ltd, Beccles, Suffolk

Contents

List of Illustrations

Preface

This volume began life as a paper presented at a conference on the Gospel of John and Christian Theology, which was organized by St Andrews colleagues Professor Richard Bauckham and Professor Alan Torrance, and held in St Andrews in July 2003. It was commissioned for a session entitled 'The Raising of Lazarus: Multidisciplinary Perspectives'. Our task was to demonstrate how a social-scientific interpretation of the Lazarus narrative could contribute to understanding the theology of the Fourth Gospel.

On an earlier occasion, in March 2003, we presented a trial version of our views to a meeting of the Context Group held in Aston, Pennsylvania. We are grateful for the feedback we received on that occasion, especially from the designated respondent, Professor Richard Rohrbaugh. We were also assisted in feedback on an earlier version of this project by scholars then in residence at the Center of Theological Inquiry at Princeton. Mr Aaron Kuecker, a research student in St Mary's College in the University of St Andrews, kindly read through the entire manuscript before its submission to the publisher, saved us from many errors and made some interesting suggestions for improvement. Any imperfections that remain are entirely our own responsibility.

In relation to our discussion in Chapter 6, of the early Christian art from Rome, we gratefully acknowledge the assistance of Princeton University for allowing us access to its Index of Christian Art. We also thank the University of St Andrews for funding a trip we made to Rome that allowed us the chance to inspect some of the Lazarus material *in situ*. Professor Robin Jensen has kindly let us use some of her own photos of early Christian sarcophagi in Rome.

During the writing of this volume we were greatly assisted in some of our research by Ms Gisela Kreglinger.

We dedicate this book to our friend Jerome H. Neyrey SJ, pioneer in the social-scientific investigation of the Fourth Gospel.

1

Lazarus, Martha and Mary: Reframing the Discussion

The story of Lazarus being raised from the dead that is told in John 11 has etched itself deeply into the human imagination wherever the Gospel has reached.[1] It has spoken to Christians of the pain of death and the hope of immortality. It has incited theologians to make sense of its meaning since the earliest centuries.[2] It has inspired popular Christian belief.[3] Artists have represented the story visually from as early as the third century CE, through the medieval and Renaissance periods and right up to the present.[4] It has also provoked a plethora of literary responses in the last two centuries, some of them construing Jesus' raising of Lazarus in ways that are in tension with a modern individualistic consciousness.[5] Even in the secular culture of the West, it has become commonplace to mention the raising of Lazarus in relation to various forms of rebirth.

---

1 We note that in this volume we will speak of Lazarus being 'raised' or 'raised from the dead', or occasionally of his 'revivification', in connection with the narrative of John 11, but not of his 'resurrection'. This is because it is presumed Lazarus will die again and the word 'resurrection' is best reserved for clear references to being raised up on the last day to a state that continues thereafter, either to life or to the result of judgement. This is in accord with the picture in John 5.28–29, where the Johannine Jesus states that the hour is coming when *all* those who are in their graves will come out of them, with those who did good to the resurrection of life (*anastasis zōēs*) and those who did evil to the resurrection of judgement (*anastasis kriseōs*).

2 See Kremer 1985.

3 See Puchner 1991.

4 See Darmstaedter 1955 and Sauser 1981.

5 See Thompson 1978. Note Eugene O'Neil's play *Lazarus Laughed*.

This book is written in the conviction that the figure of Lazarus which has exerted a potent force within Christian experience for 2,000 years will continue to do so. While our aim is to contribute to the long tradition of reflection on Lazarus, the body of existing literature by New Testament critics in this area represents a daunting challenge to any authors intending to venture into it.[6] Nevertheless, by adopting a methodology that involves the use of pertinent social-scientific insights focused especially on the nature of social identity, we aim to make a fresh proposal. Our argument will embrace not only the death and raising of Lazarus in John 11, but also the way he and his sisters Mary and Martha are presented in John 11—12 within the larger context of the Gospel. For a major discovery of our application of social identity theory to the Fourth Gospel has been that it is essential to address the total presentation of Lazarus, Mary and Martha in John 11—12 if we are to comprehend this section of the Gospel as part of its wider communicative intent. Treatments of Lazarus, Mary and Martha together are not common in the scholarly literature.

Our primary interest is the historical one of understanding what meaning the account of Lazarus, Martha and Mary in the Fourth Gospel would have conveyed to its first audience, a largely illiterate one who would have heard it read aloud to them somewhere in the Greco-Roman East late in the first century CE.[7] Yet we are also concerned with how this text can inform contemporary Christian experience and identity. For this purpose we adopt the overall view recently published by one of us arguing that to read New Testament texts within an explicitly Christian context with a focus on what their authors originally meant entails engaging in a process of intercultural communication and communion.[8] In the present study, this type of dialogue is facilitated by the fact that our central theoretical issue of identity not only allows us to investigate the original meanings of the text, but is also a matter of intense interest in so many social, ethnic and religious settings today. In other words, interpreting a New Testament text

---

6 See the bibliographies in Brown 1966, Barrett 1978, Lee 1994 and Sproston North 2001.

7 On the largely oral culture of the first-century CE Mediterranean world, see Kelber 1983, Achtemeier 1990 and Esler 2003, p. 17.

8 See Esler 2005a.

historically but within an identity framework produces results relevant to pressing contemporary concerns.[9]

In the remainder of the present chapter, after setting out our position on a number of preliminary issues of interpretation, we will canvass the main areas that scholars have identified as significant in understanding the presentation of Lazarus, Mary and Martha and indicate where our own investigation will develop or diverge from current views. At the end of this chapter we will outline the course of our argument for the rest of this book.

Preliminary Issues of Interpretation

John and the Final Form of the Fourth Gospel

Many scholars have concluded that the Fourth Gospel has been composed in a series of stages. Raymond Brown, for example, developed an elaborate theory correlating different compositional layers with the different historical phases of the 'Johannine community',[10] a theory that to some scholars seems to push the evidence too far. Sensitivity to questions of Johannine redaction in relation to the material concerning Lazarus, Martha and Mary is inevitably required. Debates about the unity of John 11.1–44 have, indeed, been evident in previous scholarship, with critics making a great variety of proposals relating to the impact of source and redaction. Thus, Brown also argued that John 11—12 was among the material added at the very last stage in that history.[11] Yet, as we shall see, even these chapters show some evidence of having had a compositional history of their own. There is, however, little consensus about the precise compositional and redactional history of this material. Jerome Neyrey considers the problem of the death of believers to have been addressed in the 'first redaction' of the source. The 'second redaction' emphasized the high Christological claims attributed to Jesus.[12] Other critics have produced

9 For an illustration pointing to the contemporary significance of the historical meaning of Paul's letter to the Romans, see Esler 2005a, pp. 273–85.

10 See Brown 1979.

11 See Brown 1966, pp. xxxv–xxxix.

12 To the source he assigns 11.1–3, 17–18, (26?), 33–34, 38–39, 43–45; to the first redaction he assigns 11.5–16, 19–24, 25b, (26?), 27–32, 35–38, 40–42; to the second redaction he assigns 11.4, 25a. See Neyrey 1988, pp. 81–93, 150.

different interpretations.[13] More recently Michael Labahn has discussed John 11 as a development from the traditions in the Secret Gospel of Mark and the special Lucan material,[14] while W. E. Sproston North has considered the Johannine account in relation to traditions found in 1 John, as well as elsewhere in the Gospel and the Synoptic accounts.[15] Nevertheless, it is not our goal to create a tradition history of the passage. It will be sufficient to recognize the surprising elements in the passage, the context of the passage and the particular emphases of the current formulation (especially where they seem to be unnecessary for the miracle story itself) in order to show how John has made use of Lazarus' raising for the purpose of reinforcing specific features of group identity.

Most interpreters consider that there was a 'redactor', an editor, who compiled the Gospel in much the form in which we now have it. But discussion rages as to whether this person is to be equated with the substantial author of the material, the evangelist 'John', or with someone after or different from him. Hypotheses as to the Gospel having passed through phases of redaction are often formulated in relation to literary aporias in the text, or sometimes in relation to thematic tensions that are observed. Yet Martin de Boer reasonably regards 'the whole of the Fourth Gospel in all of its layers as completely Johannine' and acknowledges 'that the theology of each layer has not been lost or rejected, but taken up into the subsequent editions and "recontextualized", i.e., reinterpreted through incorporation into a new edition, thereby becoming part of a "new literary entity" (de Jonge)'.[16]

Furthermore, we shall adopt the convention of referring to 'John' or the 'evangelist' as a convenient means of designating the one responsible for the final version, but fully recognizing both that the precise hand responsible for the final version may not be the same as that responsible for earlier stages of composition and also that the identification of this hand in terms of a figure in the Gospel narrative (such as the Beloved Disciple) or any particular figure in the later Johannine community or communities out of which this work arose should not be assumed.

---

13 See Wilckens 1959, pp. 22–39; Rochais 1981, pp. 113–46; Kremer 1985, pp. 83–95; and Wagner 1988, pp. 329–34.

14 See Labahn 1999, pp. 378–465. For a recent book vigorously debunking the authenticity of 'The Secret Gospel of Mark', see Carlson 2005.

15 Sproston North 2001.

16 de Boer 1996, p. 79.

We will indicate when we are referring to possible composers of earlier stages of the tradition or composition. Our starting point will therefore be this final editorial 'recontextualization' of all preceding materials of the Gospel. When we refer to the 'Fourth Gospel' or 'John's Gospel', we shall mean this final version.

Although we are not primarily interested in the history of that section of the Christ-movement for whom this Gospel was written, only in the audience for its final form, there will be occasions on which we do discuss earlier stages of its composition. When we do so, we shall make this clear.

We consider that John's Gospel was written for a particular section of the Christ-movement late in the first century CE. We do not accept the arguments of Richard Bauckham and his collaborators that the Fourth Gospel (or any of the canonical Gospels) was originally written for 'all Christians'.[17] While it is clear that each of the Gospels, including John's, eventually travelled around the various groups of Christ-followers in the first century of the movement, that is hardly the end of the story, as some of the supporters of Bauckham's hypothesis suppose.[18] We are of the view that each of the Gospels reflects a position attuned to the original local audience for which it was written. It is difficult to believe that someone writing a Gospel would not have responded directly to the needs of the audience he knew best. The whole thrust of ancient rhetorical training was to attune one's communication to the immediate audience and the suggestion, made by Bauckham,[19] that this may apply to letters but not Gospels seems to us implausible. Margaret Mitchell has recently demonstrated the widespread recognition among the early Christ-movement of the connection of each Gospel with a particular community.[20] This does not, however, preclude the possibility that the evangelists, while attending directly to the needs of their own immediate audiences, would not have been unhappy if their productions travelled further afield, in effect colonizing other members of the Christ-movement with the distinctive views of its meaning that they had expressed for their own immediate

17 See Bauckham 1998a for this thesis; for critiques of this view, see Esler 1998a, Sim 2001 and Mitchell 2005; for a defence of Bauckham's thesis, see Klink 2005.

18 For example, Rowe 2005, p. 143.

19 Bauckham 1998b, pp. 26–30.

20 Mitchell 2005.

communities. Such a result was not inevitable, however, as the fate of Mark's Gospel once it fell into the hands of Matthew and Luke reveals.

A powerful argument supporting the distinctiveness of the Johannine audience within the Christ-movement at large can be derived from those references in the Fourth Gospel that indicate an awareness of the existence of Christ-followers who are not of the group most directly addressed by John. This is most clearly indicated in passages such as John 10.14–16. In the preceding verses in John 10, John has described 'his own' using the metaphor of his sheep, whom Jesus knows by name and leads (cf. John 10.3–5). Shortly after, in a contest between Jesus and the Judeans, the latter are described as not believing because 'you do not belong to my sheep' (10.26).[21] These latter Judeans are clearly outsiders. Yet between these two descriptions Jesus refers to another group (or groups) in the following terms: 'And I have other sheep, that are not of this fold (*aulē*); I must bring them also, and they will heed my voice. So there shall be one flock (*poimēn*), one shepherd' (10.16). These are sheep – the term used for Christ-followers – for whom Jesus accepts some responsibility, but who are still to be united with '*this* fold', probably a reference to the Johannine group. These other sheep are described in a way that suggests their present existence; they do not appear to refer to future converts.[22] Our view is close to that of J. L. Martyn, who argues that the other sheep are 'Jewish Christians' belonging to conventicles known to but separate from the Johannine community,[23] except that we would not wish to identify these other Christ-followers under the label 'Jewish Christians'.

Barnabas Lindars thinks there are two groups referred to in John 10.16: Judean Christians (this fold) and 'Gentile' Christians (other sheep). He bases this in part on the reference to the scattered children of God in John 11.52 (a reference he believes to refer to the Dispersion), but there is little in the context of John 10 to support such a definition of the groups. The supposed

---

21 Our reasons for translating the word *Ioudaioi* in the Fourth Gospel as 'Judeans' in this volume and not 'Jews' appear in Appendix 1.

22 As suggested by O'Grady 1999, p. 47. Klink is of the view that the other sheep in 10.16 refers to people who will become sheep of Jesus (2005, pp. 202–3), but this view is difficult to reconcile with 10.16a.

23 Martyn 2003, p. 164.

interpretation of the 'fold' in 10.1 to refer to Judeans cannot be defining 'this fold' in 10.16, because the Judeans are hardly those who 'know' Jesus (v. 14), as John 10.26 also makes clear. Lindars does, however, add: 'But it is possible that John is thinking of the spread of heresy in the church, and the need to maintain Christian unity.'[24] Thus Lindars does rightly acknowledge that the reference in John 10.16 might indeed reflect a problem of differences within the Christ-movement. C. K. Barrett also regards the 'other sheep' not of 'this fold' as 'Gentiles', by which he means non-Judean Christ-followers, on the basis that 'John was written in the context of the Gentile mission.'[25]

Such disunity at the time of the author makes sense also of the prayer of Jesus for his followers in John 17: 'keep them in thy name, which thou hast given me, *that they may be one*, even as we are one' (v. 11; RSV, with emphasis added; see also 17.21 and, between the two Lazarus episodes, 11.52). Thus it is clear that, in addition to outsiders who are not Jesus' sheep, there are other Christ-followers who somehow must be united with the Johannine fold in order to create the desired unity of a single flock of followers. In other words, John recognizes distinctions *within* the Christ-movement. It is likely that if John seeks to address these 'other' Christ-followers at all, it is in order to persuade them of the power of the Johannine perception. The task is to bring or lead these others, something not yet fulfilled, in the way comparable to how he already leads those who are clearly known to him. The description of these as not being of '*this* fold' underlines the group consciousness of John. This is not simply to be taken as a reference to making new converts; it implies the awareness of other existing groups, which hopefully in the future '*will* heed my voice'.

Finally, other evidence for potential or actual apostasy can be found in John 13.11 and 15.2. Judas provides a further example of this for Johannine hearers or readers.[26] Thus the Fourth Gospel offers evidence of both an awareness of varied, distinct groups of Christ-followers and also a concern that some individuals and

---

24 Lindars 1972, p. 363. More generally on this interpretation of John 10.16, see the classic study of R. E. Brown 1978. His identification of *specific* groups in the Johannine purview is open to challenge, however.

25 Barrett 1978, p. 376.

26 See Piper 2007 forthcoming.

groups may now be in danger of slipping outside the boundaries of the group of true followers of Christ.

A further strong indication of the Fourth Gospel having been composed originally for a particular and local audience of Christ-followers is the unique character of some of its prose (the degree of relexicalization and overlexicalization in the discourses of Jesus especially), which most commentators neglect but which Malina in 1985 and then he and Rohrbaugh in their 1998 social-science commentary on John have rightly highlighted, characterizing such discourse as 'anti-language' stemming from some sort of 'anti-society'.[27] This is the language and social position of the Johannine group, not that of the Christ-movement in general.

The Scope of Our Investigation

The story of the raising of Lazarus is found in John 11.1–44. These are the normally recognized boundaries of the passage. In the present volume, however, we will adopt a much wider set of boundaries and consider several other parts of the Gospel that bear upon our subject. First, the geographical setting is prefigured in part in John 10.40–42, where Jesus and his disciples travel to the far side of the Jordan where John had previously baptized, meaning that Jesus is a long way from Bethany when Lazarus falls ill. Then there are references in John 11.45–54, 12.9–11 and 12.12–19 to the Lazarus episode and the way in which it inflames the Judean leaders to kill Jesus. These details are important in relation to the development of the plot of the Gospel and the progression of Jesus towards death. Finally, Jesus has a meal with Lazarus in Bethany, where Martha waits upon him and Mary anoints him (12.1–8). Not only is this incident vital on its own terms, as we will see, for the presentation and role of this family, but it needs to be interpreted in relation both to the anointing of Jesus in John 19 and to what happens after his death in John 20.

---

27 See Malina 1985 and Malina and Rohrbaugh 1998, pp. 4–11, 46–8 and *passim*.

The Significance of the Lazarus Narrative

When one considers how Lazarus is depicted in the Fourth Gospel, it may at first sight seem strange that he has had such a profound impact on the Christian imagination. To begin with, there are some grounds for regarding him as a minor character in the Fourth Gospel. Even though the Lazarus story occupies a sizeable section of narrative in this Gospel, his role is limited. While we will return to the whole issue of Johannine characterization later in this chapter, it is worth noting some important data here. Lazarus only appears in John 11 and 12; he is not a recurring character like the disciples or Nicodemus. Most notable, however, is the circumstance that he never says a word, not even a word of thanks or a prayer of faith after Jesus has raised him. Martha and Mary speak, but their brother does not. While Lazarus is, as it were, 'out of commission' for much of John 11, it is noteworthy that even at the meal described in John 12.1–8 he says nothing. This silence stands in stark contrast to the occasions of speech attributed to the man whom Jesus cures of blindness (a lesser miracle) in John 9 – speech both with the leaders of the Judean people (9.8–17, 24–34) and with Jesus himself (9.35–39). In addition, Lazarus of Bethany only appears in this Gospel.

Yet there are countervailing considerations, which suggest that the story of the raising of Lazarus does have a good claim to be considered a key text in the Fourth Gospel. The very fact that he is named is significant, since many of the people with whom Jesus interacts to their benefit in this Gospel pass unnamed – for example, the Samaritan woman in John 4 and the man born blind in John 9.[28] This is probably due to the significance that the evangelist attaches to Lazarus, as we will explain later in this volume. In part, however, this may also reflect the sheer enormity of the event. It is difficult to imagine a more dramatic miracle than to raise someone from the dead. In addition, although there are other accounts of Jesus raising the dead in the Gospels, such as the daughter of Jairus in Mark 5.21–43 (with the parallel passages, dependent on this one, in Matt. 9.18–26 and Luke 8.40–56) and the raising of the son of the widow of Nain (described as a *neaniskos*, meaning a youth or young man) in Luke 7.11–17, Lazarus is the only named individual whom Jesus

28 This point is well made by Hakola 1999, p. 234.

raises. In addition, in the other two accounts the focus falls more on the parents of the deceased, whereas in the case of Lazarus we appear to be dealing with an adult of full age, where the question of his parentage is, unusually for John, irrelevant[29] and where his status attracts the hostile attention of the Judean authorities. Finally, whereas the daughter of Jairus had just died, Lazarus had been dead for four days, by which time the processes of bodily decomposition in a hot climate would have meant not only that his corpse had begun to smell, but that his very appearance had begun to change.

Throughout the ages, adult Christians have found Lazarus as the only example in the New Testament of someone like them who had been raised from the dead, the fate that they had been taught lay in store for all the faithful (even though they probably realized Lazarus must have died a second time to await the general resurrection at the end of time). Is it possible that the power of Lazarus in the Christian imagination owes its explanation to the force of its image of 'rebirth' for adult humankind that this narrative from the Fourth Gospel alone portrays?

Tempering such a view is the consideration that we must not forget the agent of this rebirth: Jesus himself. Lazarus may have been raised but what does this say about the one whose intervention secured his rebirth? Someone, indeed, who himself was soon to experience resurrection! Whose raising or resurrection is in view? Is John conveying a message about the fate of the faithful or the person and identity of the Christ? Or both? Are the Christian faithful more interested in the former alternative and Christian theologians in the latter? To what extent is the emphasis on *a display of power* by Jesus, with raising from the dead merely the arena in which that power can be shown off to greatest effect?

---

29 Contrast the telling of the story of Lazarus with the Johannine healing of the blind man in John 9.1–41 in which his parents figure prominently and the crucifixion where Jesus' mother is given a significant role, uniquely in John (19.25–27).

Lazarus, Martha and Mary in Current Discussion

The Raising of Lazarus and the Narrative Structure of the Fourth Gospel

A convenient entry point for examining current discussion of the Lazarus account is the popular view that the Fourth Gospel falls naturally into two sections: the first section comprising Chapters 1—12 and the second Chapters 13—20. Following the lead taken by C. H. Dodd in 1953, it has become customary to refer to the first as 'the Book of Signs', with the second section constituting the (Book of) Passion.[30] The designation 'the Book of Signs' derives from the statement in John 12.37: 'Even though he had done so many signs (*sēmeia*) in their presence, they did not believe in him.' It is even possible that underlying John 1—12 is a 'Signs Source', which may have existed in written form.[31] Without entering into the scholarly discussion about this alleged source, it is easy to identify six miracles that seem to constitute 'signs'. These are the changing of water into wine at Cana (2.1–11), which is described as 'the first of the signs' (*archē tōn sēmeiōn*, 2.11); the healing of the royal official's son (4.46–54); the healing of the paralytic at the pool (5.1–9a); the feeding of the five thousand (6.1–15); the cure of the man born blind (9.1–7); and, lastly and possibly as a climax, the raising of Lazarus. Scholars enthusiastic to discern a more satisfying number of *seven* signs add Jesus' walking on the sea (6.19–21), but this differs from the six just mentioned in significant respects.[32] Each of these six *sēmeia* (a) begins with a disclosure of human need; (b) involves Jesus remedying this need miraculously; and (c) reveals some new dimension of the divine presence in Jesus.[33]

The importance of this sign involving Lazarus also derives from its placement as the last of the sequence of six signs in the Fourth Gospel. Sequentially, it serves as the climax to the wonder-working of Jesus.[34] Whether or not it is derived from a Signs Source and held a climactic position within that source already, the story

30 Dodd 1953, p. 289.

31 For the debate, see Kysar 1975, pp. 13–37; Becker 1969–70; Fortna 1970 and 1988; Byrne 1991, pp. 17–21 and Van Belle 1994.

32 So Byrne 1991, p. 18.

33 Byrne 1991, pp. 19–20.

34 See, for example, Stibbe 1994, pp. 38–40.

in its current formulation shows editorial links to the first sign at Cana, especially in the conscious editorial *inclusio* formed by the references to glory in 2.11 and 11.40. Malina and Rohrbaugh also note another connection – how the signs begin with a wedding and end with a funeral.[35] John means the Lazarus story to be the sign towards which the series builds.

The precise location of this sign in the Fourth Gospel at the turning point from public ministry to the Last Supper and Passion is also significant. There is an ongoing debate as to whether the raising of Lazarus is the conclusion of the signs marking the public ministry of Jesus or whether it is already to be seen as part of the Passion account.[36] In fact, Chapters 11—12 are transitional in many respects. The last of the signs, the raising of Lazarus, both marks the end of the public ministry of Jesus,[37] and also constitutes the catalyst for the final determination of the Judean leadership to arrest and execute Jesus (11.45–54). *It effectively replaces the role of the Temple action in the Synoptic Gospels in this respect* (which John inserts towards the start of his Gospel, in 2.13–25). Moreover, John not only makes the raising of Lazarus the explanation for the concern of the authorities (see also 12.9–11), but he also proffers this event as the explicit explanation for the crowds hailing Jesus at his entry into Jerusalem (12.17–19). Typical of Johannine irony,[38] an event that portrays the giving of life is made the event that motivates the authorities to execute Jesus.

The raising of Lazarus from the dead is the most impressive miracle Jesus works in the Fourth Gospel, the most notable of the signs. Among the signs, moreover, only the Lazarus story places the miracle at the end, the grand finale, of the narrative.[39] Not surprisingly, for critics interested in the composition history of this Gospel, the earliest formulation of this sign has been a subject of considerable speculation.[40] Thus Schnackenburg discussed and in part accepted the hypothesis that the Johannine story had links with the tradition of the rich man and the poor

35 Malina and Rohrbaugh 1998, p. 193.

36 See the discussion by Labahn 1999, pp. 381–2.

37 Hakola 1999, p. 228.

38 On Johannine irony, see Duke 1985.

39 So Stibbe 1994, p. 42.

40 For a brief consideration of the reconstructions of Bultmann, Wilckens and Fortna, see Schnackenburg 1980, pp. 318–21.

Lazarus found in Luke 16.19–31.[41] Barnabas Lindars argued that an early exorcism account lay behind the narrative.[42] D. Burkett has advocated the theory that the present narrative derives from the combination of two distinct accounts of the story.[43] Yet our interest (in line with the approach set out above) lies rather in understanding the particular emphases to be found in the final version of the account as we now have it.

One aspect of that final form deserving notice is the dominance of narrative in John 11.1–44. Unlike some other signs, such as the healing of the sick man at the pool of Bethsaida in John 5 and the feeding of the five thousand in John 6, the raising of Lazarus lacks an extensive discourse connected with it. Nevertheless, a set of dialogues permeates this passage in its current form. C. H. Dodd noted the uniqueness of this passage in the Fourth Gospel with respect to the way in which it interweaves narrative and discourse. As a continuous narrative, its length is only exceeded by the Passion Narrative.[44]

The Significance of the Raising of Lazarus

Christological Interpretations

The declaration in John 11.25–26 seems to lie close to the heart of what is portrayed dramatically in the narrative: 'I am the resurrection and the life; he who believes in me, though he die, yet shall he live, and whoever lives and believes in me shall never die' (RSV). Rudolf Schnackenburg has identified the two most important themes – the role and character of Jesus Christ and the character of the salvation being offered to the believer – in his comment that 'A word of revelation in the centre of the chapter gives it [the sign] its literal interpretation (vv. 25–26). Its Christological (v. 4) and soteriological (v. 40) significance are also briefly mentioned in the introduction and at the climax of the narrative.'[45] This twofold emphasis also chimes with a statement that the evangelist presents as programmatic for his meaning in the Gospel as a whole:

41 Schnackenburg 1980, pp. 340–5.
42 Lindars 1992.
43 Burkett 1994.
44 Dodd 1963, p. 228.
45 Schnackenburg 1980, p. 316.

> Now Jesus did many other signs (*sēmeia*) in the presence of the disciples, which are not written in this book; but these are written that you may believe that Jesus is the Christ, the Son of God, and that believing you may have life in his name. (20.30–31; RSV)

Scholarly views extend across the spectrum from the strongly Christological to the soteriological, but the preponderance of opinion regarding which theme dominates is probably fixed on the former point. As will emerge through the course of this volume, however, we tend to find the emphasis more at the soteriological end, although without denying the Christological dimensions of Jesus' interactions with Lazarus, Martha and Mary.

Many critics give priority to the role and function of Jesus Christ, to Christology. Marking a highpoint of this approach, C. F. D. Moule comments: 'it is that Son of God who occupies the whole attention of the evangelist. *Do not ask what sort of life it is; ask only who bestows it*'.[46] Christological interpretations frequently fix upon the glory associated with Jesus Christ in the Fourth Gospel. The raising of Lazarus clearly seems to share in the function of all of the signs that was expressly attributed to the first of them at Cana: to allow Jesus to manifest his glory (2.11). Brown, in a richly elaborated treatment,[47] argues that the miracle has been made to serve several purposes in the Fourth Gospel. He notes that the theme of glory not only forms an inclusion around this episode (11.4, 40), but also links the first and last signs (11.40 and 2.11). The conversations in John 11 serve to draw out the implications of the 'sign' concerning Lazarus and for many critics those implications lie mainly in the area of Christology. Thus the conjunction of the event with Jesus' declaration to Martha that 'I am the resurrection and the life' (11.25) has led many commentators to view the significance of the raising of Lazarus in the Fourth Gospel as a means to reveal divine glory (11.4, 40).[48] Many of these themes come together in the view of Siegfried Schulz, who believes that the raising of Lazarus from the dead is theologically and Christologically overtaken by the

---

46 Moule 1975, p. 123 (emphasis original).
47 Brown 1966, pp. 420–37.
48 Brown 1966, pp. 431 and 436.

expression 'I am' and that the detailed description of the raising of Lazarus serves to glorify the One who became human.[49] For Schulz, the placement of this miracle at the end of the revealer's earthly ministry means that John wanted to provide an effective closure to the picture of the power and effectiveness of Jesus. The story of Lazarus proclaims the might of the prince of light who intervenes when everything seems beyond hope.[50]

Other commentators, while focusing on Christology, insist upon the extent to which the narrative of Lazarus also speaks of the humanity of Jesus and of his impending death. One of those whose emphasis is thus slightly different, yet no less Christologically oriented, is Andrew Lincoln, who finds the burden of the episode to lie upon *prefiguring the death of Jesus*, the one who gives life, and anticipating 'the decisive restoration of life to the life giver himself'.[51] Brown also proposes that the miracle prefigures the death of Jesus.[52] Other scholars see the evangelist reinforcing the humanity of Jesus specifically by writing to 'correct' Gnostic and docetic influences that were allegedly abroad in his environment.[53]

Soteriological Interpretations

Other critics, however, emphasize the importance of the Lazarus narrative as bearing upon the experience and destiny of those who believe. Thus, one popular approach is to interpret the story as demonstrating that Jesus is the *source of life* that conquers death by means of the resurrection of the just at the end of time. Thus C. K. Barrett has written: 'The meaning of the narrative for John is as simple as the narrative itself . . . it is an anticipation of what is to take place at the last day.'[54] With somewhat more emphasis on 'belief', Ulrich Wilckens sees the theological point of the evangelist to be comparable to John 20.31, where the evangelist describes his purpose in writing to be 'that you may believe

49 Schulz 1983, p. 159.
50 Schulz 1983, p. 160.
51 Lincoln 2000, p. 151; compare also Lee 1994, pp. 224–26.
52 Brown 1966, p. 431.
53 For example, Wagner 1988, pp. 451–6.
54 Barrett 1978, p. 322.

that Jesus is the Christ, the Son of God, and that through believing you may have life in his name'.[55]

It is interesting to note that Jacob Kremer, in a work that includes a consideration of the reception-history of John 11.1–46, comes out strongly in favour of an interpretation linked to soteriology, especially as relevant for the original audience of the Fourth Gospel. Thus, he regards John as concerned both to present Jesus' power over death and to lead his audience to have faith in Jesus, a concern strongly influenced by the problems of that first audience.[56] We will return later (in Chapter 6) to consider the evidence for our interpretation from that moment in the reception-history of the text represented by the paintings of Lazarus in the Roman catacombs. Also foreshadowing a theme of this volume, Kremer asks whether the fact that Jesus is described as loving Martha and her sister and Lazarus (John 11.5) might indicate the evangelist had his audience is mind, as those whom Jesus loves.[57]

This view brings us close to those (more strongly) soteriological interpretations that are evident in the occasional descriptions in Johannine scholarship of Lazarus (like Nathanael, Nicodemus or the beloved disciple) as a 'symbolic', 'representative', or 'ideal' figure. These terms are used to indicate that such a character seems to have the potential for an idealized or representative function, while at the same time lacking credible external reference as a historical figure (e.g., by not appearing in the Synoptic Gospels).[58] Brendan Byrne has recently proposed a 'representative' function for Lazarus, who 'is a character with whom anyone can identify'.[59] Yet rarely, if ever, do critics (with Kremer as an honourable exception) see Martha and Mary as representative figures. Nor, more importantly, do they subject the meaning of 'representative' to adequate scrutiny nor indicate what they mean by it within a particular model or theoretical approach.

55 Wilckens 1959, p. 33.

56 Kremer 1985, p. 38.

57 Kremer 1985, p. 50.

58 For a general discussion of actual and 'symbolic' characters in the Fourth Gospel, see Koester 2003, pp. 34–9.

59 Byrne 1991, pp. 106–7.

A New Social-Scientific and Theological Approach to Lazarus, Mary and Martha

Lazarus, Mary and Martha as Prototypes of Identity for Christ-Followers

It is precisely at this point that we aim in this volume to inaugurate a new approach to Lazarus, Mary and Martha in the Fourth Gospel – by exploring the way in which they serve a 'representative' function, but only after using a social-scientific theory to develop a suitable model. While we assume that the Gospel was written in a Mediterranean social script of the sort initially proposed by Bruce Malina and whose usefulness (as a heuristic model expressed at a fairly high level of abstraction) requires no further demonstration,[60] we will propose a model specifically attuned to the essential features of the Lazarus narrative. From the array of social-scientific ideas and perspectives on offer, we will deploy that part of social psychology known as social identity theory, in particular the extent to which individuals can be prototypical or exemplary of the identity of a group. We will show that traditional scholarship has undervalued key features of the passage that such a model, when applied to the textual data, reveals to be highly significant. In addition, not only does this approach allow us to offer a fresh interpretation of what the material relating to Lazarus, Martha and Mary would have meant to its original audience, we will also outline how this type of interpretation can contribute to eliciting the theological significance of the narrative concerning Lazarus, Martha and Mary. That is, we will consider how it bears upon the ways in which modern-day Christians understand themselves and their destiny in relation to God and the cosmos.

We are not the first to bring the social sciences to bear upon the Fourth Gospel. Yet we submit that while those who have undertaken such interpretation have offered valuable insights into the text (many of which we will adopt), they have nevertheless struggled to do its historical meaning full justice and have had little, if anything, to say of its theological potential. In 1988 Jerome Neyrey noted the importance of the experience of the death of

---

60 See the defence of this type of model use from a Weberian perspective in Esler 2005d.

believers for understanding this passage – a point with which we share a measure of agreement – but he analysed the passage in terms of stages of redaction (focusing on Christological development) that he linked to Mary Douglas' group-grid model.[61] There are two problems with this. First, the Douglas group-grid model is one of limited utility, which few, if any biblical scholars, would use today. Second, the uncertainties surrounding the redactional history of the Fourth Gospel make it a hazardous exercise to attach too much confidence to particular stages of redaction or to tie one's interpretation to them.

Bruce Malina and Richard Rohrbaugh, in a commentary published in 1998 that pays particular attention to the general character of Mediterranean culture and to the specific issues of 'anti-society' and 'anti-language' in John, have commented upon the significance of the death story and of the family relationships that are depicted in the Lazarus narrative, as well as issues of honour in relation to Jesus and his Judean opponents.[62] We consider that issues of 'insider' identity, within the broad context of first-century CE Mediterranean world and the specific setting of Johannine community, are indeed central to the passage, but that these are most revealingly uncovered when Lazarus and his sisters are understood as prototypes for this group of Jesus-followers within the theoretical framework of social identity theory.

Group Prototypes and the Question of Characterization

By focusing on Lazarus, Martha and Mary as prototypical Christ-followers, we inevitably enter the question of characterization in the Fourth Gospel.[63] To many this may seem an unpromising venture. Franz Overbeck, for example, once remarked that the characters in this Gospel are but 'a mirror for the manifestation of an alien Being and are of no further significance'.[64] Here we see how a strongly Christological view can overwhelm other aspects

---

61 Neyrey 1988, pp. 81–93, 115–212.

62 Malina and Rohrbaugh 1998, pp. 193–201.

63 On this subject, see the extremely helpful essay by Hakola (1999). For valuable insights into the characters of the Lazarus story, see Sproston North 2001.

64 Overbeck 1911, p. 303 (cited in Hakola 1999, p. 223).

of the Fourth Gospel. For Louis Martyn, on the other hand, the characters have a much more important role. In his celebrated approach to this Gospel, he argued that it constituted a drama on two levels, with the characters witnessing both to the events of Jesus' own time and ministry and to the situation of the audience for whom the work was written.[65] On Martyn's view, the characters spoke directly to John's late first-century CE audience and represented issues and events known to them from their own experience, such as a painful exclusion from the synagogue.

What of Lazarus, Martha and Mary? We must first counsel caution in what type of characterization is to be expected in a text from the ancient Mediterranean world. In particular, we should not expect the same degree of psychological introspection familiar to us in the works of modern novelists, like George Eliot, Henry James, D. H. Lawrence or E. M. Forster. They were writing in a period when a pronounced individualistic consciousness had developed in the West and where the psychological exploration that would culminate in the works of Freud, Jung, Adler and so on was providing a progressively richer understanding of the human psyche. In the far more strongly group-oriented ancient world people were much less likely to reveal their inner selves. In addition, although methods of probing the inner person did exist, they were not on the same scale as those to which we are accustomed. In a culture such as this, the important thing was to live in accordance with group values and behaviour, not to carve out a distinctive new mode of existence for oneself (of the sort that we would see as making for an interesting character). In general, honourable men and women lived in accordance with the roles society laid down for them. For all these reasons, the characters in ancient works of fiction or in epic poems and drama often appear to portray character in a rather stereotypical form.

What about the Fourth Gospel? Alan Culpepper has observed the characters in John's Gospel are 'individualized by their position in society and their interaction with Jesus. This means that they may easily become types. They are not so individualized that they have much of a "personality."'[66] This is completely accurate, yet it is exactly what one would expect from a group-oriented, cultural context such as this! To come to an appreciation

65 Martyn 1979.

66 Culpepper 1983, p. 145.

of the characters in the Fourth Gospel, accordingly, it is a futile exercise to expect the subtleties of modern characterization or to bemoan their absence. Instead, we must recognize the distinctive nature of the cultural context in which John portrayed them as he did and explore the function they have in this distinctive setting. We submit that our recourse to a social identity approach that argues for Lazarus, Martha and Mary as prototypical of group identity allows us a new purchase on this important question of Johannine characterization.

When we investigate these figures from this perspective we are led to posit a role for them that is much more ample than is usual in scholarly discussion. Thus, as far as Raimo Hakola is concerned, Lazarus is but 'a marginal agent'. He suggests that the 'characterization of Lazarus is minimal, and his function is strictly connected to the plot and major themes of the Gospel'. According to Hakola, Lazarus only moves towards having a genuine personality when the Gospel comes to be read and interpreted in new contexts.[67] In other words, Lazarus had little significance for the *original* audience of the Gospel. Furthermore, Hakola does not recognize that we need to examine the whole family of Lazarus and his two sisters, not just Lazarus himself, to appreciate the meaning they would have communicated to John's audience.

Theology

During the course of this volume we will also have occasion to draw out something of the theological significance of the narrative of Lazarus, Martha and Mary. We will do so within the approach to New Testament theology set out recently by one us.[68] Ever since Johann Philipp Gabler inaugurated a distinction between (historically derived) biblical theology and dogmatic theology on 30 March 1787,[69] the dominant method for bringing the results of the historical criticism of the New Testament into connection with contemporary Christianity has been via frameworks derived from systematic theology. This process involves selecting certain

67 Hakola 1999, p. 224–5.

68 Esler 2005a.

69 For the text of Gabler's address, see Sandys-Wunsch and Eldredge 1980; for a critical discussion of Gabler's proposal in its historical and theological context, see Esler 2005a, pp. 12–17.

historically recovered data from the texts (typically data embodying ideas that are regarded as transcending the particular historical exigencies for which that particular New Testament text was written) and integrating them with ideas and perspectives drawn from systematic theology. The approach that will be utilized here diverges from this one by proposing instead that when we read the New Testament authors in a manner directed to enriching Christian experience and identity today, we should understand the process as one of intercultural (and hence critical) dialogue and communion with them. The aim here is not to filter out some data for inclusion in the constructions of systematicians. Rather, we propose engaging with the original meaning of a particular New Testament text or narrative in its historical specificity as a precious communication from our ancestor in faith who produced it, which should be addressed on its own terms and its own forms, not broken up and fed into forms of conceptuality alien to its original intent. In adopting this course, we are entering into 'communion' with the author, a communion that can be modelled in various ways. We will provide further details of this perspective later in this volume.

Conclusion

We have now addressed central issues relating to the manner in which John portrays Lazarus and his revivification, and his sisters Martha and Mary in this Gospel. We have also discussed existing scholarship and outlined a new and social-scientific way of understanding these issues that we will propound in the remaining chapters of this volume. We must now proceed to outline the social-scientific model that we consider useful in making sense of the narrative concerning Lazarus in John 11, both historically in terms of its meaning for the first audience of this Gospel, and theologically in relation to its ongoing significance for Christian life and faith within a framework of intercultural communication and communion with John. We will do this in Chapter 2.

In Chapter 3 we will argue that although the problem of what, if any, sources John used is a very difficult one, it is useful to explore the way he has interacted with existing traditions of the Christ-movement in terms of the 'processing of the past'. In Chapter 4 we will argue that the Fourth Gospel presents Lazarus,

Martha and Mary as a family prototypical of those whom Jesus loves. Chapter 5 will present our case for the raising of Lazarus as prototypical of Christ-followers. In Chapter 6 we will consider certain portrayals of Lazarus in the early Christian art of the Roman catacombs as endorsing our view that the raising of Lazarus does speak in a prototypical way to Christians. Chapter 7 will contain our conclusions, setting out our reflections on the continuing theological role of Lazarus, Martha and Mary for Christian experience and identity . In Appendix 1 we will briefly set out the basis for translating the words *Ioudaios* or *Ioudaioi* in the Fourth Gospel as 'Judean' and 'Judeans' and not 'Jew' or 'Jews', while in Appendix 2 we will defend our text-critical reading of John 12.3 that entails the argument that myrrh and not nard was the spice used by Mary in anointing Jesus.

2

Social Identity and Prototypes:

A Social-Scientific Model for Historical and Theological Application

Prerequisites for a Social-Scientific Model Relating to Lazarus, Mary and Martha

We begin with the characteristics of this Gospel that are relevant to our choice of model. First, as noted in the previous chapter, we consider that the group (or, possibly, the ensemble of groups of a similar type) for which it was written, were quite distinctive and different in many respects from other groups in the Christ-movement. Thus we demur from the provocative thesis of Richard Bauckham that this Gospel was written 'for all Christians', a thesis that has attracted considerable opposition.[1] Second, we are of the view that it was written late in the first century CE for Christ-followers who were existing in a state of tension with the outside world, which encompassed Judeans and non-Judeans.[2] That environment was predominantly Judean, given the extent to which John goes to inscribe a new form of identity for the Christ-movement distinct from Judean ethnic identity.[3] We do not consider feasible the suggestion that its author had an audience

---

1 Bauckham 1998b and 1998c, and the critiques in Esler 1998a, Sim 2001 and Mitchell 2005.

2 For our reasons for referring to *Ioudaioi* as 'Judeans' and not 'Jews', see Appendix 1. For a case against using the word 'Gentile' of non-Judeans (essentially because it is a way of referring to outsiders from a Judean perspective that such people themselves did not use as a self-designation, preferring instead an expression of ethnic identity such as 'Egyptian', 'Greek' and so on), see Esler 2003, p. 75.

3 See Esler 2006b. This theme begins as early as John 1.11–13.

in mind that directly addressed non-Christ-followers.[4] Second, since Christ-followers at this time were organized in small groups located in cities throughout the Mediterranean region and meeting in domestic contexts, we consider such to be the context from within which this Gospel emerged.[5] We propose that if John envisaged his Gospel would travel further afield, he would have hoped that it would influence other groups of Christ-followers to whom it reached to adopt the views of the Johannine group. As we have mentioned in Chapter 1, the Fourth Evangelist does seem to acknowledge the existence of other groups of Christ-followers that were not in full communion with the Johannine group, with the evidence for this including the sheep imagery in John 10 and the signs of division in the Johannine letters. In spite of this position on the connection between this Gospel and its *original* audience, however, we consider that, at the theological level, the meaning of the Lazarus narrative transcends the particular time and place in which it was created and says something about the experience of Christians in all times and places. Later in this chapter we will set out a way of understanding its theological impact.

The features of the Gospel just mentioned indicate that social identity theory, as developed by Henri Tajfel and John Turner in the University of Bristol, England, in the 1970s and 1980s and developed since by a large number of social psychologists, will prove useful for considering the Fourth Gospel. Broadly speaking, this theory focuses on the way in which the members of one group (or social category) derive a sense of identity, of who they are, from belonging to that group, in contrast to other groups (other social categories) to which they do not belong.

The Fourth Gospel states that the things in it are written so that 'you may believe that Jesus is the Christ, the Son of God, and that believing you may have life in his name' (20.31). In other words, this Gospel explicitly looks to events in the past as the foundation for belief and life in the present and the future. For this reason, an investigation focusing on questions of identity must embrace the past, present and future. Fortunately, as we will see, social identity theory, which initially investigated social phenomena almost as

---

4 As suggested by Burridge 1998, p. 144 and Barton 1998, p. 193.

5 For the domestic context of the early Christ-movement, see Moxnes 1997, and Osiek and Balch 1997 and 2003.

if they were frozen in time, has recently become interested in the question of time and the temporal progression in which a group finds itself. In addition, the growing study of collective memory, deriving mainly from sociology, also offers important resources as to how any group deals with the past for the sake of the present and the future, and this area is easily capable of assimilation with the recent interest in time shown by social identity theorists.

Our last prerequisite is that the model is capable of addressing a narrative that relates events concerning particular individuals, Lazarus and his two sisters, Martha and Mary, and of relating those (remembered) events to the experience of the group (or closely related groups) for whom and to whom John was writing. Here the fact that social identity theory includes in its ambit a consideration of how real or imagined persons serve as prototypes and exemplars of the group identity offers a promising line of investigation.

We will now address these issues in more detail, to produce a composite model linking social identity, collective memory and group prototypicality. As we will see, this model serves a historical purpose in assisting us to understand the message that John sought to convey to his original audience. But it can also be adapted to a framework for discerning the relevance of such results to modern-day Christian experience and identity that builds upon notions of intercultural (and critical) community and communion with John, our ancestor in faith, whose writing continues to resonate in our hearts and minds.[6] We will conclude the present chapter with a brief exploration of this theological dimension, before proceeding to apply the model to the material in the Fourth Gospel on Lazarus, Martha and Mary.

Social Identity Theory Generally

The Key Concepts

Since one of the present authors has recently applied social identity theory in detail to Paul's letters to the Galatians and Romans,[7] only a brief summary of its general nature is necessary here. The

---

6 See Esler 2005a for a new approach to New Testament theology built on interpersonal and intercultural community and communion.

7 See Esler 1998b and 2003.

foundation of this theory is that the allocation of people to different groups (even on a purely random basis) almost immediately results in processes of comparison between the groups and discrimination by members of one group against the members of another. Faced with this phenomenon, Henri Tajfel argued in a seminal essay that groups needed to establish a positively valued distinctiveness from other groups so as to provide their members with a positive social identity.[8] By 'social identity' he meant that part of the sense of self, the identity, of the individual members that derived from their belonging to the group in question. Social identity did not constitute the entirety of the identity of each member, but in certain situations it becomes salient. This formulation means that this theory is both psychological, in that it interests itself in individuals, and also social, in that it considers how a group manages to install itself in the minds and hearts of its members, thus affecting their views and behaviour. Responding to the location of this theory in the area of intergroup comparison and discrimination, Tajfel identified three dimensions of group belonging. First there was the 'cognitive' dimension, meaning the recognition of belonging to a group; second was the 'emotional' dimension, meaning the positive or negative connotations of belonging and, thirdly, there was the 'evaluative' dimension, referring to attitudes members hold towards insiders and outsiders.[9]

A phenomenon that frequently accompanies ingroup/outgroup differentiation and requires some consideration here is that of stereotyping. According to social identity theorists, stereotypes are social categorical judgements, perceptions of people based on their group memberships (not on their character as unique individuals). 'When we stereotype people', according to Rupert Brown, 'we attribute to them certain characteristics that are seen to be shared by all or most of their fellow group members.'[10] Stereotypes are used in the setting of intergroup relations, often (not always) to describe outgroups. They are not immutable and constant, not fixed mental images lodged in members' heads, but vary in accordance with the vagaries of any particular social

8 See Tajfel 1972. See Hogg and Abrams 1988 for a useful outline of social identity theory.

9 Tajfel 1978, p. 28.

10 Brown 2000, p. 290.

context and the state of intergroup relations. As they are mental perceptions, they vary depending upon the situation of the perceiver. This has the result that there can be disputes over the validity of stereotypes within and between groups and such disputes are a normal part of political and historical processes through which groups and society at large must move.[11]

Subsequent research has shown that not all groups engage in the processes of intergroup comparison elaborated upon by Tajfel and others working in this area. Nevertheless, Hinkle and Brown have demonstrated that the theory is appropriate where two conditions are met: first, the society in which the relevant groups are located is collectivistic rather than individualistic in character, and, second, that the group must exhibit a comparative outlook.[12] Both of these conditions are satisfied in relation to the Fourth Gospel. All cultures in the ancient Mediterranean world were group-oriented, and the groups for whom John was writing were caught up in a strong differentiation between insiders heading for eternal life and outsiders who were not.

An extension of social identity theory is 'self-categorization theory', initially developed by John Turner.[13] Whereas the former theory concerns itself with intergroup phenomena, the latter is interested in phenomena *within* groups. The theory suggests that individuals categorize themselves in terms of social categories and then describe, define and evaluate themselves in terms of those categories. Central to this approach is the distinction between social identity (self-definitions based on social category memberships) and personal identity (self-definitions based on personal or idiosyncratic attributes). Turner relied on experiments which indicated that a person's self-concept varied in particular group situations, notably by movement along a continuum from pronounced personal identity at one end to pronounced social identity at the other. An important stimulus to self-categorization theory was the recognition that where people define themselves in terms of a shared category membership, they tend to stereotype themselves in terms of such membership, and in so doing enhance the sense of identity shared with ingroup members,

11 See Oakes, Haslam and Turner 1994, pp. 83, 211–13.

12 Hinkle and Brown 1990.

13 See Turner, Hogg, Oakes *et al.* 1987 and Turner 1999.

while heightening the sense of contrast between themselves and members of outgroups. Most importantly:

> Where social identity becomes relatively more salient than personal identity, people see themselves less as differing individual persons and more as the similar, prototypical representatives of their ingroup category. There is a depersonalisation of the self – a 'cognitive re-definition of the self' – from unique attributes and individual differences to shared category memberships and associated stereotypes.[14]

Beliefs and Social Identity

Bearing upon the processes of social identity (and its closely related cousin, self-categorization), and highly relevant to the subject of this volume, is Daniel Bar-Tal's recent expansion of the theory to cover group beliefs.[15] This research represents a step beyond the theories of Tajfel and Turner in the direction of recognizing that social identity is not based solely on the mere fact of categorization, but that beliefs held by the members also provide a rationale and character to group existence. Group beliefs are 'convictions that group members (a) are aware that they share, and (b) consider as defining their "groupness"'. Such beliefs are additional to the fundamental belief, namely, that the group *is* a group, and give a particular character to 'we-ness and uniqueness' experienced by the members.[16] Group beliefs include values and norms (referring to the ideals of the group and its ideas on appropriate behaviour for the members), goals (meaning beliefs as to valued or desired future states for the group) and ideology (here meaning an integrated set of beliefs constituting a programme or a theory of order).[17] Bar-Tal notes that group beliefs 'are usually held with great confidence because they are considered to be facts and verities'.[18] Yet usually a group will consider some of its beliefs to be more central than others in characterizing and defining who they are: '*The more central group beliefs are considered to be*

14 Turner 1999, p. 31.
15 See Bar-Tal 1998.
16 Bar-Tal 1998, p. 94.
17 Bar-Tal 1998, pp. 95–101.
18 Bar-Tal 1998, p. 101.

prototypic in group characterization and therefore are called basic group beliefs.'[19]

Not every belief shared by members acquires the status of a group belief. Members of a group may, for example, all entertain a particular view about how the world was created which is even shared by outgroups. Accordingly, Bar-Tal has proposed three conditions for isolating *group beliefs* from other beliefs. First, they must be functional for group formation and maintenance, especially by differentiating between the ingroup and outgroup. Second, they must be salient, here meaning that they must hold the attention of group members because of their prominence and distinctiveness. Third, the 'epistemic authorities' of the group must regard them as group beliefs and support them. By 'epistemic authorities' Bar-Tal has in mind those sources of knowledge who exert determinative influence on the formation of knowledge within the group, such as religious leaders. 'Group members attribute high confidence to beliefs coming from epistemic authority, consider those beliefs as truth, and adopt them as part of their own repertoires.'[20]

Time and Collective Memory in Social Identity Theory

Although time has long been of interest to anthropologists and sociologists,[21] social identity theorists had rather neglected it until quite recently. This position has now begun to change.[22] In 1996 Susan Condor noted that although most empirical social psychological research had produced an image of social life composed of discrete moments and contexts, this circumstance was oddly in tension with Henri Tajfel's own interest in how social phenomena such as intergroup differentiation, prejudice and conflict endured and developed over time. Condor correctly insists that to generate such a perspective it is necessary to understand social life as a temporal trajectory rather than as a static set of positions.

---

19 Bar-Tal 1998, p. 102 (emphasis original).

20 Bar-Tal 1998, pp. 108–9.

21 For a survey of recent contributions by cultural anthropologists in the area of time, see Munn 1992. On sociological approaches to time, see Adam 1990 and 1994.

22 For a fuller account of time in social identity theory than is possible here, see Esler 2003, pp. 19–39.

Social life is a reality in which human agents acquire identities, ideas and practices and hand them on to others, often transforming them in the process.[23] Just as individuals experience themselves 'as coherent beings-over-time',[24] so too groups regard themselves as ongoing processes, extending across past, present and future. That we possess identities is based on our ability to relate fragmentary experiences across temporal boundaries: 'Even momentary self-images involve a simultaneous awareness of the present (self-in-context), the past and the anticipated future . . . A sense of identity – of being oneself – hence necessitates both retroactive and proactive memory.'[25] Thus we understand the groups of which we are members as historical phenomena, originating in the past and stretching forward into the future. To explain how groups provide their members with a serial connectedness with other group members, Condor quotes D. Carr:

> . . . my social existence not only puts me in contact with a co-existing multiplicity of contemporaries: it connects me with a peculiar form of temporal continuity . . . which runs from predecessors to successors. This sequence extends beyond the boundaries of my life, both into the past before my birth and into the future after my death . . . the *we* with whose experience the individual identifies can both pre-date and survive the individuals that make it up.[26]

Marco Cinnirella has further explored the temporal aspects of social identity in an essay published in 1998.[27] Cinnirella utilizes earlier research (from outside the social identity tradition) that develops the notion of 'possible selves'.[28] These are 'the ideal selves that we would very much like to become. They are also the selves we could become, and the selves we are afraid of becoming.'[29] Thus, 'possible selves' essentially represent the beliefs held

23 Condor 1996.
24 Condor 1996, pp. 302–3.
25 Condor 1996, p. 303.
26 Carr 1991, pp. 113–14; cited in Condor 1996, p. 306.
27 Cinnirella 1998.
28 This research was by Markus and Nurius 1986 and 1987.
29 Markus and Nurius 1986, p. 954.

by an individual as to his or her self in the past and present and how it might change in the future, together with an estimate of the probability that different possible selves will be realized.[30] In this phrase Cinnirella is employing the notion of cognitive alternatives, meaning different ways of imagining a current state of affairs. One particular concern of Cinnirella is to develop social identity theory in a form that will allow it to address *past* social identities and the manner in which past, present and future may be reconstituted to create meaningful 'stories' at the level of both the individual and the group.[31]

Remembering is the most important means by which group members bring past persons, their predecessors or ancestors, and events into recollection in the present. They remember people or events they have personally experienced. But they also remember people or events they have learnt about from others. As Edward Shils notes: 'Memory is the vessel which retains in the present the record of the experiences undergone in the past and of knowledge gained through the recorded and remembered experience of others, living and dead.'[32] Thus we use memory even to cover phenomena occurring before we were born, as when Americans remember their War of Independence, or Australians and New Zealanders remember the Gallipoli landings of 25 April 1915 when the Anzac tradition was born.[33] Many of our memories are 'collective', that is, they are derived from the groups to which we belong.[34] This was the thesis argued by Maurice Halbwachs in the period leading up to World War Two, and it is becoming increasingly influential in the present time, with Jan Assmann of the University of Heidelberg having done much to bring it to

30 Cinnirella 1998, p. 229.

31 Cinnirella 1998, p. 243.

32 Shils 1981, p. 50. His treatment of memory in this volume occupies pages 50–2.

33 'Anzac' is the acronym for 'the Australian and New Zealand Army Corps' that had its baptism of fire on the beaches of Gallipoli, at the mouth of the Hellespont, in the ultimately unsuccessful campaign in 1915 to capture Istanbul from the south.

34 See Halbwachs 1980. Halbwachs died in Buchenwald in 1945. It is interesting to note that Shils, writing as recently as 1981, *supra*, does not mention Halbwachs.

prominence.[35] Collective memory encompasses a range of related phenomena, including the situations that mobilize memory, the process by which this happens and the content of what is remembered.[36] Collective remembering is central to the experience of a community.[37] Even though members of a group or community know that they themselves did not participate in certain past events affecting the group, they still identify with group members from the past (even if they are dead), as when they recall what their forefathers did in distant former times.[38] It is clear that analysis of memory and collective memory, the subject of important research by sociologists such as Edwards Shils and Maurice Halbwachs, is capable of being readily integrated with social identity theory, now that it has begun to address the question of how groups understand and experience themselves as entities extending through time.

Yet the past, especially the meaning and relevance of remembered figures and events, is often a battleground between rival groups. Collaboration between anthropologists and historians has recently shown the potency and prevalence of 'the processing of the past' and has highlighted the universal struggle to control voices and texts from the past in numerous settings in order to maintain claims concerning group status and identity.[39] Within the framework of social identity theory, this phenomenon points

---

35 See Assmann 2000 and 2002 [1992]. Assmann prefers the description 'cultural memory' (*kulturelle Gedächtnis*) for his version of this idea. This embraces two areas, that of 'memory culture' (*Erinnerungskultur*) and 'reference to the past' (*Vergangenheitsbezug*). Memory culture refers to the means by which a society preserves cultural continuity by protecting its collective knowledge from generation to generation by the use of cultural mnemonics (which includes material culture); this allows later generations to reconstruct their cultural identity. Reference to the past, on the other hand, reassures members of a society of their group identity and supplies them with an historical consciousness (that is, their sense of a unity with the past and of their own particular situation in the present) by recreating the past.

36 Billig, 1990, p. 60.

37 Middleton and Edwards 1990, p. 10: '. . . *he who controls the past controls who we are*' (emphasis original).

38 Billig 1990, p. 62.

39 The notion of 'the processing of the past' derives from Cohen 1994, pp. 4, 245.

to the need to assess the extent to which, in any given environment, processes of intergroup comparison and discrimination are linked to rival interpretations of memories of the past. We will return to this topic at some length in Chapter 3.

Group Prototypes

Running through much psychological research has been the idea that information about social categories is stored in the form of prototypes which are thought to express each category. A 'prototype' is a summary representation that is considered to capture the central tendency of the category and derives from multiple experiences with category members.[40] A prototype of a group of people will be a representation of a person thought to typify the group; that is, someone who is 'maximally representative of the shared social identity and consensual position of the group'.[41] Such a prototype will not be a current or actual member of the group, but rather the image of an ideal person who embodies its character. On the other hand, social psychologists refer to an actual person who may embody the identity of a group as an 'exemplar'.[42] A basic group belief, which we have already encountered, refers to a belief held by a group that is prototypic for the group. It is a belief central to how the group characterizes and defines itself.

Prototypes resemble stereotypes in being judgements concerning social categories. Accordingly, prototypes share with stereotypes the fact that they are not fixed and immutable. Rather, they vary with the changing context in which a group finds itself.[43] In a situation of extreme conflict, for example, those regarded as prototypical or exemplary of a group may well be characterized by stubbornness, courage and aggression, whereas once peace becomes a possibility, the group is likely to see these qualities as hindrances and select prototypes or exemplars more attuned to the new situation in which it finds itself. Thus, Winston Churchill, who had been outstandingly successful as a wartime leader, did not last very long as the British Prime Minister after the end of

40 See Smith and Zarate 1990, p. 245.

41 Haslam 2001, p. 66.

42 Smith and Zarate 1990, p. 246.

43 See Haslam 2001, pp. 66–7.

World War Two. The context-dependent nature of prototypes means that, just as with stereotypes, there can also be disputes over the nature and validity of prototypes within and between groups.[44] Yet it is helpful to distinguish between prototypes and stereotypes. Stereotypes are usually directed at outgroups and encapsulate the attitudes of the ingroup toward the identity of outgroup members. They are often accompanied by the view that the members of the outgroup are all similar to one another along the lines of the stereotype – this is the so-called 'outgroup homogeneity' effect.[45] A prototype, on the other hand, mainly refers to how an ingroup sees itself. It is usually positive in nature and its existence does not lead members of a group to abandon their conviction that they are all distinctive individuals – this is the so-called 'ingroup heterogeneity' effect.

In the vast majority of cases, exemplars and prototypes will be known by a proper name. Yet this is not necessarily the case. It is possible to imagine a situation in which an unnamed person has performed some feat, an act of conspicuous valour on a battlefield for example, and is remembered by the group as prototypical of its values. Yet the purposes of prototypicality will be served far more easily and effectively if the figure has a name, since this will make him or her far more memorable for the group. Collective memories will be far more resilient if they are attached to specific names.

Group Prototypes, Time and Collective Memory

It is now necessary to integrate our discussion of prototypes and exemplars in social identity theory with the views just expressed on the role of time and collective memory in this theory. This is an area where there has been, as yet, little theoretical elaboration by social psychologists, although the fact that some of them have begun analysing historical documents (even if so far only from the recent past) is an encouraging sign of growing interest in this area.[46] We have already noted Marco Cinnirella's suggestion that

---

44 For this characteristic of stereotypes, see Oakes, Haslam and Turner 1994, pp. 211–13.

45 See Brown 2000, pp. 285–90.

46 See Reicher and Hopkins 1996.

groups sometimes understand themselves and their situation by reference to 'possible social identities', meaning those identities that they believe they have had in the past or consider that they may have in the future. Such a suggestion highlights the intersection between a group's (context-dependent) sense of itself and how it is oriented to time. This induces us to make a proposal of fundamental importance for how we will interpret the Lazarus narrative in the Fourth Gospel: *since the representation of social categories is often achieved by the use of prototypes and exemplars, it is likely that the postulation of possible past or future social identities will also employ such means.*[47]

Abundant empirical evidence confirms this proposal. Groups very commonly attach their identities to outstanding members from the past, now dead, but whose remembrance lives on among the membership. Within a social identity framework, a person aiming at leadership of a group in a given context needs to be maximally representative of the shared social identity and consensual position of the group, that is, to approximate as near as possible to a prototype or exemplar of the group.[48] Similarly, a figure from the past will be accepted as a group prototype or exemplar if he or she is regarded as having represented the group identity to the maximum extent. This may happen if the figure concerned is maximally representative of one or more group beliefs – including its values and norms, goals and ideology. Thus, among of the people of Afghanistan, Shah Masood, the highly successful guerilla (nicknamed 'the Lion of the Panshir') who stood up to the Soviet invasion and the Taliban, and who was murdered in September 2001, is coming to be treated as someone who exemplifies the whole nation. Winston Churchill already serves a similar role among the British, and Charles de Gaulle among the French. To Christians, Jesus is an exemplar who straddles past, present (cf. Matt. 28.20) and future, although his role is much greater than this, given his additional status as an object of faith along with the Father.

On the other hand, if a person belongs to the legendary past

---

47 For an exploration of this proposal in relation to the figure of Abraham in Romans 4, see Esler 2003, pp. 171–94.

48 For a detailed exploration of this approach in relation to Paul's communicative strategy in Romans 7, especially his use of the 'I-voice', see Esler 2003, pp. 222–42.

of a people, say an Abraham or a Roland,[49] whereas the ingroup members who accept his or her real existence will esteem the person as (what we are calling) an exemplar, a detached observer will employ the concept of prototype, since the subject is an imagined not a real person. In the figure of Arthur as 'the once and future king' we have a prototype of Britishness who encompasses the past and the future.[50]

Marco Cinnirella has observed that the choice of prototypes and exemplars will be affected by the temporal orientation of the ingroup. He cites, as an example of an orientation to the past, the way in which, during a 1996 European football championship, elements of the British tabloid media used images and discourse from World War Two in relation to England's match against Germany (with English soccer players dressed in military attire, for example).[51] This phenomenon induces us to expect that groups originating in cultures that treasure the past – for example, those that engage in the veneration of ancestors – and that are not oriented to the future in the manner typical of modern Western society will *a fortiori* choose as prototypes people from the past, especially real or imagined former members. There is little doubt that Mediterranean culture in the first century CE was traditional in this sense, with ancestors and ancestral practices being revered everywhere. In addition, its prevailing concepts of time were more focused on the present and the past than on the future.[52]

To raise the question of prototypes or exemplars being selected from among outstanding former members of a group constitutes one facet of adopting an emphasis on social life as a temporal trajectory rather than as a static set of positions, which, as we have just seen, constitutes a recent elaboration of social identity theory. In this new perspective, social life is a reality in which members of various groups assume identities, ideas and practices and transfer them to others, frequently transforming them in the process.[53] People generally appreciate that the groups to which they belong are phenomena in history, stretching backwards in time and reaching forward into the future.

---

49 For the problems in the way of asserting a historical basis for Abraham in the second millennium BCE, see Van Seters 1975.

50 This is the title of the novel by T. H. White.

51 Cinnirella 1998, p. 232. The British team lost the game.

52 See Malina 1989a, reprinted in Malina 1996, pp. 179–214.

53 Condor 1996, pp. 289–91.

All this leads us to propose that the collective memory of a group is frequently stored in and, at times, manipulated through appeal to, or the creation of, exemplary or prototypical figures from the past. These figures, who will inevitably represent group beliefs, are employed to mobilize memory for particular purposes in the life of the community in the present in ways that are central to its ongoing experience and its understanding of what it will be in the future. Group prototypes and exemplars from the past tell the members who they are, what they should believe and who they should become. They represent the sheer factuality of belonging to a group like this, the emotional dimensions of such belonging and the extent that they are differentiated from outgroups (usually by superiority over them) in having heroes such as these. In short, prototypes and exemplars epitomize the experience and value of membership. One senses the presence of all of these aspects, for example, in the attitude of the Judeans who have come out to John the Baptist: 'We have Abraham as our father' (Matt. 3.9; Luke 3.8). We can add to this, however, that prototypes and exemplars provide invaluable models for self-categorizations by group members whenever social identity is salient. By aligning themselves as closely as possible with these figures from the past, the current members approximate to prototypical representatives of their ingroup category.

Again, however, we must remember that the context-oriented nature of prototypical and exemplary figures cautions against any absolute, static or constant understanding of their force and effect. As already noted, in any social setting individuals and groups are at odds over what people and events in the past are significant in the present and over the nature of any claimed significance. These disagreements are likely to be most extreme in the common situation where different groups spring from the same tradition with its stock of prototypes and exemplars. Where this happens, the past can become a field of fierce social contest, with each group claiming 'ownership' of these heroes (real or imagined from the past) and enlisting them in support of its vision of reality. This is an example of the 'processing of the past' mentioned above. Prototypes and exemplars then assume a central role in the processes of intergroup comparison and discrimination. Thus, the heroine in the Book of Judith arguably constitutes an attempt by its author, using a fictional character, to redefine what it meant to be an Israelite in the period 150–50 BCE.[54] In the New Testament, Abraham is a frequent focus of such activity. Even in relation to the statement concerning Abraham just mentioned, John the Baptist immediately acts to undercut the Judeans' boast of Abrahamic descent by pointing to the possibility of any entirely different lineage from this illustrious ancestor: 'I tell you, God is able from these stones to raise up children to Abraham' (Matt. 3.9; Luke 3.8). Similarly, Paul seeks to enlist Abraham as the ancestor of non-Judean Christ-followers in both Galatians and Romans in ways that would have been regarded as outlandish, if not scandalous, by Judeans not connected with the Christ-movement.[55]

The Broad Applicability of Social Identity to the Fourth Gospel

The broad relevance of social identity theory to the Fourth Gospel is easily demonstrated. The text is directed to a very distinctive group that sees itself existing in a state of pronounced tension with some other outgroups. The evangelist refers to these outsiders collectively as the *kosmos*, a word he uses nearly 80 times and very often with the meaning 'society alienated from God'.[56] Such a description represents an example of stereotyping of outgroups. On many occasions he also designates certain outsiders as *Ioudaioi*, a subject on which there is now a very large body of secondary literature.[57] Perhaps the most damning reference to *Ioudaioi* comes in John 8.44 when the Johannine Jesus describes certain Judeans as having had the Devil as their father.[58] Although ancient Mediterranean culture was group-oriented in a way that

---

54 For the Book of Judith interpreted in this light, see Esler 2002.

55 On the presentation of Abraham in Galatians, see Esler 2006c. Paul's position in Romans is, however, less extreme than in Galatians, inasmuch as he makes clear in Romans 4 that Abraham is also the ancestor of Judeans and Judean Christ-followers, something that was left highly obscure in Galatians – see Esler 2003, pp. 180–94.

56 See Elliott 2000, p. 863.

57 See Appendix 1 for references to a selection of this discussion.

58 For a discussion of the exchange between Jesus and these Judeans in John 8.31–59 in terms of the Mediterranean cultural pattern of challenge-and-response, see Esler 1994, pp. 84–90.

readily encouraged the activation of forces of social comparison and discrimination between groups, the Fourth Gospel constitutes a notable example of this process.

So replete, indeed, is this Gospel with material relating to the profound differentiation between the wider society and the followers of Jesus, beginning as early as John 1.10–12, that Bruce Malina has usefully adopted from sociolinguistics the phrase 'anti-society' to designate the latter and 'anti-language' to describe the extraordinarily repetitious language employed by Jesus in his discourses.[59] These penetrating insights have been fruitfully developed by Malina and Richard Rohrbaugh in their social-scientific commentary on this Gospel.[60] John 15.19 well illustrates these dimensions of the text: 'If you were of the *kosmos*, the *kosmos* would love its own; but because you are not of the *kosmos*, but I chose you out of the *kosmos*, therefore the *kosmos* hates you.'

The cognitive, emotional and evaluative aspects of belonging to a group, which Tajfel highlighted, are all very much alive in the Johannine picture. While all of John's intended readers were individuals, the social identity, that is, those aspects of their sense of self which they derived from belonging to a group such as this, would have been a powerful one, especially if its salience in their lives had been promoted by events such as expulsion from the synagogues, which the Johannine Jesus predicts will be their fate in John 16.2. External pressures such as these frequently induce members of groups to categorize themselves more in terms of their group memberships than the personal and idiosyncratic components of their sense of self.

The relationship of beliefs to the social identity derived from belonging to the Johannine group is also apparent in the Fourth Gospel and, as we will see, in John 11 especially. This part of the text highlights beliefs relating to mutual love, faith, resurrection and eternal life. These are central enough to qualify as 'group beliefs' within the meaning set out above. They are certainly functional for group formation and maintenance in that they differentiate the ingroup from outgroups and they are sufficiently prominent and distinctive to keep a firm grip on the attention

59 Malina 1985.
60 Malina and Rohrbaugh 1998.

of ingroup members. In addition, they are all advocated by the 'epistemic authority' of this group, Jesus himself. We will suggest below, in fact, that the Christological dimensions of John 11 primarily serve to substantiate these beliefs as group beliefs by providing them with an unassailable epistemic warrant.

Time, Memory and Identity

John situates his audience in an all-encompassing chronological framework. This begins before the creation of the cosmos, with the mutual existence of God and the Word (John 1.1–2; 17.24). It enters a critical phase with certain past, but comparatively recent events – the arrival of Jesus, his formation of a group of followers and his departure and the coming of the Counsellor (*paraklētos*; 14.16, 26; 15.26; 16.7). This timespan continues in the present, with the ongoing experience of the Counsellor. Finally, it extends into the future, to Jesus' preparation of a place whither he will take his own (14.1–4) and to the general resurrection – to life (eternal life, presumably) for those who have done good and to judgement for those who have done evil (John 5.28–9). The Johannine group is one which has a past, a present and a future,[61] and the identity it provided to its members must be seen in this perspective. By using the genre of Gospel, however, rather than, say, an apocalypse speaking of the end times, John has been able to provide some information bearing upon the future of the group, while being necessarily more ample in the representation of vital elements of the group's past. The Gospel form allows the evangelist to establish a sense of connection between his listeners/readers and the ingroup representatives who have roles in the narrative. This was the case even though his audience would have assumed that some of those characters, Jesus most notably, or most of them (if the Fourth Gospel is dated to the 90s) had already died when the Johannine audience first encountered this Gospel. The audience knew that they were part of a group that pre-dated them in the form of the characters in the narrative referred to by John. The ingroup characters in the Fourth Gospel served to provide its original audience with examples from the

61 It is, however, the future element that has been underplayed by many commentators who stress a 'realized eschatology' in the Fourth Gospel.

times of the group's formation, with modes of human life available within a group like this, in short, with 'possible selves'.

By composing such a text, the evangelist was supplying his group with the stuff from which collective memories are made. He was equipping them with a permanent *aide-memoire* of their first predecessors in the group and their experience, which would be available to nourish the life of the community in the present and the future. He was shaping and mobilizing their collective memory for particular purposes relevant to their ongoing experience and to their understanding of who they were and would become. Yet at this time there were other interpretations of this period in existence in the communities of Christ-followers scattered around the Mediterranean – certainly the Gospel of Mark, and possibly also those of Matthew and Luke – that provided different (and probably rival) accounts. The way that John processed the past reflected competition among the various groups constituting the Christ-movement. They each sought to speak with the most authentic voice of the times of its origin and the truth of its message in order to maintain their identity and status.

This brings us to the final issues from our model, the nature of prototypes and exemplars and how they feature in the collective memories of a group in ways adapted to expressing or modifying its social identity. At this point we can merely state that the text provides rich data for investigation within such a perspective, as we will see in later chapters of this volume.

So far in this chapter we have been concerned to set out and assess the usefulness of certain social-scientific theories in understanding the meaning John conveyed to his original audience. But how can we employ insights so derived from a historical analysis of the Gospel in order to assist present-day Christians who wish to enrich their own experience and identity and to deepen their beliefs in how God deals with men and women? This brings us to the theological dimension. Here we will rely on the broad approach to New Testament theology one of us has set out at length recently.[62]

62 See Esler 2005a.

Intercultural Communion with John, our Ancestor in Faith

There can be no underestimating the cultural, as well as chronological and geographic, gap that separates us from those, including John, who produced the 27 documents of the New Testament. Yet we should not be paralysed by this gap, since we are now familiar with the possibility of communicating with people who are culturally different from us, that is, with the possibility of intercultural communication, using techniques to help us shed some of our ethnocentricity in these engagements. At the same time, a recognition of the cultural distance necessitates that we always maintain a critical stance in relation to what these people might be saying to us. In some respects, their acceptance of slavery for example, it is clear that the ways of those who produced the New Testament are not our ways.

Nevertheless, we are able to model our relationship with the New Testament authors like John. When we attempt to understand in the fullest historical detail what message they conveyed to their contemporaries we are attending to them in a manner for which Martin Buber's 'I–thou' relationship provides an appropriate basis. We are engaging in a form of dialogue which, like all true dialogue, allows the possibility of disagreement. At its best, such dialogue, in spite of its intercultural dimension, embodies profound interpersonal communion. If it is suggested that all this entails searching for the 'authorial intention', which is for many a quite illicit notion, we will reply that this catchphrase only has relevance to 'literary' texts. When the New Testament is being read in a specifically Christian and theological context, it is a fundamental category error to view it as a 'literary text' for which the intention of the author is unimportant. Instead, the New Testament documents, including the Fourth Gospel (most clearly in 20.31), make direct demands upon us and push us to adopt certain beliefs and patterns of behaviour. If we were reading a novel today and we discovered a similar strategy on the part of its author, we might well throw down the novel in disgust. Clearly, a novel might draw upon pressing issues that feature in the imaginative universe it creates. Our point is that *if the novelist was pushing us to accept a programme he or she was mounting in relation to these issues* we would regard the novel as flawed.[63] Yet this is precisely what John tells us he was doing in 20.31. Moreover, if an interlocutor objects that the notion of interpersonal communion makes no sense if one of the parties is dead, we will reply that communications from deceased relatives and friends are regularly treasured in our memories in a sufficient manner for such communion to achieve a vivid reality. Taking the discussion further (although it is not necessary for the point) entails appealing to a high theology of the communion of saints present in the Church from the ancient period.[64] Put simply, when we read John's Gospel for an expressly Christian purpose, to have its message fertilize our Christian life and identity, we are entering into intercultural communication and communion with John. We seek to absorb his meaning – as one who is alive in our memories or even in some more profound ontological sense – in the full force of its historical specificity. While retaining our critical faculties in relation to what we hear him saying, we will let the power of his words energize our existence because of rather than in spite of their strangeness to us. His message shaped the identity in-Christ of his own local audience and now it can shape ours.[65]

Conclusion

We must now begin to apply this model that integrates social identity theory with sociological ideas on collective memory to the text. Central to our argument will be a case for Lazarus, Martha and Mary as prototypes of the identity of Johannine Christ-followers in the first century CE and, within the theological framework just set out, for contemporary Christians. We will

---

63 For a fuller exposition of the non-literary character of the Gospels and the importance of authorial intention in the communication of their messages, see Esler 2005a, pp. 88–118.

64 See Esler 2005a, pp. 229–54. Esler makes clear, however, that Christians who are uncomfortable with such a high theology of the communion of saints will find in memory adequate support for the type of intercultural communication and communion he has in mind (see Esler 2005a, pp. 217–28).

65 The material in the last two paragraphs summarizes some of the main themes in Esler 2005a.

also argue that early support for our approach exists in Christian art from the third and fourth centuries CE, in particular, the depictions of Lazarus in the frescoes and sarcophagus reliefs from the catacombs in Rome.

3

Johannine Processing of the Past in Relation to Lazarus, Mary and Martha

Contesting Memory and Processing the Past

In setting out our model in Chapter 2, we noted that in any given context individuals and groups are likely to be in dispute over what people and events in the past are significant in the present and over the nature of any claimed significance. Memory is the primary field for such a contest. As Jeffrey Olick has pointed out, 'memory is never unitary, no matter how hard various powers strive to make it so. There are always subnarratives, transitional periods, and contests over dominance.'[1] In relation to such contests, Francesca Polletta, speaking of how Martin Luther King is variously remembered in the US Congress, has observed that collective memory as it is deployed in relation to claims to the stewardship of an insurgent past can be a crucial terrain for fighting out claims for leadership between groups.[2] Wherever groups spring from a common tradition that has a repertoire of exemplary and prototypical figures (including both the founder and his immediate followers), these disagreements may be quite extreme. Thus the past and how it is remembered become a battleground, with the competing groups claiming 'ownership' of (real or imagined) heroes from the past and 'processing' them in ways that will support their rival visions of reality. These processes are evident when one considers the subjects of this volume – 'Lazarus', 'Mary' and 'Martha' as they are presented in

1 Olick 2003, p. 8.

2 Polletta 2003, p. 220.

Chapters 11 and 12 of John's Gospel – in comparison with how these figures (and other persons) and the incidents in which they appear are portrayed in the Synoptic Gospels.

It is worth reiterating here that this represents a new methodological approach to the Fourth Gospel. For we are not about to compare John with Matthew, Mark and Luke as an exercise in source criticism (although we will occasionally have to express some views on the question of sources). Nor are we attempting to say something about the historical Jesus (although we will need at times to weigh up the historicity of some of the traditions). Furthermore, it goes without saying that in undertaking such a comparison we are diverging from narrative critical approaches, which can proceed solely with reference to what *John* has written.

What is our purpose then? We are certainly interested in the final form of the Fourth Gospel as we have it. Nevertheless, because our methodology involves the assessment of how John develops and maintains an identity for the members of his version of the Christ-movement, in large part through an exploration of the distinctive manner in which he has contested shared memories concerning Jesus and his first followers, it is essential that we look to other evidence for the evolving collective memory of the movement close to him in time. For distinctiveness is a relative concept – something is distinctive only in comparison with other data. For our purposes this other data is found, for the most part, in the Synoptic Gospels.

As we made clear in Chapter 1, our focus of interest in this volume comprises the entirety of the material in the Johannine Gospel that features Martha and Mary and Lazarus; they figure explicitly in the section from John 11.1 to John 12.19 and, we will argue, their presence is implied in connection with what happens to Jesus' body in John 19. The dominant feature of this material for the purpose of the current discussion is the way the evangelist integrates the story of the raising of Lazarus (whose anointing, importantly, and for reasons we will explain below, is not described) in John 11 with the anointing of Jesus – in this Gospel performed by Lazarus' sister Mary – in John 12.1–8 and then by Joseph of Arimathea and Nicodemus in John 19.38–42. In addition, we will need to consider how the raising of Lazarus contributes to bringing about the death of Jesus and thus serves the purpose of Johannine plot development. In our view, the integration of the accounts of the raising of Lazarus and the anointing of Jesus *by Mary* provide important clues for interpreting the rationale for and manner of the evangelist's manipulation of the collective memory of the Christ-movement in the interests of advocating his particular vision of its identity.

The main comparative data encompass four areas. First, there are accounts of other revivifications of deceased persons by Jesus in the Synoptic Gospels.[3] Second, there is the passage concerning Jesus' visit to Martha and Mary in Luke 10.38–42 and, third, the mention of one 'Lazarus' in Luke 16.19–31. Fourth, we have the tradition of Jesus being anointed by an unnamed woman in Mark (with a close parallel in Matthew) and the very different anointing of Jesus by an equally unnamed woman in Luke 7.36–50. We will now deal with each of these four bodies of material in turn, with our aim being in each case to engage in a comparison with the material concerning Lazarus, Martha and Mary in the Fourth Gospel within the framework of social identity and collective memory set out in the previous chapter. First we will consider similarities between the Synoptic material and the relevant features in John 11—12 and then move on to the question of the differences. The real interest lies with the differences, given that we are concerned with the distinctive way John has processed the past and manipulated collective memories of the Christ-movement in his presentation of Lazarus, Martha and Mary.

Similarities with the Synoptic Tradition

Jesus' Raising of Other Persons from the Dead in the Synoptic Tradition

Parallels to the raising of Lazarus in John's Gospel can be drawn with the raising of Jairus' (unnamed) daughter in Mark 5.22–43 and the widow's (equally unnamed) son at Nain in Luke 7.11–17, but not to the characters in these passages. The second account is from Luke's special material. In both of these cases, admittedly, the person was only recently dead and had not yet been buried,

3 There is another revivification in the alleged 'Secret Gospel of Mark', but see below for recent suspicion concerning this alleged document.

but they still share with John 11 the picture of a Jesus who could produce raising of the dead.

The 'Secret Gospel of Mark', allegedly discovered by Morton Smith in a letter attributed to Clement of Alexandria (*c.* 200 CE), also contains a revivification narrative. We mention this document here because others have brought it into the discussion. The recent study by S. C. Carlson suggests that this document was conceived as a modern hoax.[4] This document, purportedly to be located between Mark 10.34 and 35, describes how Jesus effected a revivification from the dead (at the request of his unnamed sister) of an unnamed wealthy young man in Bethany.[5] The man is then said to 'love' Jesus. As Moody Smith notes, if this document were genuine, it could represent an earlier version of the Lazarus story or something very like it,[6] since in John 11 Jesus in Bethany raises a man from the dead at the behest of his sisters. However, Carlson's analysis demonstrates that serious doubts now attend the likelihood that this tradition is authentic.

---

4 See Carlson 2005, especially pp. 68–71 and 81–6 with respect to the revivification story. For a defence of its authenticity, but based on a much narrower range of evidence than that considered by Carlson, see the recent article by Hedrick and Olympiou (2000). They argue for its authenticity on a number of grounds, but especially in reliance on colour photographs of the letter of Clement taken after Smith's visit by the then librarian of the library where the document was supposedly found. Carlson responds to their findings at several points in his book.

5 See Smith 1973 on the 'Secret Gospel of Mark'. Smith 'translates' the relevant passage of this document as follows: 'And they come into Bethany. And a certain woman whose brother had died was there. And, coming, she prostrated herself before Jesus and says to him, "Son of David, have mercy on me." But the disciples rebuked her. And Jesus, being angered, went off with her into the garden where the tomb was, and straightway a great cry was heard from the tomb. And going near Jesus rolled away the stone from the door of the tomb. And straightway going in where the youth was, he stretched forth his hand and raised him, seizing his hand. But the youth, looking upon him, loved him and began to beseech him that he might be with him. And going out of the tomb they came into the house of the youth for he was rich.' (Smith 1973, p. 447)

6 Smith 1999, pp. 216–17.

Mary and Martha in Luke 10.38–42

Mary and Martha only appear elsewhere in Luke 10.38–42, although they seem to have no male relatives, as none is mentioned as receiving Jesus into the house or in attending to him when he is there. The shock inflicted on first-century Mediterranean values by the Lucan Jesus leaving his disciples behind (Luke 10.38) to visit two women, apparently alone, to whom he is not said to have been related, has been analysed recently by Jane Boyd and Philip Esler.[7] Although Luke does not name the village in which they lived, the geographical sequence in which he places this incident, forming part of Jesus' journey to Jerusalem that began at Luke 9.51, suggests it was located in Galilee or Samaria.[8] In Luke 10.38–42 it seems likely that Martha is the older sister, as she is the one who receives Jesus into the house. Martha, famously, attends to the meal while her sister Mary sits at Jesus' feet and listens to his teaching. In response to Martha's complaint that Jesus is unconcerned that Mary has left her to serve alone, Jesus replies, 'Martha, Martha, you are anxious and troubled about many things; one thing is needful. Mary has chosen the good portion, which shall not be taken away from her' (10.41–42; RSV).[9]

There are certain similarities between Luke's Martha and Mary and John's. First of all, John also seems to present Martha as the older sister. The principal sign of this is that when Jesus is on his way back to Bethany, it is Martha who goes to meet him (presumably because he has sent a messenger to her house), whereas Mary only learns of his arrival later.[10] In addition, it is Martha who serves at table during the meal in chapter 12 (John 12.2)! The second similarity is that Martha is the down-to-earth sister, whereas Mary is given to more florid displays of devotion to Jesus, either sitting at his feet to hear him teach (as in Luke) or anointing his feet with precious ointment (as in John).

---

7 See Boyd and Esler 2004, pp. 22–30.

8 Also see Brown 1966, p. 422.

9 See Boyd and Esler 2004 for the argument that in his 1618 CE painting of *Kitchen Scene with Christ in the House of Martha and Mary*, Velázquez has depicted a very disconsolate, seventeenth-century Sevillean serving-girl in the foreground whose unhappiness is compounded by her imagining this biblical scene in which Jesus himself had devalued the activity of someone such as her.

10 See John 11.20 and 11.28.

Lazarus in Luke 16.19–31

What about Lazarus? One of the surprises of John 11 is the fact that a close relationship between Jesus and Lazarus seems to be presupposed from the start, even though no earlier reference to Lazarus or his sisters can be found in the Gospel. While it is possible that the initial recipients of the Fourth Gospel already had knowledge of Martha and Mary from traditions outside of the Gospel, can the same be held to be true for a figure 'Lazarus of Bethany'? Not surprisingly, some scholars are attracted to finding a link with Luke's special material for Lazarus as well as the sisters, based on the fact that the only other 'Lazarus' in the Gospel tradition is the beggar of that name found in Luke 16.19–31 who was taken up to the bosom of Abraham when he died.

But do the Lucan Lazarus and the Johannine Lazarus have anything more in common than their name, which is a shortened form of Eleazar, a name that ossuary inscriptions show to have been common in New Testament times?[11] Eleazar is also the name of the son of Aaron and priestly leader of the Levites responsible for care of the sanctuary (Num. 3.32). He was with Aaron when Aaron died on the mountaintop and assumed the vestments of Aaron (Num. 20.25ff.). This common background does little, however, to elucidate the portrayals of either the Lazarus of Luke 16 or the Lazarus of John 11—12. Nor does it offer a link between the two.

One intriguing connection depends on what is said at the end of the Lucan account. Here the rich man suggests that if Lazarus is sent from the dead to speak to his sinful brothers they will repent (Luke 16.27–30). But Abraham replies, 'If they do not hear Moses and the prophets, neither will they be convinced if some one should rise from the dead' (Luke 16.31). It could be argued, therefore, that in John 11 the evangelist has confirmed the truth of what Abraham says – by bringing a man called Lazarus back from the dead who fails to convince some of the Judeans (cf. John 11. 46). In short, 'Did John turn Luke's parable into a story concerning a raising from the dead?'[12] But this suggestion presupposes John's familiarity precisely with this ending of the Lucan story probably

11 Brown 1966, p. 422.
12 Smith 1999, p. 217.

in literary form and his responding to it. The actual reference to someone rising from the dead in Luke 16.31 comes, however, in a section (16.27–31) that appears to be a secondary feature in the parable's development.[13] This in itself does not preclude John's knowledge of the story, but further arguments given below will suggest that this is unlikely.

Another possible link to Lazarus in the Third Gospel has been identified by Michael Labahn. He argues that the name Lazarus, a figure known to early Jesus-followers, has also possibly introduced from Luke an ethical dimension to the story used by the Fourth Gospel. By employing the name Lazarus, he suggests that one might be encouraged to think in terms of Jesus' love for the poor and (also from the parable in Luke 16.19–31) of judgement upon the world, even though the Fourth Evangelist certainly introduced additional themes.[14] This seems an improbable scenario. Apart from Labahn's reliance on the 'Secret Gospel of Mark',[15] whose authenticity is disputed as we have mentioned above, we must query how far one can have confidence that a distinguishing feature of the name 'Lazarus' (one that would have contributed to the understanding of such a prototype by early Jesus-followers) is his status as one who is destitute.[16]

First, John gives mixed signals about whether previous familiarity with Lazarus should be presupposed. Even though Jesus'

---

13 For the widely held view that 16.27–31 is an appended conclusion to the parable, see the discussion in Scott 1989, pp. 141–59.

14 Labahn 1999, pp. 456–7, 464–5. Labahn does not, however, consider Lazarus a *persona dramatis* or representative figure in the Fourth Gospel on the grounds that the evangelist is more concerned with the fate of Lazarus than with his person (p. 390).

15 While cognizant of the problems surrounding the 'Secret Gospel of Mark', Labahn speculates that these various traditions may indicate an early formulation of a revivification story in which the ill man was unnamed. He then suggests that the name Lazarus was added under the influence of an early version of the parable in Luke 16 in which a poor man Lazarus was taken up to Abraham.

16 Our results are at some variance also with the recent study by Hunter (2002), in that he argues that 'the community of the Gospel of John is a "community of the poor" that is profoundly defensive in its relationship to those outside the community' (2002, p. 250). He argues his case primarily in relationship to Judas and Nicodemus rather than Lazarus.

love for Lazarus implies earlier contact in terms of the ministry of Jesus, the evangelist's introduction of Lazarus as 'A certain man, Lazarus of Bethany, was ill' (John 11.1) does not seem to presuppose any earlier acquaintance of *the readers/hearers* with the figure.[17]

Second, the absence of any clues to the destitution of Lazarus in the Johannine narrative, and indeed the presence of contrary indications, cast in doubt John's having associated such connotations with Lazarus. Specifically, while the Lazarus in Luke 16 seems too destitute to have a burial worth mention and seems to be without any human support, being targeted even by stray dogs, the Lazarus in the Johannine story has been wrapped and placed in a tomb, probably after anointing. Such tombs cost money. Moreover, these sisters are far from destitute themselves, with one of them having access to costly ointment with which to anoint Jesus later (John 12.3). The topic of the destitute is certainly raised in the anointing episode in John, but is dealt with in a way that is closer to Matthew and Mark than to Luke. It is here that Jesus declares, 'The destitute you always have with you, but you do not always have me' (John 12.8; cf. Mark 14.7 and Matt. 26.11). According to Malina and Rohrbaugh, such a saying is typical of limited good societies, meaning that you never solve the problem of destitution.[18] These considerations must surely suggest that the name Lazarus no longer (if ever) preserved for John connotations of destitution and of Jesus' love for the destitute.[19]

The Anointing of Jesus

There are two distinct stories of a woman anointing Jesus in the Synoptic Gospels, in Mark 14.3–9 (compare Matt. 26.6–13) and in Luke 7.36–50. Although these are very different, there are similarities between both of them and the account in John 12.1–8.

The important features of the Marcan passage are as follows. It

17 Rightly, Sproston North 2001, p. 121.

18 Malina and Rohrbaugh 1998, pp. 204–6. Malina and Rohrbaugh suggest that Mary of Bethany must be a rather wealthy mistress of the house.

19 For another theory of the link between Luke's story of Lazarus and John's story of Lazarus, see Busse 1992 and the reservations of Hakola 1999, pp. 234–5, n.26.

was two days before the Passover and the Feast of the Unleavened Bread: 'And while he was at Bethany in the house of Simon the leper, as he sat at table, a woman came with an alabaster flask of ointment of pure nard, very costly, and she broke the flask and poured it over his head' (14.3; RSV). Some of the disciples were angry and reproached the woman, since the perfume could have been sold for more than 300 denarii and the money given to the destitute (*ptōchoi*; 14.4–5). As Mark had earlier indicated that 200 denarii would have been enough to provided a meal for 5,000 men (Mark 6.37, 44), we can see the scale of the problem. But Jesus defended the woman, telling them to leave her alone, on the grounds that they would have the destitute with them always but not him, that she had anointed his body beforehand for burial and that what she had done would be told in the whole world in memory of her. Immediately afterwards, Judas Iscariot went off to the high priests in order to betray Jesus (Mark 14.10–11; cf. Matt. 26.14–16).

The Lucan narrative (Luke 7.36–50) occurs during the Galilean ministry of Jesus in the house of Simon (a Pharisee). It is worth noting that the raising of the son of the widow of Nain occurs in the same section of this Gospel (7.11–17), so that we have a similar order of events to John 11 and 12, namely, a raising to life by Jesus, other events and dialogue, and then a meal at which Jesus is anointed. In Luke, a sinful and unnamed woman with 'an alabaster jar of ointment' (7.37; RSV) weeps on Jesus' feet, dries them with her hair and then anoints them with the oinment. Simon has critical thoughts towards Jesus, because he has not realized she is a sinner, but Jesus rebukes him and forgives the woman.

The relationship between the accounts of the anointing in Mark and Luke, especially the marked differences between them, has prompted a variety of explanations, which we must briefly note, as they bear upon how John treats this incident. A. Legault, adapting an idea of P. Benoit, proposed that two separate incidents had occurred.[20] One incident occurred in Galilee at the house of a Pharisee, which consisted of a penitent sinner entering and weeping in Jesus' presence, with tears falling on his feet that she hastily wipes away. No anointing with perfume occurred in this scene. This lies behind the Lucan version. The second

20 Legault 1954.

incident occurs in Bethany in the house of Simon the Leper where a woman (named Mary) uses her expensive ointment to anoint Jesus' head as an expression of love for him. Raymond Brown followed Legault here, especially for the reason that the positing of two incidents had the advantage of respecting the totally different nature and purpose of the two scenes in Luke and Mark. But Brown was unwise to favour this explanation. The simplest solution to doublets or triplets of this type is to assume that one incident underlies them all. Thus, C. H. Dodd argued for one basic incident lying behind all three accounts.[21]

There is, in addition, a compelling reason why Luke could not have tolerated the version in Mark: its insouciance towards the destitute, that is beggars (*hoi ptōchoi*). Luke, as Philip Esler has argued,[22] has a very well developed theology of poverty that fixes upon the fact of Jesus proclaiming good news to *ptōchoi*, as in Luke 4.18; 6.20; 7.22; 14.13 and 21; 16.20 and 22; 18.22 and 19.8. Luke must have found it impossible to reconcile Jesus' easy dismissal of the needs of the destitute and the waste of enough money to give 7,500 men a meal with the concern his Jesus expresses for the needs of beggars. On the other hand, he must have been attracted by the powerful imagery of a woman who comes into a room and anoints Jesus. His solution to the dilemma is to bring the story back into the Galilean ministry of Jesus, to change the woman into a penitent sinner who is thus weeping, to remove any reference to the value of the ointment she is using and to eliminate reference to the relationship between its value and the needs of the destitute. Even so, he still retains 'Simon' as the name of the home-owner.

In John 12.1–8 the meal takes place in Bethany (as in Mark). Although the particular house is not specified, it is probably that of Lazarus, Martha and Mary, since Martha (and Martha alone) serves at table, Lazarus is reclining at table and Mary is mentioned as present, without any explanation. Similar to the Marcan account, a woman (here specified as Mary) anoints Jesus with expensive perfume to the value of 300 denarii. Judas complains that the perfume could have been sold and the money given to the destitute. Jesus defends the woman, saying (to Judas presumably)

21 Dodd 1963, pp. 162–73.
22 See Esler 1987, pp. 164–200.

to leave her alone, for the perfume is for his burial and they have the destitute (*ptōchoi*) with them always, but not him. Judas is angry and there is an aside to the effect that he was the one to betray Jesus, which is somewhat similar to the Marcan detail of his departure immediately after the anointing to betray Jesus. As in the Lucan account, however, the woman anoints Jesus on the feet, not the head, and, most strikingly, wipes his feet with her hair.

Conclusion on Similarities

From a consideration of how these four areas of evidence in the Synoptic Gospels are similar in many respects to what we find in John 11 and 12, it is difficult not to conclude that there are common traditions being used by various evangelists here or that they have influenced one another in some way or another. J. N. Sanders argued that John actually represented a version independent of Luke (and of Mark too) with as good or better a title to be closest to the facts,[23] but this seems less likely than that one evangelist knew the other or, perhaps more likely, they both had access to some similar oral traditions. Certainly John is not working wholly independently of other traditions. These similarities seem to indicate some connection between the Johannine tradition on the one hand and the Lucan and Marcan traditions on the other. Specifying the nature of any such influence or dependence, whether it is simply because one has read the Gospel of another or is aware of versions of the Gospels or the traditions that led to them in forms that are no longer available to us, is virtually impossible to say and upon which we do not wish to speculate. Over all attempts to find a direct dependence of John on Luke, or of Luke on John,[24] or of John on Mark,[25] we pronounce the verdict known in Scottish law, 'Not proven.'

It is clear from all of these comparisons that John's use of any sources or traditions is far from slavish. This is, in part, what makes it so difficult to reach firm decisions about his sources. The differences are at least as pronounced as the points of similarity.

---

23 Sanders 1954–5.
24 See Coakley 1988 and Shellard 2002.
25 See Bauckham 1998c.

These differences are, moreover, of particular interest in revealing his determination to reshape the memory of the group to serve the needs of his addressees in the present.

Differences from the Synoptic Tradition: Johannine Processing of the Past

Mary and the Bethany Connection

We begin with a detail of the text that is very often the subject of comment. After stating at the beginning of Chapter 11 that 'Now a certain man was ill, Lazarus of Bethany, the village of Mary and her sister Martha', John continues: 'It was Mary who anointed the Lord with ointment and wiped his feet with her hair, whose brother Lazarus was sick' (11.2). To C. K. Barrett, speaking of the anointing by Mary, it is clear that the evangelist 'is able to presuppose that his readers were already familiar with it; this implies that they were Christians and knew the Synoptic tradition'.[26] To many critics, on the other hand, this is an awkward feature. Typical is the remark of Brown: 'This verse is clearly a parenthesis added by an editor: it refers to a scene in ch. xii that has not yet been narrated . . .'[27]

We consider both of these views unfounded. To our mind, John 11.2 represents an audacious attempt by the evangelist to rework the collective memory of the Christ-movement. He achieves this by integrating his unique story of Lazarus, Martha and Mary, a brother and his two sisters, itself a congeries of pre-existing elements and Johannine creation for which there exists no precedent in the tradition, with a story well known to Christ-followers of his time – the anointing of Jesus by a woman with very expensive perfume in Bethany shortly before his death. It is difficult to understate the significance of John taking the tradition of a woman, whose very name was unknown, who anointed Jesus shortly before his death (which we find in Mark 14.3–9, also in Bethany but localized in the house of Simon the Leper) and identifying this woman with Mary, sister of Martha and Lazarus

26 Barrett 1978, p. 390.

27 Brown 1966, p. 423.

(John 11.2; 12.3).[28] There is no reason to think that this connection was already known to his readers; we consider it more likely that he invented it for the purpose of his Gospel and introduced it at 11.2 to pave the way for 12.1–9. Nor should we follow Brown in seeing John 11.2 as a parenthesis added by an editor. Rather, it reflects a deliberate decision by the evangelist of great moment for the message he wished to communicate in this section of the Gospel.

It is significant that John specifies Bethany as the village of Lazarus, Martha and Mary (11.1; 12.1). Presumably, he chose Bethany as the village of Lazarus because of its attachment to the story of the unnamed woman that we find in Mark 14.3–9. But, again, the significance of this selection should not be underestimated, since it involves supplanting Simon as the host of the meal in Bethany shortly before Jesus' death where a woman anointed him – as known in the tradition recorded in Mark.[29] This aspect of the Marcan account of Jesus' last days in and around Jerusalem may well go back to an early Jerusalemite source (possibly as early as the 40s of the first century).[30] If so, John's replacement of Simon with Lazarus and his sisters stands out even more starkly as a manipulation of the collective memory of the group.

The Reasons for John's Integration of the Raising of Lazarus and the Anointing of Jesus

Why has John linked the stories of the raising of Lazarus and the anointing of Jesus before his death? If John knew Luke, he may have been aware of the fact, as noted above, that in that Gospel there is an account of Jesus raising a young man (7.11–17) followed soon after by his anointing passage (7.36–50). Yet we do not consider that this sequence, which, if John was aware of it, may have established a very general background for the narrative

28 For John 11.2 as reflecting knowledge of Mark, see Bauckham 1998c.

29 We discount the unlikely suggestion of Sanders (1954–5, p. 39) that Simon was the father of Lazarus, Martha and Mary (and his even more unlikely view that Judas was the brother of Lazarus, Martha and Mary [1954–5, p. 41])!

30 See Esler 2005b.

links he crafted, in itself constitutes a sufficient explanation for them, especially as Luke provides no correspondence between the *dramatis personae* in the two incidents. We need a more particular explanation and there is a persuasive one to be discerned in the underlying similarities in the two Johannine accounts. We will now deal with these.

John wanted to include a narrative describing someone being raised from the dead whom (for reasons unknown to us) he called Lazarus and whom he was presenting as the brother of Martha and Mary, two women who were already lodged in the memory of the Christ-movement. Meanwhile, there already existed the tradition of the anointing of Jesus (in at least two different forms but probably derived from one incident). So why, then, does he link the raising of Lazarus and the anointing of Jesus?

The reason for this, in our view, is that it was essential to the way John was to present the story of Lazarus and his sisters both that Jesus loved them (John 11.3, 5, 36) *and also that they loved him*. This is not simply reflected in the fact that Lazarus is described as the 'friend' (*philos*) of Jesus in John 11.11, but in the whole tenor of the narrative of John 11. We will have more to say of this mutual love and its implications for group identity in later chapters of this volume. At this point, however, it will suffice for us to note that in this context John's fixing upon the story of the woman who anointed Jesus is readily explicable. For it is easy to appreciate how a woman could passionately and dramatically demonstrate her love for Jesus by such an act. That is to say, John saw the woman's anointing of Jesus as a powerful token of love that he could reuse for this own narrative purposes. Indeed, he strengthens this aspect of the incident by combining both the express reference to the value of the perfume (similar to the Marcan version) and the very physical behaviour of Mary in wiping his feet with her hair (similar to the Lucan version).

Tina Beattie offers a fine insight into Mary's devotion when she juxtaposes her anointing of Jesus' feet with Peter's initial refusal to let Jesus wash his feet later in the Gospel (John 13.80). Beattie suggests that Peter's concern is for himself, not for Christ. Peter has 'an inappropriate concern for the status quo' and desires 'to protect hierarchical relationships of dominance and servitude' in an exaggerated display of commitment that masks his failure to understand discipleship. Mary, however:

> manifests a forgetting of self and a profound sensitivity to another. She makes connections and has an awareness of the hidden meanings in the events around her. Sensing the darkness to come, she reaches out to Christ and wordlessly demonstrates her compassion and her understanding.[31]

That John had Mary and not Martha do the anointing is explicable as reflecting the tradition where Martha was the more practical of the two sisters and not easily given to extravagant gesture or display. That was Mary's role – even as witnessed in John 11 itself, since Mary falls at Jesus' feet (11.32) but Martha does not (11.20–21). It is possible that the reference to Mary sitting *at the feet* of Jesus in Luke 10.39 (or a tradition similar to this that was in circulation) provided the crucial clue to later thinking that she must have been the one who anointed his feet, a connection not made by Luke but possible for anyone aware of these traditions,[32] as John shows he was in both 11.32 and 12.3. But reflecting on the exuberant character of the act of the woman in anointing Jesus brings us to the second reason why John has brought the two incidents together.

The importance John attached to Mary's anointing of Jesus, with Jesus himself relating the perfume she used to his coming burial, is reflected in a curious feature of John 11, namely, that John tells us nothing whatever about the anointing and burial of Lazarus. While we are duly cautious of arguments from silence, this feature does call for some explanation. For there can be no doubt that loving sisters like Martha and Mary would have anointed and wrapped the body of their brother Lazarus before seeing him laid in the tomb. This would have been a duty of fundamental importance to them. Even today in non-Mediterranean countries, those who have experienced the death of an unmarried brother will know how naturally it comes to his sisters to wish to attend to his body before burial, for example by visiting the funeral parlour in order to dress their brother in particular clothes before he is placed in the coffin. In Mediterranean countries, where the heat makes quick burial necessary and where the corpse may be carried directly from the family home to the grave,

31 Beattie 1997, p. 174.

32 Again, see the helpful discussion of Sproston North (2001, p. 119).

these considerations apply *a fortiori*. The strong interest shown in the Gospels concerning the decent burial and anointing of Jesus indicates how seriously this duty was taken.[33]

Martha and Mary must have anointed and wrapped the body of their brother Lazarus and seen him laid in the tomb, as, indeed, the reference to the bandages he is wearing when he emerges from the tomb (John 11.44) shows they did. Yet John is completely silent on their having done this. While the original audience of this Gospel would have assumed that Martha and Mary had expressed their love of Lazarus by anointing him, and probably realized that Mary's anointing of Jesus was stimulated by a similar love, the evangelist has not wanted explicitly to describe the anointing of Lazarus, let alone present it as a homologue to that of Jesus. Why?

In our view, John has omitted to mention or describe the anointing of Lazarus by his sisters because he did not want to distract attention from the anointing that Mary was to perform on Jesus later in his Gospel. This allowed John to emphasize the extent to which Mary became a prototype for the devotion of the Christ-follower to Jesus, a theme which would have been weakened if he had described Mary (and her sister) as treating their brother in too similar a manner.

By having Mary display to Jesus a devotion at home in the loving relationships of sisters and brothers, John created a powerful context in which he could develop this particular family as prototypes of the identity of the Christ-movement, a subject to which we will return in the next chapter.

Once he has established this connection between the account of the raising of Lazarus and the anointing of Jesus, John is then in a position to solve other problems raised by the latter story. We now know the identity and origin of the woman who anoints Jesus' feet. We also see a clear motivation for her doing so. By associating her with an immediately preceding 'Lazarus' episode in his Gospel, John provides the preceding history that is lacking in earlier versions of the anointing story. In the Synoptic accounts, the action of the unnamed woman who anoints Jesus comes largely out of the blue. Luke links the event to the forgiveness

---

33 See Matt. 27.57–61; Mark 15.42–47; 16.1; Luke 23.50–56; 24.1; John 19.38–42.

of the woman's unspecified sins (Luke 7.47–50), but otherwise a clear motivation is absent even there. The Johannine writer, however, is able to suggest that Jesus has long been a friend of this entire family. Moreover, and apart from the love that animated the relationship between Jesus and the family already, Jesus has just raised Mary's brother from the dead. Jesus' raising of Lazarus effectively provides a specific reason for the devotion that Mary shows only a short while later at the meal in John 12. Is it any surprise then that she responds in such an extraordinary way?

On the basis of this analysis we may briefly revert to the fact noted earlier that some scholars, such as Brown, have found the introduction of Mary as the one who anointed Jesus in John 11.2 rather awkward, because the event has not yet been narrated. We are now in an even better position to reject this view and to affirm how vital is this note in setting up such connections between the Lazarus episode and the anointing. We are also now able to investigate the Johannine account of the anointing of Jesus (John 12.1–8) in greater depth.

Distinctive Features of John's Portrayal of the Anointing of Jesus

We can further explicate the issue of the anointing in relation to certain oddities in the Johannine version of this account. We have already offered an explanation for the following notable features: the location in the house of Mary and Martha, the presence of Lazarus, and the anointing by Mary. But this still leaves the following unusual aspects of the way John has modified the collective memory of the Christ-movement in this account crying out for comment: (1) the time reference to six days before Passover; (2) the reference to Mary having taken a pound of ointment rather than coming from outside with a solitary 'flask'; (3) her putting the ointment on Jesus' feet and wiping the feet with her hair (shared in part by Luke in weeping over his feet, wiping her tears and then anointing the feet); (4) the house being filled with fragrance; (5) the dispute with Judas and the specific reference to him as a thief – in contrast to the objection to the anointing being raised by 'others' in Mark, Pharisees in Luke, disciples in Matthew; (6) Jesus' defence of Mary in terms of 'let her keep it for the day of my burial', (7) the omission of any reference to the woman's deed being known wherever the Gospel is preached in all the world, as in Mark and Matthew, yet the inclusion of a reference to Jesus' burial, as against Luke. We will now deal with these features, treating some together for convenience.

Six Days Before the Passover

In the Synoptic Gospels Jesus eats the Passover meal on the evening before he is crucified (Matt. 26.19; Mark 14.16; Luke 22.13), so the Synoptic Passover is Thursday evening/Friday, with Jesus being executed on the Day of Passover itself.

In Mark and Matthew, the meal at the house of Simon the Leper appears to occur two days before the Passover, so probably on Tuesday evening (Mark 14.1–3; Matt. 26.1–6). In the Fourth Gospel, on the other hand, Jesus is executed on the afternoon before the Passover, at the time the Passover lambs were being slaughtered in preparation for the meal (John 19.14). This means that the Johannine Passover starts on Friday evening and coincides with the start of the Sabbath, the last day of the week. It also means that the Johannine last supper (on Thursday evening) is not a Passover meal.

John also differs from Mark and Matthew in his timing of the meal at which Jesus was anointed in Bethany. John locates the anointing (in an unusually precise fashion) six days before the Passover, not two days prior to it. This indicates that the meal at which the anointing by Mary occurred took place on the first day of the week (the Sabbath always marking the last day of the week). Raymond Brown aptly notes that the Sabbath must have come to an end, otherwise Martha would not have been able to wait on table.[34]

The reason that John situates the anointing on the first day of the week (six days before the Passover), in contrast to the two days before the Passover noted in Mark and Matthew, is not clear and has frequently puzzled scholars. What is the purpose of such a precise and distinct reference? If John is manipulating collective memory, as we have suggested, why is he doing so here? It is doubtful that John has stretched the time frame between the anointing meal and the last supper because he has other important activities of Jesus that he wishes to record between the two

34 Brown 1966, p. 447.

events. In narrative terms, little happens between John 12.11 and the last supper with the disciples (John 13.1ff.) that requires so many intervening days – and certainly nothing that would require such a precise time reference.

Although it is not possible to be certain, we suggest that the significance of the anointing meal occurring on the *first day of the week*, Sunday to us, should not be overlooked. At the anointing meal, we have the reunion of (the raised) Lazarus with his sisters and with Jesus in the context of a communal meal. They are gathered at table, presumably in the house of the Lazarus family, because Martha is serving. The first day of the week has significance because it will also be the day on which Jesus is discovered to have been raised, exactly one week later: 'Now *on the first day of the week* Mary Magdalene came to the tomb' (John 20.1). Oddly, John even refers to the raised Jesus being reunited with his disciples in terms of the first day of the week: 'On the evening of that day, *the first day of the week*, the doors being shut where the disciples were, for fear of the Judeans, Jesus came and stood among them . . .' (John 20.19). The oddity is that the evening would normally be the start of a new day, but John persists in relating it to the first day of the week. This is the occasion when he breathes upon them and appears to impart the Holy Spirit. He also gives them the commission of 'boundary maintenance' – the forgiveness and retention of sins (John 20.23). It is difficult to escape the view that John is closely and deliberately linking the critical events in the beginnings of the new movement of Christ-followers with 'the first day of the week', when Jesus was raised. We propose that the evangelist has strikingly prefigured these events and their significance in the gathering of the Lazarus family with Jesus on the first day of the week, a meal at which Mary displays lavish devotion to Jesus, thus anticipating the honour to be shown in due course to the glorified Lord. This is probably intentional, and it provides a clear motive for the Johannine manipulation of the collective memory concerning the time of the anointing meal. Raymond Brown, indeed, has already suggested that the repetition of the phrase 'the first day of the week' in John 20.1 and 20.19 is linked to the celebration of the Lord's Supper on the first day of the week (Acts 20.7; Cf. 1 Cor. 16.2).[35] This

35 See Brown 1966, p. 1019.

suggestion coheres closely with our proposal that the anointing meal in John 12 has overtones of Sunday table-fellowship.

The Anointing and Its Significance

At the outset of our discussion of the anointing of Jesus by Mary, we must note that we consider that the received text of John 12.3 is wrong in an important respect. We need here only summarize our reasons for our view on the correct reading, since we have set out our detailed argument in Appendix 2 to this volume. The text that occurs in most edited versions (including that of the United Bible Societies and Nestle-Aland) is this: *Hē oun Mariam labousa litran murou nardou pistikēs polytimou ēleipsen tous podas tou Iēsou kai exemaxen tais thrixin autēs tous podas autou: hē de oikia eplērōthē ek tēs osmēs tou murou.* The RSV translates this as follows: 'Mary took a pound of costly ointment of pure nard and anointed the feet of Jesus and wiped his feet with her hair; and the house was filled with the fragrance of the ointment.' On our view, however, the correct text for 12.3a is: *Hē oun Mariam labousa litran murou pistikēs polytimou ēleipsen tous podas tou Iēsou*; in other words, the word *nardou* (nard) was not in the version the evangelist dictated to his scribe and has been added later. Our case rests ultimately upon the non-appearance of *nardou* in P66, Codex Bezae and the Old Latin. In addition, we translate John 12.3a like this: 'Mary, when she had taken a pound of ointment, of best quality, a precious lotion, anointed the feet of Jesus' – where 'best quality', translating *pistikēs*, refers (in our view) to myrrh of the best available type. Myrrh will reappear, with aloes, in John 19 for use in the anointing of Jesus for burial carried out by Joseph of Arimathea and Nicodemus.

What then are we to make of Mary's wiping Jesus' (ointment-laden) feet with her hair and Jesus' apparent encouragement in verse 7 to her to keep the ointment for the day of his burial? Mary, it must be noted, is not mentioned in connection with the anointing at Jesus' burial in John 19, an important subject to which we will return below. And, in any case, how could she keep the ointment if she had already used it? Moreover, although the feet of guests were often washed (by a slave for example), they were not usually anointed with ointment nor wiped with someone's hair.[36]

36 Malina and Rohrbaugh 1998, p. 205.

To answer these questions and to explain these puzzling features we will consider the story in relation to its narrative progression, beginning with what Mary does and its immediate result.

John says that 'Mary, when she had taken (*labousa*) a pound (*litran*) of best quality [myrrh], a precious lotion, anointed (*ēleipsen*) the feet of Jesus and wiped (*exemaxen*) his feet with her hair; and the house was filled with the fragrance (*osmēs*) of the lotion (*murou*)' (12.3). We must initially mention two aspects that contrast with the description in Mark. First, as just noted, whereas in Mark the perfume used is nard, we consider that in John it is myrrh. Second, Mark says the woman brought in the perfume in an alabaster flask which she broke and then poured over (*katecheen*) his head; here the perfume clearly takes very liquid form. Luke has the flask but, in line with his concern to avoid a conflict with this theology of poverty, eliminates any reference to the precious nature of the perfume (cf. *alabastron murou*; Luke 7.37). In John, on the other hand, there is no reference to a flask; perhaps the perfume was more viscous.[37] The word *litra* was used as a measurement for weight (as in the translation above), but could also be used to measure volume.

How do we explain the Johannine picture? Because the setting in John is uniquely in the home of Lazarus, Martha and Mary, there is no reason to think that this was all the perfume available. Mary may well have 'taken' (*labousa*) it from a larger supply in the house; indeed, that is the natural way to interpret this word in John 12.3 and there is little to be said for C. K. Barrett's blank denial of this possibility.[38] This is very different from the Synoptic accounts, where the woman comes in from outside with an alabaster jar of perfume, but it is perfectly conceivable in John's unusual narrative. We will see below how this explanation helps to explain the reaction of Judas in the Johannine version.

---

37 Brown notes (1966, p. 448) that myrrh existed in the ancient world in the form of a powder or liquid; probably, however, it had been mixed with some substance like olive oil. Also note the discussion in Zangenberg 2006 forthcoming.

38 Barrett states: 'To suggest that only a small part of the ointment had been used and that the rest might be preserved is not only to miss the spirit of the narrative but also to ignore v. 3c.' (1978, p. 414) We explain further below how closely the notion of Mary only using part of the ointment does cohere with the narrative and see no basis for his reference to v. 3c.

Why does Mary anoint Jesus' feet – as in Luke's account, but not in Mark (where the woman pours out the perfume on his head)? Raymond Brown suggests that this element highlights the connection between Mary's prophetic anointing and Jesus' burial, for one would anoint the head of a living person; but it is conceivable that the feet of a corpse might be anointed in preparation for burial.[39]

We are of the view, however, that Mary's anointing Jesus' *feet* is rather to be explained by reference to what occurs later in the Gospel and, indeed, elsewhere in the Johannine corpus. Such attention to Jesus' feet is of a piece with what we have previously noted in John 11.32 (where Mary falls at his feet, though Martha failed to do so earlier in the passage) and with a possibly traditional picture of Mary sitting at his feet while he taught (cf. Luke 10.39). But another factor may also be in play here. Mary's anointing of Jesus' feet may be preparing the way for the foot-washing later, which forms such a prominent and distinctive feature in John 13, a possibility already raised by John Painter.[40] What Mary does instinctively as an act of devotion with expensive ointment, the disciples will be instructed to do later for one another using the common substance of water. In this respect, therefore, Mary becomes prototypical of the movement. In addition, it is intriguing to note that in 1 John 2.20, 27 one finds the distinctive rite of 'anointing' (*chrisma*) being known and presumably practised within a Johannine community. Did this practice also find its origins in the Johannine picture of how Mary had treated Jesus?

In both John and Luke, but not Mark, the woman wipes Jesus' feet with her hair. In Luke she uses her hair to wipe her tears from his feet and then anoints them with the perfume. In John she applies the perfume to Jesus' feet and then wipes them with her hair. We must not miss the significance of this; to explain this unusual feature, with Raymond Brown,[41] simply as a 'crisscrossing' of other traditions is quite unsatisfactory. *For the effect of Mary wiping Jesus' ointment-bearing feet with her hair is that her head has been anointed via the body of Jesus.* She has quite

39 Brown 1966, p. 454.

40 Painter 1993, p. 375: 'It seems likely that some comparison between the two "footwashings" was intended.'

41 Brown 1966, p. 451.

literally been anointed (in the usual way, with respect to the head) with the very ointment that she has used for Jesus.

The full significance of this 'anointing' emerges when taken with the next feature in the passage, namely, that 'the house was filled with the fragrance (*osmēs*) of the perfume (*murou*)'. At this point the audience of this Gospel were likely to recall the reference to a smell that occurs shortly before this in John's Gospel, namely, Martha's (typically practical?) warning to Jesus when requested that the tomb of Lazarus be opened: 'Lord, by now he smells (*ozei*), for it is the fourth day' (John 11.39). There is a strong contrast between the terrible smell that Martha feared from the decaying corpse of Lazarus, which would not have been much diminished by the anointing he must have received at the hands of herself and Mary, even though John fails to mention this for the reasons noted above, and the sweet smell of the perfume that Mary applies to Jesus' feet in her act of anointing him.

For Mark and Matthew the woman's anointing provides a reference to the Gospel being preached throughout the world (Mark 14.9; Matt. 26.13). In contrast, for John, the 'spread' of this event is to the Lazarus–Martha–Mary household. Some critics have argued that there is a parallel between these two consequences of the anointing in the very process of dispersal. Thus Raymond Brown cites the Midrash Rabbah on Ecclesiastes 7.1, which says: 'The fragrance of a good perfume spreads from the bedroom to the dining room; so does a good name spread from one end of the world to the other.'[42] Rudolf Bultmann, moreover, insisted that verse 3 conveyed the idea that the fragrance filling the house was symbolical of the *gnosis* filling the whole world.[43]

Yet these views are mistaken in seeing the benefits of anointing spreading throughout the world. John's picture represents a contrast to what we find in the Synoptic Gospels, not a parallel. John does not have a universalist vision of salvation. He believes that evil will continue in the world and will be a reality that believers have to face (John 17.15) but that eventually Jesus will take his own out of the world to his Father's house (14.2–3).[44]

Let us focus for a moment on why the benefits of the anointing are not so widely available as Bultmann suggested. In John 12 is

---

42 Brown 1966, p. 453.
43 Bultmann 1971, p. 415.
44 See Piper, 2007 forthcoming.

it clear that the fragrance of the anointing fills the *house* of the beloved Johannine Christ-followers, but does it extend beyond this circle? The house in John 12 clearly represents a group of insiders, just as earlier in John 10 the sheepfold for which Jesus cared was clearly distinct from the threats that were to be found outside the fold. Later John will talk about his own in terms of being in the world but distinct from it (John 17.9–16). He will also return to the imagery of the 'house' in John 14.1–3. In this context his followers are promised a place in the Father's house, and Jesus will come and take them to himself and to the 'rooms' he has prepared for them. Their 'removal' from this world appears to be in view, which again strongly suggests that the 'house' in John 12 is not a metaphor for the world at large. In John 12.3 the vision is limited – the smell spreads only throughout the house, not beyond it. In other words, it is the community of Christ-followers (typified by this family in a particular house), not the world at large, who enjoy the benefits of the anointing. They obtain a kind of air/spirit-borne anointing themselves, in a domestic context that was typical of the early Christ-movement. This represents a fine example of the extent to which John will go in modifying an element in the collective memory of Christ-followers. By this means, therefore, the prototypical family share in this anointing – just as the disciples will later have a share in their feet being washed by Jesus. John has cleverly adapted the anointing story to create a reference to Christ-followers, rather than exclusively focusing on Jesus and his burial. The significance of the anointing for the Johannine community is underlined.

This brings us to Judas, who asks why the ointment was not sold for 300 denarii (the same number that appears in Mark) and the money given to beggars (*ptōchois*; John 12.4–5). But Judas (the evangelist tells us) was not concerned for the destitute; he was a thief who used to take what was put into the group's money box which he looked after (John 12.6).

To understand his reaction properly we must first consider Jesus' reply to him: 'Therefore Jesus said, "Leave her alone, *hina eis tēn hēmeran tou entaphiasmou mou tērēsē*. The destitute you always have with you, but you do not always have me"' (John 12.7–8). The Greek words in this quotation, which represent the version in the best manuscripts, can be translated in a straightforward way as a purpose clause: 'in order that she may keep it for the day of my burial'. Yet commentators have been troubled by this interpretation for two reasons: first, how could Mary keep for Jesus' burial ointment she had just poured on his feet, and, second, although Jesus is anointed in John's Gospel, this occurs at the hands of Joseph of Arimathea and Nicodemus, not Mary (John 19.38–42). Thus we have D. Moody Smith, for example, describing these words as 'a harsh contradiction', for 'how could she keep it when she has just poured it out?'[45] The same problem is reflected in some lesser manuscripts, which read 'she has kept', a reading that Raymond Brown considers to be the correct interpretation, even if it is not the original reading.[46] On this view, Mary was not keeping the ointment for some future use but was keeping it until now to 'embalm' Jesus. P. Schmiedel conjectured that we should substitute *poiēsē* for *tērēsē*, meaning 'in order that *she might do* this for my burial',[47] which would again make Mary's action referable to the time of the meal in the house at Bethany. C. K. Barrett finally, unable to make sense of the Greek, essentially admitted defeat in relation to the clause under discussion.[48] In our view, however, the proper interpretation is the same as the natural translation of the Greek in the best attested manuscripts: 'in order that she may keep it for the day of my burial'. We will now explain why.

Our view depends on the interpretation we have proposed above – that we should understand John to mean that more of the costly perfume was available to Mary elsewhere in the house. First of all, the incident with Judas now makes much more sense. In Matthew, Mark and Luke there is reference to an alabaster jar; which conveys a strong sense of the finite nature of the perfume used. On the other hand, the *litra* of perfume which John mentions, a measure of weight or volume, without mention of its vessel, conveys no such finitude; in fact, such an expression sits more comfortably in a context where what was taken formed only part of a larger stock. Second, in the accounts of Mark and Matthew (Luke not including any objection about the use of expensive perfume but only about the sinner who performs the act), the emphasis is on the 'loss' ([*apōleia*]; Matt. 26.8; Mark 14.4). A complaint about the 'loss' involved in the woman's anointing makes good sense if there is no more of such perfume where that

45 Smith 1999, pp. 234–5.
46 Brown 1966, p. 449.
47 Nestle-Aland 1993, p. 290.
48 Barrett 1978, p. 414.

came from. In John, Judas makes no mention of 'loss', which, again, coheres with the existence of a larger supply from which the amount applied to Jesus was taken. Third, Judas is described here as the keeper of the valuables and as a 'thief'. If all the perfume has been used up, it will not benefit Judas at all to raise his objection. It is spilt milk, so to speak. Or sour grapes. But if there is more perfume at hand, Judas' objection takes on another dimension. Judas is actually making a bid to be given at least a comparable amount of perfume to sell and 'give the proceeds to beggars'. So when Jesus commands that Mary be left alone 'so that she might keep it for his burial', he is in fact making Mary rather than Judas custodian of the amount that remains. On this basis there is a stronger reason for the dispute with Judas other than his being simply piqued by Jesus' rebuke.

Yet, having reached this view, we encounter an objection to it – that if there is a further supply of ointment in the house, ointment that is being safeguarded by Mary for the day of Jesus' burial, then why does Mary not appear with it in John 19? For Raymond Brown this represents an insuperable problem to the interpretation of the Greek clause in question in John 12.7.[49] Yet not only do we consider John does intend his audience to understand that Mary was custodian of a larger measure of ointment that she was keeping for the purpose of Jesus' burial, but that an examination of this point allows us to resolve some other seemingly peculiar features of John's Gospel.

We will begin our argument on this point with the proposal that John's account of the burial of Jesus certainly eliminates some difficulties that appear in the Synoptic accounts, and particularly in Mark. It is important to note that in none of the Synoptic Gospels is the body of Jesus ever anointed after his death. Mark describes how the women come to anoint Jesus but are forestalled by his resurrection (Mark 15.42–47; 16.1). A frequent objection to Mark's account of the women going with the spices to the tomb is that it would be rather late to think of anointing the body of Jesus by the 'third day'. Luke does not completely break with Mark here, since he retains the visit of the women to the tomb on Sunday morning (Luke 24.1). Although Luke does have a preparation of the spices on the Friday (Luke

49 Brown 1966, p. 449.

23.50–56), this does little to soften the notion of bringing spices to a now-decomposing corpse. Matthew, alone of the evangelists, mentions burial but neither anointing nor an attempt at anointing of Jesus' body (Matt. 27.57–61). It is likely that he omits the planned Sunday morning anointing because he is aware of this problem, a suspicion strengthened by the fact that he retains a visit to the tomb at this time by women (Mary Magdalene and the other Mary), but not for the purpose of anointing but so they can see it (Matt. 28.1). To all this we must add that in Matthew and Mark the anointing of Jesus by the woman at Bethany is the only anointing Jesus receives and in each case this gives his statement that she has anointed his body for burial a particular relevance (Matt. 26.12; Mark 14.8). Luke, as we have already explained, lacks even this proleptic anointing for burial because of the way he completely recasts the incident to avoid Jesus seeming to be insouciant to the needs of the destitute (Luke 7.36–50).

In contrast to the difficulties apparent in the Synoptic accounts, John has a tidy story whereby Jesus' body is well prepared prior to burial (19.38–40), 'as is the burial custom of the Judeans'. Jürgen Zangenberg has recently demonstrated how John's account does indeed accord with what is now known of Judean burials in Palestine in the first century CE from recent archaeological evidence.[50] Moreover, only John specifies the amount – 'a mixture of *myrrh* and aloes, about a hundred pounds' weight' (*migma smurnēs kai aloēs hōs litras hekaton*).[51] Myrrh and aloes were widely used as funeral spices.[52] We have already noted our view (the argument for which appears in Appendix 2 of this volume) that myrrh is the spice John has in mind in John 12.3 (in the word *pistikēs*). John thereby creates a unique verbal link back to the anointing story. We should not underestimate the force of this connection: these are the only two instances of the word *litra* in the New Testament and the word does not appear at all in the Septuagint. Mary's 'pound' of myrrh prefigures the 100 'pounds' of myrrh and aloes.

---

50 See Zangenberg 2006 forthcoming.

51 According to Raymond Brown (1971, p. 940), the word 'smyrna' (σμύρνη) is a fragrant resin used by the Egyptians in embalming, while aloes (ἀλόη) is a powdered aromatic sandalwood used for perfuming bedding or clothes, but normally for burial.

52 Zangenberg 2006 forthcoming.

This explanation, however, still leaves unanswered the question of why Mary is not mentioned in John 19 as the agent of Jesus' anointing. John follows the tradition that the body of Jesus was requested by Joseph of Arimathea and granted by Pilate (19.38). Joseph appears to be a known figure. John does not explain, as the Synoptic Gospels do, that Joseph was a respected member of the Sanhedrin, but he does mention that Joseph was 'secretly' a disciple of Jesus. This idea is not foreign to the Synoptics, which variously call him a 'disciple' (Matt. 27.57) or one 'looking for the kingdom of God' (Mark 15.43; Luke 23.51). In comparison, John seems to 'downgrade' Joseph of Arimathea by describing him as an ambivalent 'secret disciple'. As Bassler, supported by Zangenberg, notes, there is an air of ambiguity about both Joseph and Nicodemus.[53] Almost certainly John is aware that Joseph was known as a member of the council, because it is scarcely credible that Pilate in the Gospel accounts would have granted the body to anyone who was not deemed 'trustworthy'. Put another way, it would be completely incredible to think that, in this Gospel, Pilate would grant the body to any member of Lazarus' family or permit any member of Lazarus' family to have access to the body. After all, for John, Lazarus' raising is precisely the catalyst for the arrest of Jesus. Even Lazarus is sought by the authorities (12.10). Moreover, this is the family that identifies Jesus with resurrection. Pilate could hardly find a less 'safe' group to whom to deliver the body than the Lazarus family.

Yet it would be considered to be 'safe' to deliver the body to members of the Sanhedrin. So in place of one person, John has two. Just to be doubly safe, he brings in Nicodemus, a ruler of the Judeans, as well as preserving the traditional reference to Joseph of Arimathea. Moreover, the only Sanhedrin members that would be interested in having the body of Jesus would presumably be those who already had some interest in him. Yet if they are not to be suspected of some plot of deception, then they have to be both interested and sceptical at the same time. Joseph and Nicodemus fit the bill precisely. Joseph is placed in the somewhat dubious category of a 'secret' disciple. Nicodemus has never been shown very clearly to be a disciple at all, but is shown to be 'secretly' intrigued in John 3 and fair-minded in John 7.50–51. So John

53 Bassler 1989, p. 641; Zangenberg 2006 forthcoming.

gives us two male respected figures who are responsible for the burial of Jesus, neither of whom is so committed to Jesus as to be likely to be involved in any deception.

If this is the intention behind John's portrayal, however, how does one explain the extravagant quantity of myrrh and aloes brought by Nicodemus? Is he now, suddenly and without explanation, a fully-fledged Jesus-enthusiast – and thereby also compromised as a 'safe' figure to whom the authorities would entrust the body? If Nicodemus went out and purchased the spices from his own funds, then it would seem so. Yet if he were simply the bearer of spices provided by some other devoted follower who would not be allowed to be present in person (namely, Mary), then our earlier understanding of Nicodemus' role (perhaps set up for this very purpose) is preserved. How do we know whether this is the case? We have already drawn attention to the verbal links with the anointing story and to the possibility of Mary keeping further myrrh for Jesus' burial. In addition, John carefully notes that Nicodemus was 'bearing' the mixture. He never indicates that Nicodemus was the source or the purchaser. That Nicodemus might be presumed to have contact with a wealthy Bethany family near Jerusalem is hardly inconceivable. To make the point even more firmly, it is worth noting how John treats Joseph of Arimathea. In Mark (15.46) Joseph bought a linen shroud for Jesus' body. In John, unlike the Synoptics, there is no expensive shroud at all. Jesus is just wrapped in cloth wrappings (19.40). No significant financial outlay on Joseph's part is stated or presumed. Might not the same be true of Nicodemus? John records nothing that would cause us to believe otherwise. Even the unused tomb in which Jesus was laid appears not to have been purchased. John describes it simply as useful because it was 'close at hand' (19.42).

We have argued that extraordinary devotion here on the part of Nicodemus is both unexpected and quite contrary to the need at this point in the narrative for the body to be given to figures deemed respectable in the eyes in the authorities. It is our suggestion that John has laid the foundation not only for the preparation of the body at Jesus' burial by way of the earlier story of the anointing; he has also alerted us to the source of the ointments eventually to be used. If this interpretation is correct, then Mary's 'absence' from the burial is not complete, however understandable it may be in terms of the narrative that Pilate resist any direct presence on the part of the Lazarus family. Just as Jesus instructed, she did indeed 'keep it' for the day of his burial.

Conclusion

The result of this discussion is that although John has certainly availed himself of some traditions in his picture of Lazarus, Martha and Mary, he has also demonstrated great freedom in the way he has recast them to paint a particular picture of the past and to form and mobilize an abiding collective memory.

In later chapters we will explore how these figures mattered greatly for the manner in which John wished to shape the identity of those to whom he was writing. We will propose in the next chapter that their significance to the evangelist propelled him in the direction of depicting these three siblings as prototypical of the love within the movement – the love received from the Father and the Son and bestowed on one another. We will also devote a chapter to the vital aspect of the prototypicality of Lazarus – that he was raised from the dead.

4

Lazarus, Martha and Mary as Prototypes of Those Whom Jesus Loves

Prototypes, Exemplars and Group Identity

We noted in Chapter 1 that Lazarus has sometimes been cited in Johannine scholarship as a 'symbolic', 'representative' or 'ideal' figure, although rarely are such terms adequately explained, let alone modelled. For many scholars, a regular point of debate is whether such characters are 'real' or merely 'symbolic' or 'ideal'.[1] In addition, only rarely are Martha and Mary regarded as representative figures, as we have seen in Chapter 1 above.

The model of prototypes within social identity theory, however, puts the discussion on another footing altogether. We are interested in people from the past who are thought to typify the group, that is, those who are maximally representative of its shared social identity. We have referred above to a real person of this sort as an 'exemplar' and to an imagined or fictional person as a 'prototype'.

Yet this distinction makes little difference to the identity of the group. Its collective memory will be fed by the recollection of these figures whether they had historical existence or not. Groups in the pre-critical period tended to assume that heroes from the past, like Abraham or Judith, Roland or Arthur, had been actual

1 For a defence of the historicity of the Bethany family, see Sanders 1954–5. For a quest of the historical Lazarus, concluding that Lazarus, Mary and Martha were the former High Priest Eleazar, Miriam and Martha of the Boethus family, see Baltz 1996.

persons. The historical existence of such figures was nevertheless largely irrelevant to their role as serving to embody a particular group identity. Accordingly, it is of little moment in the current discussion whether the Lazarus, Martha and Mary of whom John speaks were historical or not. The difficulty of reconciling Luke's portrait of Martha and Mary, who apparently had no living brother (Luke 10.38–42), with John's equipping two sisters of the same name with a brother named Lazarus is obviously a stumbling-block to his historical existence. By the same token, perhaps a pair of sisters called Martha and Mary had really been disciples of Jesus, given their appearance in both Luke and John.

Nevertheless, although hereafter we will employ the language of prototype and prototypicality rather than that of exemplarity in connection with Lazarus, Martha and Mary, this will have little bearing on what we have to say about them (which would just as easily suit them if they had actually been followers, and hence better regarded as exemplars of the group). In this chapter our aim is to explore Lazarus, Martha and Mary as prototypical Christ-followers, in the special sense of those whom Jesus loved (and loves). First, we will discuss the textual data bearing on these issues. Second, we will weigh up the implications of John's portrayal of these figures in the light of the model of social identity we have presented in Chapter 2. Third, we will indicate areas of theological significance that arise from our discussion within the framework of intercultural dialogue and communion, also set out in Chapter 2.

The Case for Lazarus, Martha and Mary as Prototypes of Those Whom Jesus Loves

Lazarus, Martha and Mary

We are looking for evidence that Lazarus, Martha and Mary typify the Johannine group. It is worth noting that occasionally even scholars who have not considered that community issues comprise the major emphasis of the episode have nonetheless noted how Lazarus is 'representative' of later Jesus-followers.[2]

---

2 For example, Brown 1966, p. 431. This is but one of many themes that Brown uncovers in the passage.

Yet there are two hurdles to be overcome in attributing to Lazarus prototypical (or even 'representative') significance. First, there is the circumstance that John does not explicitly label Lazarus as a 'disciple' or 'follower' of Jesus. Nor is he part of any list of disciples in the Synoptic Gospels, so that his place as a disciple cannot be assumed on the basis of external tradition. This is in spite of the fact that the word *mathētēs*, of a disciple (of Jesus), appears some 70 times in the Fourth Gospel (with *sunmathētēs* appearing at John 11.16), while the verb *akolouthein*, 'follow', is used in a semi-technical sense of 'following' Jesus on nine occasions.[3] Second, Lazarus does not seem to have responded to Jesus in faith in ways typical of this Gospel. There are answers to both of these objections, and we will return to them when we have summoned positive evidence for the prototypicality of Lazarus.

Lazarus is first mentioned in John 11.1–3:

> Now a certain man was ill, Lazarus of Bethany, the village of Mary and her sister Martha. It was Mary who anointed the Lord with ointment and wiped his feet with her hair, whose brother Lazarus was ill. So the sisters sent to him, saying, 'Lord, he whom you love (*phileis*) is ill.' (RSV)

A number of remarkable features of this passage require comment. First and foremost is the fact that the statement that the Lord loves Lazarus represents the inaugural occasion in the Gospel in which Jesus is said to love anyone, either by use of the verb *philein*, as here, or *agapan*, another verb meaning 'to love' in the Fourth Gospel. This is highly significant. Hitherto the evangelist has used several expressions involving 'love'. God is said to love the world (*agapan*; 3.16), the son (*agapan* at 3.35 and *philein* at 5.20) and 'me', meaning Jesus (*agapan* at 10.17). Human beings love darkness, and certain Judeans fail to love Jesus (*agapan* at 3.19 and 8.42). The Judeans in Jerusalem have no love (*agapē* at 5.42) in them. Up to this point there is no indication of any particular people that Jesus loves. *But now we learn that Jesus loves Lazarus*. We very soon find out, moreover, that actually 'Jesus loved (*ēgapa*) Martha and her sister and Lazarus' (John 11.5). *So Jesus loves the whole family*! Soon after Lazarus is described

3 John 1.37; 38, 40, 43; 8.12; 10.27; 12.26; 21.19 and 21.22.

as Jesus' 'friend' (*philos*; 11.11). When Jesus wept at the death of Lazarus, the Judeans there observed, 'See how he loved (*ephilei*) him' (John 11.36). These descriptions are reinforced by the unusually strong and frequent emotions attributed to Jesus in 11.33, 35, 38. This love seems to have been reciprocated, as indicated by the information about Mary's anointing of Jesus in John 11.2, which notably disturbs the chronological progression of the narrative by looking forward to the full account of this event in John 12.1–8, in part to underline the depths of love involved in such devotion (as we argued in the previous chapter).

The significance of these references to the love Jesus had for Lazarus and his sisters emerges from John 13 onwards. The critical verse is 13.1: 'Before the feast of the Passover, when Jesus knew that his hour had come to depart out of this world to the Father, having loved his own (*agapēsas tous idious*) in the world, he loved (*ēgapēsen*) them to the end.' The love which Jesus has for his own (*hoi idioi*), thus announced in general terms, thereafter becomes a dominant theme in the Fourth Gospel. To be 'loved' by Jesus is what is set out (amidst some initial resistance from Peter) in the foot-washing account in John 13.2–16. Jesus gives them a new commandment that, just as he has loved them, they should love one another (13.34; 15.12). The one who keeps his commandments is the one who loves him, and such a person will be loved by the Father and by him (14.21, 23). Jesus has loved them as the Father loved him (15.9). The Father has loved them because they have loved Jesus and have believed that he came from the Father (16.27). The world will know that the Father has loved them just as he had loved Jesus (17.23). There is even a particular disciple whom Jesus loved (13.23; 19.26; 20.2; 21.7, 20). Finally, Jesus asks Peter if he loves him more than the others do (21.15, 16, 17). Thus 'love' is a key identity-descriptor for believers in the Fourth Gospel. 'Love of one another' is the 'new' commandment that Jesus imparts and is what marks the identity of the community, even ostensibly for the outside world (John 13.34–35).

Within this context, Lazarus and his sisters emerge *as both the first people described as loved by Jesus and as the only ones who are named,* with 'the disciple whom Jesus loved' remaining nameless throughout the Gospel. In short, Lazarus, Mary and Martha are prototypes of Jesus' 'own people' (*hoi idioi*), both in the sense of typifying this social category and, indeed, in being the first in time to do so. We say 'prototypes' to allow for the possibility that these are constructed figures, whereas 'exemplars' would probably be more appropriate if they were real people. The fact that they are named and that Jesus manifests his love for them in the most dramatic means possible admirably adapts them to permanent lodgement in the collective memory of this group.

The circumstance that Lazarus is never mentioned again in the Fourth Gospel after 12.9–10 (a statement referring to the authorities planning to put Lazarus to death, after his revivification!) and 12.17–18 (explaining that the crowd response to Jesus at the entry into Jerusalem was the result of learning about the raising of Lazarus) does not weigh against this result. Nor does the absence of mention of Lazarus' sisters after John 12.2–3 present a telling objection. For, as we have just seen, critical issues (those concerning the love characteristic of the Christ-movement in particular) raised with respect to Lazarus and his sisters are in fact carried forward as issues (often in relation to the disciples) in John 13—21. Second, it is not our contention that Lazarus and his sisters are the *sole* prototypes for members of the Jesus-group offered by the Fourth Gospel, although this is a matter on which there might be dispute.[4]

Another aspect of John 11 confirms the prototypicality of Lazarus, Mary and Martha. The sisters use the word *Kurios*

---

4 Thomas actually figures as an 'anti-prototype': 'Jesus said to him, "Have you believed because you have seen me? Blessed are those who have not seen and yet believe"' (John 20.29; RSV)! Whether (or in what sense) the Beloved Disciple can be considered prototypical is an interesting question. The Beloved Disciple as purported author certainly enjoys a unique status in comparison with other disciples in the Fourth Gospel. The author clearly intends him to have a high status in the Johannine Jesus-group, but this need not mean that he was typical of the group or that subsequent Jesus-followers would be expected to emulate his role. The refusal to name the Beloved Disciple, in contrast to the other disciples, hardly assists in the process of identification with him (see pp. 9, 34, 84–5). The real problem in regarding the Beloved Disciple as prototypical is that whereas the status of Lazarus, Martha and Mary as loved by Jesus is accompanied by other characteristics or phenomena with which the evangelist's addressees could identify, this cannot really be said of the Beloved Disciple. Bauckham argues that even as a disciple he is different in kind from the other disciples – an ideal witness or author, but not the ideal disciple; see Bauckham 1993, pp. 33–44.

('Lord'), in the vocative, six times in this passage (John 11.3, 21, 27, 32, 34, 39). Although it can simply mean 'Sir', the indications of intimacy between them and Jesus (cf. 11.5) and Martha's eventual confession strongly suggest that this is to be taken as 'insider language' (as also in 11.12 on the lips of disciples). Moreover, the narrator's use of *Kurios* as a reference to Jesus in John 11.2 is quite remarkable. Only John 4.1, referring to Jesus' baptizing, and John 6.23, referring back to Jesus' breaking of bread and giving thanks, depict a comparable narrator's use of *Kurios* prior to the resurrection narrative. Bultmann and Schnackenburg therefore consider 11.2 a gloss of the ecclesiastical redactor or a later editor.[5] Their instinct here is certainly correct that such a reference highlights for the reader the significance of the episode for believers. But the most probable interpretation is that this usage constitutes insider language. It confirms that the sisters are prototypical of the insider group and that in this episode they enact attitudes and behaviour appropriate for the group as a whole in relation to Jesus, their Lord. The evangelist's use of 'Lord' in a confessional/insider sense in John 11.2 vividly reveals that in telling the story of Lazarus and his two sisters the evangelist is also speaking about the experience of his audience contemporary with him. The sacred past and the present of the community are fused in the recognition of the members of the group from both periods that Jesus is Lord.

So far we have been considering the general position in relation to Lazarus and his sisters. Now we will focus on Lazarus alone, before returning to Martha and Mary later in this chapter.

Lazarus

Since the only two males who are said to be 'loved' by Jesus in the Fourth Gospel are Lazarus and 'the disciple whom Jesus loved', there have been some critics who have suggested that we should assume the identification of these two figures.[6] Grounds for such a hypothesis include the following: (a) apart possibly from 1.35, 37, 40, 'the disciple whom Jesus loved' never makes an appearance until *after* the Lazarus episode (first in 13.23); (b) both

---

5 Bultmann1971, p. 176 n.2; Schnackenburg, 1980, p. 322.
6 See discussions in Charlesworth 1995, pp. 185–92, 288–91.

figures may be associated with the environs of Jerusalem (cf. possibly 18.15–17);[7] (c) the question is raised in John 21.20–23 as to whether the Beloved Disciple would die, which is a natural question to pose in the case of the revivified Lazarus; (d) the Beloved Disciple is never otherwise named; and (e) both have relatively 'passive' roles.[8] As Raymond Brown notes, however, it is difficult to believe that the same person spoken of anonymously as the Beloved Disciple in chapters 13—21 has already been mentioned by name in chapters 11—12, and this must pose a serious obstacle to any such theory.[9] If they are to be considered therefore distinct figures, as seems highly likely, then what are the implications of their shared status as particularly 'beloved' by Jesus? For Lazarus to share such a status with the Beloved Disciple must certainly elevate his significance in the Fourth Gospel. It also highlights the point that the significant feature in our consideration of Lazarus' prototypicality is not 'discipleship' but 'being loved by Jesus'. This important issue of discipleship, noted above as a possible objection to the prototypicality of Lazarus, must now be discussed.

The essential point seems to be that the evangelist attributes a status to Lazarus, that he is loved by Jesus, which is greater than that of 'disciple'. Immediately after the introduction of 'Lazarus of Bethany' in 11.1–2 the evangelist makes clear that an *ongoing personal relationship with Jesus* is presupposed, as reflected in the data showing Jesus' love for him mentioned above. In addition, in the second episode that refers to Lazarus – in John 12.1–2 – Lazarus appears in table-fellowship with Jesus, presumably at his home in Bethany. This places him in very select company and probably suggests that he is the host of the gathering. Lazarus' close relationship, and that of his sisters (which we will consider below), to Jesus contrasts sharply in this passage with the only disciple named as present at this meal, Judas Iscariot. This serves to illustrate the point that being a disciple is not a necessary or sufficient basis for membership of those perceived by John as Jesus' true followers. At John 6.66–71 Jesus had indicated that

7 But note that Helen Bond (2004, pp. 134–5) suggests that this refers to Judas and not the Beloved Disciple.

8 For other arguments, see Stibbe 1992, pp. 77–82, 154–8. Stibbe sees Lazarus (the Beloved Disciple) as an historical eyewitness, the source of a primitive 'Bethany gospel'.

9 Brown 1966, p. xcv.

even membership of the Twelve was not sufficient, since one of the Twelve was to betray him. But the point is made far more clearly after the Lazarus episode – in John 15.13–15. Here Jesus announces to those who were at supper with him, who are his disciples (John 13.5, 22, 23, 35; 15.8), that they are his friends (*philoi*), if they should do what he commands them, and that he will no longer call them servants (*douloi*), but friends (*philoi*). This suggests that, although they were his disciples, they had not had the status of his 'friends' until this point. Being labelled a disciple was not essential, but the friendship of Jesus was what counted. Lazarus was already his friend (John 11.11), but hitherto they were not, nor will they be unless they keep his commandments. Similarly, the Beloved Disciple has this status, but again by virtue of Jesus' love, not by virtue of his discipleship. For John, writing to an audience long after the events in question, it no doubt made good sense for an ongoing relationship in love with Jesus to be the basis of group membership (even for those who have not seen him; John 20.29), rather than discipleship which might have been seen as closely tied to actual association with Jesus during his earthly mission. And of this relationship Lazarus was, in every sense, a prototype.[10]

For the Lazarus stories combine an image of domesticity with something further. Intertwined with the 'family' relationship is the relationship of 'friendship'. The concept of friendship was important in ancient Mediterranean cultures.[11] While a family member is a natural 'insider' (to whom one owes the obligations of kinship), a 'friend' is a potential outsider who is drawn into an insider relationship. The ties are voluntary rather than obligatory. Sometimes friendship could depict patron–client relationships, but more often it depicted a voluntary relationship among equals. Thus Jesus, who in John 11.5 is said to have loved Mary, Martha and Lazarus, refers to Lazarus as his 'friend' in John 11.11. In this story, Jesus is not depicted as a relative but as a friend of the family. The nature of this friendship, however, is one that has made him effectively like one of the family.

---

10 Thus Lee misses the mark when she argues with respect to Lazarus that no character in symbolic narratives in the Fourth Gospel is 'so clearly to be understood as a disciple'; see Lee 1994, p. 199.

11 See, for example, the essays on friendship in Greco-Roman settings in Fitzgerald 1997.

This does not appear to be simply a minor feature to account for Jesus' role in the story. Friendship is a theme that has surprisingly little explicit development in the New Testament as a model for relationships amongst Christ-followers. Friends are not entirely ignored in the Gospels, however, and a valuable study of this has been done by Alan Mitchell.[12] Luke and John particularly make frequent use of the term *philos*, friend. Often it is simply a term of address, 'I tell you, my friends, do not fear those who kill the body, and after that have no more that they can do' (Luke 12.4) or in a parable when the host at the banquet comes and says, 'Friend, go up higher' (Luke 14.10). While friends are therefore *mentioned* in the Gospels from time to time, it is rare to find it as a *theme* developed in its own right. Even parables about friends are rare in the Gospels, in contrast to parables about slaves and masters and even about family relationships.

For John, however, the friendship model is made a more explicit example for relationships between Christ-followers. It actually becomes in John more generalized as a way of describing disciples. This occurs in John 15, which begins with the imagery of the vine as a way of showing how integral the relationship is between Jesus and his followers. This metaphor, however, gives way to the explicit theme of friendship in verses 12–15. Here he does two things. First, he affirms in verse 14 that his followers are his 'friends' if they do what he commands them. What he commanded them back in verse 12 was to love one another as he loved them. Friendship is based on practical love, as the Lazarus story shows. This is a model for the community of followers. Second, he gives them the supreme example. There may be a condition imposed on them being his friends. But he has first concretely acted to be theirs. In verse 13 he explains, 'Greater love has no one than this, that someone lays down his life for his friends.' Sacrifice for friends is the supreme sign of true friendship. This is indeed where a true friend *may be* closer than a brother (cf. Prov. 18.24: 'There are friends who pretend to be friends, but there are friends who stick closer than a brother'). The final word on this is when he declares that he no longer calls his disciples servants or slaves, for the servant does not know what his master is doing; but 'I have called you friends' (John 15.15). They now

---

12 Mitchell 1992.

know what he knows. They are not reliant for teaching from him as they were previously, which is important because he is about to leave them. This description in John 15 makes it possible that Johannine Christ-followers also called *one another* 'friends', in the sense of true friends who behave almost like kin. We find concrete evidence of this in the Johannine letters. In 3 John 15 (in Gaius' letter to an unknown church), the closing benediction records 'Peace be to you. The *friends* greet you. Greet the *friends*, every one of them.' Johannine Christ-followers could therefore not only use the paradigm of being brothers and sisters, but also use the paradigm of being friends. The integration of the two, begun in the Lazarus story, is perhaps a later Johannine attempt to explain what fictive kinship might look like.

The fact that Lazarus is named demands closer consideration, and not simply by contrast with the disciple whom Jesus loved, who remains anonymous. Some critics have found significance in the meaning of the name of Lazarus, a Greek formulation representing the shortened Hebrew form for 'God helps'. If this did occur to the evangelist – and it is quite relevant to the narrative and Johannine theology – then the main surprise is that nothing much is made of this, and that he offers no explanation of the name for his Greek-speaking readers.[13] Indeed if the name were chosen only for its Hebrew meaning, it could have been equally applicable to the unnamed figures whom Jesus helps by his wonder-working, such as the man at the pool in Jerusalem in John 5 and the blind man in John 9. The evangelist does not seem compelled to provide a name, much less an encrypted name, for other people whom Jesus has healed. Why, then, should the evangelist provide a name at all for Lazarus, if this is not typical of the Johannine healings? Even being loved by Jesus does not require a named individual, as the Beloved Disciple demonstrates.

Does the attribution of a name to Lazarus serve a function, apart from being a product of tradition (an issue to which we will return below)? Some have argued that the presence of a name discourages identification with others. On this view, proposed by Raymond Brown, if one wishes to stimulate later members of the Jesus-group to 'identify' with the figure in the narrative, then the

---

13 So Sproston North 2001, p. 121. Bauckham notes it was the fourth most common male name among Palestinian Jews between 300 BCE and 200 CE; see Bauckham 1996, p. 678.

particularity of a specific name inhibits such a widening of application.[14] We consider this position to be entirely erroneous. We have argued above that exemplars and prototypes, which typify the identity of a group and thus provide members with models to imitate, in most cases carry a name, since human memory attaches itself more easily to people who are named than to anonymous figures. Thus first-century Judeans readily identified with Abraham. A named individual, like Abraham or Moses, whether historical or not, is the most effective means to ensure prototypicality.

The significance of the naming of Lazarus, however, is not merely to be deduced from the model we are using but is, in fact, confirmed by explicit comment in the Fourth Gospel, very shortly before the Lazarus episode. In John 10 the image of the shepherd and his sheep is used as an image for the relationship between Jesus and members of the group loyal to him. The sheep hear the voice of the shepherd; 'and he calls by name (*phōnei kat' onoma*) his own sheep (*ta idia probata*) and leads them out' (10.3). Commentators have long related this theme to the episode of Mary in the garden in John 20.16, where recognition comes at the point of Jesus addressing her by name. Fewer commentators, however, have noticed the phenomenon in John 11.43, where Jesus cries (*phōnei*) with a loud voice, 'Lazarus, come out!' In the more immediate context of John 11, the hearing of his voice and being called by name (John 10.3) is acted out. Jesus' naming of the man thus highlights his role as one of Jesus' 'sheep'. In addition, just as in John 10.3, Jesus is referring to his 'own' (*idia*) sheep, so Lazarus clearly fits into the social category soon after referred to as Jesus' 'own' (*idioi*) in the world whom he loved (John 13.1). There is also a parallel with John 5.28–29, but we will consider that passage later, in connection with the raising of Lazarus.[15] Additional

---

14 For such an argument with respect to the 'Secret Gospel of Mark', see Brown 1974, p. 480. Brown also speculates that hostility to women might have accounted for the absence of names for the women in the 'Secret Gospel of Mark'.

15 Reinhartz notes the parallels between John 5.25–29, 10.3 and 11.43–44 and comments not only upon the significance of the naming, but also the emergence from an enclosure in each case. She also makes a link with the blind man in John 9, arguing that he hears Jesus' voice without seeing Jesus and emerges from darkness; see Reinhartz 1992, p. 95. Also see Hakola 1999, pp. 233–5.

evidence of a consciousness of the significance of names in the Fourth Gospel can be found in the frequent references to doing a thing in someone's name or even believing in Jesus' name (1.12; 2.23; 3.18).[16]

Having discussed these considerations that are specific to Lazarus, we must now mount our case with respect to Martha and Mary.

The Case for Mary and Martha as Prototypical

There are other named figures in John 11.1–44 in addition to Jesus and Lazarus. Thomas is mentioned briefly in a section that is only loosely linked to the storyline of the miracle itself (11.16). This may have interpretative significance, as we shall see. Mary and Martha are, however, central figures in the narrative of Lazarus' raising. As Brown notes, Mary and Martha seem better known than Lazarus, as indicated by the order of names in John 11.5 ('Jesus loved Martha and her sister and Lazarus') and by the way Lazarus is introduced in relation to them in 11.1–2.[17] Since they too are explicitly described as loved by Jesus in terms very similar to Lazarus (John 11.5) and are thus the second and third persons in the Gospel who fall within this category that will receive extensive elaboration in Chapters 13—21, it is difficult to resist the conclusion that they are also prototypical of Johannine Christ-followers in this respect.

Scholarship has moved towards some measure of 'rehabilitation' of these characters, particularly with regard to the assessment of Martha's confessional statements in 11.21–27. In John 11.27 Martha says to Jesus, 'Yes. Lord; I believe that you are the Christ, the Son of God, he who is coming into the world' (RSV). Given the absence of any confessional statements at all from Lazarus, the statements of his sister become important for pursuing the theological interpretation of the evangelist. Yet while some scholars have highlighted the inadequacy of Martha's confession – as a foil against which the evangelist enables Jesus to develop a correct perspective – Sproston North draws attention to an increasing tendency to present Martha as 'the ideal of

16 On this, see Malina and Rohrbaugh 1998, pp. 247–8.
17 Brown 1979, p. 192.

Johannine faith'.[18] It is surely significant that in Martha's statement in 11.27, the titles 'Christ' and 'Son of God' are precisely the titles joined and applied by the evangelist himself in the programmatic saying in John 20.31 that looks back on the Gospel as a whole: 'But these are written that you may believe that Jesus is the Christ, the Son of God, and that believing you may have life in his name' (RSV). Martha's reference to Jesus as 'he who is coming' (John 11.27) seems to refer to the crowd's response to the feeding in John 6.14 ('This is indeed the prophet who is to come into the world' [RSV]) and also to prefigure the crowd's declaration at the Jerusalem entry in John 12.13 ('Blessed is he who comes in the name of the Lord' [RSV]). Mary also plays an important role, albeit not a confessional one. The devotion of the sisters, not only to Lazarus but also to Jesus, is acted out in Mary's anointing of Jesus in John 12.3. In this latter episode (the meal in John 12.1–8), Mary is actually more prominent than her brother Lazarus. And it is plainly significant that Mary's anointing of Jesus' feet in John 12 is soon to be followed in John 13 with the distinctive Johannine practice of foot-washing, a practice the disciples initially resist but not unlike that which Mary instinctively performed without instruction.

While these considerations constitute impressive support for the prototypicality of Martha and Mary, there are some qualifying factors. Even though the Christological declarations of Martha and the devotion of Mary should not be devalued, one might question whether these are the main focus for either the raising of Lazarus narrative or the story of the anointing at the meal. In both episodes, the women could be considered important as catalysts. In John 11, they are the ones who make Lazarus' plight known to Jesus and who bring out the nature of Jesus' love for the one whom he is about to raise. They emphasize the delay in Jesus' arrival, another key point in building the tension of the narrative and, we shall argue in the next chapter, in interpreting the event. The discussion with Martha is the occasion for the important statements attributed to Jesus in John 11.25–26. The affirmation given by Martha in 11.27 may actually be a *response* in relation to the more contentious and difficult statements that

---

18 Sproston North 2001, pp. 43–4 (especially with respect to John 11.27).

Jesus has just uttered. It is an acceptance of what Jesus has said, moving the story forward, and is arguably not the focal point either of narrative or interpretation. Even in John 12, Mary's anointing, described concisely in 12.3, serves as the catalyst for the dispute with Judas, which occupies 12.4–8.

In spite of these countervailing factors, however, it remains the case that Martha's confession in John 11.27 is the ideal confession of the insider,[19] and Mary's act of devotion is used to frame the episodes (cf. John 11.2; 12.3)[20] as well as prefiguring Jesus' own washing of the disciples' feet in John 13.[21]

The naming of the women also highlights their importance. It introduces a significance for them that is denied even the Samaritan woman in John 4 and the woman taken in the act of adultery, an independent passage usually inserted in John 8.[22] Scholars have struggled to explain why indeed John has named Mary and Martha. While their featuring in traditions available to John (an issue considered in the previous chapter) may have constituted a remote cause, some more proximate reason is needed for their prominence in the Fourth Gospel where, after all, the woman who anointed Jesus' feet is finally given a name (in contrast to Mark 14.3–9; Matt. 26.6–13 and Luke 7.36–50). In our view, the naming of Martha and Mary, both of whom typify characteristics central to the identity of John's vision of the Christ-movement, serves, as with Lazarus, to enhance their capacity to function as prototypical figures.

Having considered the particular issues surrounding the prototypicality of Lazarus and then his two sisters, it is worth reflecting for a moment on the extent to which we should consider them together as a prototypical family of the Christ-movement.

---

19 So Malina and Rohrbaugh 1998, p. 199.

20 Cf. also John 11.32: 'When Mary came where Jesus was and saw him, she fell at his feet . . .'

21 Rightly resisting attempts either to discredit the faith response of one sister at the expense of the other or to view both unsympathetically, see Hakola 1999, pp. 238–9. He notes how both are 'becoming models of true discipleship'.

22 With regard to the different levels of understanding shown by the Samaritan woman and Martha, see Neyrey 1998, p. 99.

A Prototypical Family

We submit that the evangelist effectively creates a family of characters with prototypical significance. This family is loved by Jesus. As we have noted already, this is a valued insider designation. The 'Lazarus family' and the Beloved Disciple are the only specific individuals so designated in the Fourth Gospel. Even though God's love for the world has been made clear from early in the Gospel, the 'Lazarus family' is the *first* specific set of individuals to be noted as loved by Jesus in the Fourth Gospel. In addition, taken together, they embody relationships of love to Jesus and to each other, insider confessions about Jesus, the kind of devotion to Jesus that is ultimately to be shown to each other, and the reassurance regarding life even in the face of death. No single figure embodies it all. Lazarus makes no confession and performs no act of devotion, yet he is central to concerns about the life that Jesus gives in John 11. Martha is the one who makes the confession;[23] Mary is the one who displays love in an act of extravagant devotion. For their part, the disciples of Jesus struggle in all these respects, in contrast to this unusual, named family – not identified with disciples[24] – who embody it all precisely at the point in the Gospel when the die has been cast for the Passion. Even the family meal shortly before the Passover in John 12.1, given an unusually precise date in relation to the Passover by the evangelist,[25] antedates the significant last meal with the disciples to follow in 13.1. The family anticipates, often in more perfect form, what the disciples struggle to understand in the chapters that follow.[26]

It is noteworthy that the Lazarus family is not exhorted to

---

23 Neyrey rightly notes also that Martha as well as Mary displays hospitality in her service of Jesus (cf. John 12.2); see Neyrey 1988, p. 83.

24 Thus we are reluctant to describe Lazarus as a beloved *disciple*; *contra* Neyrey (1988, pp. 83, 92).

25 Our suggestion of the reason for the precise dating of the meal in John 12.1–8 six days before the Passover (12.1), linking it to early observance of the Lord's Supper on Sunday, the first day of the week, appears in the previous chapter of this volume.

26 The absence of any of this family in the Johannine Passion and resurrection narratives is not problematic if they have already come to terms with Jesus' resurrection in John 11 and his death in John 12, once again in contrast to the disciples.

display love towards one another, such as Jesus will promulgate as a command later in the Gospel. Their family relationship and the concern of the sisters for their brother provide 'natural' examples of such love. In contrast to the disciples, the Lazarus family is prototypical of love for one another. It is also prototypical in its love for Jesus as depicted by Mary's 'natural' initiative at the anointing. By way of contrast, later (in John 21) Peter will be intensively examined regarding his 'love' *for* Jesus. The context for many of the statements of Jesus' love for disciples has an hortatory edge. Even the Beloved Disciple is *instructed* to undertake the care of Jesus' mother. But not so for Lazarus, Martha and Mary.

It is worthwhile to explore a little further features of the portrayal of Lazarus, Martha and Mary relevant to the Johannine understanding of Jesus-followers. The use of a 'family' as a prototype is itself striking. In the first place, it is a very carefully constructed family. It has siblings of both sexes but no parent.[27] In view of Johannine thinking that believers are 'born from above' the absence of a parental figure in John 11 depicts an appropriate Johannine model for membership within Jesus-groups. Not only are parental figures absent, however, so are references to ancestors. Craig Koester follows Bruce Malina in noting how the Fourth Gospel, like other ancient sources, often ascribes the characteristics of ancestors and places of origin to its characters.[28] The most obvious examples are found in Jesus' dialogue with the Samaritan woman in John 4 where Samaritans are described as those whose fathers worshipped on 'this mountain' (4.20). Later, in John 8.39, the Judeans declare their ancestor with the words 'Abraham is our father.' The absence of such ascriptions in the current passage therefore becomes a point of interest, perhaps indicating how the Lazarus–Martha–Mary group derives its characteristics not from ancestors, but from their association with Jesus, as loved by Jesus. In the collective memory of this group of Christ-followers, this is the family that represents the earliest stage of the movement. In effect, they become the hallowed ancestors, in a fictive but an important sense.

27 Contrast this with the other revivification miracles in the Gospels, which emphasize the parent–child relationship – the raising of Jairus' daughter (Mark 5.21–43 parr.) and the raising of the widow's son at Nain (Luke 7.11–17).

28 Koester 2003, p. 35, citing Malina 1989b and 1992.

In the second place, however, employment of any kind of 'family' model is all the more extraordinary in view of the hesitation of this Gospel, relative to the other canonical Gospels, in employing fictive kinship language openly with respect to the disciples. Jesus does not *explicitly* use designations of fictive kinship for his followers (in the sense of calling them his own 'brothers' or even 'brothers' of one another) until after the resurrection in the Fourth Gospel (John 20.17; 21.23).

More generally, however, the relationship of disciples to Jesus does not invoke explicit kinship categories.[29] Even at the last supper, the disciples are described as 'slaves' (John 13.16; cf. 15.20). It seems significant therefore in the Farewell Discourse in John 15.15 (despite v. 20 to follow) that Jesus states that his disciples are 'slaves' no longer, but rather are 'friends' because they now have been told by Jesus the intentions of his Father. There is no doubt that the category of 'friend' surpasses that of 'slave' and is perhaps a step towards the closer kinship language used more openly after the resurrection. Yet, as noticed above, it is precisely the description 'friend' that has already been used of Lazarus (John 11.11). Lazarus thus anticipates the later elevation of status of the disciples, while the word also corresponds to the very unusual use of 'friends' as a designation for believers that one finds in 3 John 15 ('The friends greet you. Greet the friends, every one of them'), the closing greeting of that epistle.

---

29 In the Prologue John 1.12–13 ('children of God') prefigures the common parentage, although Judeans more widely considered themselves children of God. The more distinctive use of 'born from above' or 'born of spirit' in John 3 develops this in a more oblique way, but still stops well short of what one finds in Mark 3.31–34 where 'brothers and sisters' becomes an explicit description of the community of followers. The Beloved Disciple represents a special case when Jesus specifically entrusts his mother to this disciple at the cross (John 19.26–27), saying to his mother 'Woman, behold your son!' and to the Beloved Disciple 'Behold, your mother!' The Beloved Disciple thereafter took Mary into his home.

Lazarus, Martha and Mary and the Identity of the Johannine Community

The time has now come to assess these features of John's Gospel in relation to the model of social identity we outlined in Chapter 2. The heart of our interest in this volume is the question of the identity of the audience for whom John was writing and the continuing relevance of his narrative for present-day Christians. This means we are focusing on who John's addressees thought they were by belonging to this particular section of the Christ-movement and on how the Johannine vision of Lazarus, Martha and Mary might deepen and enliven the sense that contemporary Christians have of who we are. We will deal with the historical dimension in this section of this chapter and the contemporary dimension in the next.

We are concerned with the 'social identity' of John's audience, meaning that part of their identity that they derived from belonging to such a group. Admittedly, this would not have comprised the total identity of the individuals concerned. Yet we know very little about the individuals concerned (except perhaps for a few scraps of information to be gleaned from 1, 2 and 3 John) and, in any event, if the community was, or recently had been, under pressure (for example, from local Judeans; cf. John 16.1–4), this would have made the sense of belonging to the group more salient (at least for those who remained in the group).

One's sense of identity, be it individual or social, encompasses past, present and future. We perceive ourselves to exist in a chronological continuum that begins with the progenitors of the group from which we derive our identity, such as the founders of our tribe or nation, the distant ancestors of our family or those responsible for inaugurating a socio-religious faith and lifestyle to which we adhere. Myths of origin are frequently told to explain to current members of particular groups how they came into being and acquired the distinctive identity that they now share. John's treatment of Lazarus, Martha and Mary represents just such an enterprise. For he portrays them as the first to enter into a relationship with Jesus, one of mutual love, that would emerge later in the Gospel as central to the existence and destiny of all the disciples of Jesus. There can be no doubt that John wanted the original audience of the Fourth Gospel to view this as vital for their identity as Christ-followers in their present existence. By recounting the raising of Lazarus John also introduced into this picture a potent reminder of what the future would hold for those who had faith. We will return to this topic in the next chapter of this volume.

Henri Tajfel observed that social identity embraced cognitive, emotional and evaluative dimensions. In relation to the Johannine treatment of Lazarus, Martha and Mary, the cognitive dimension is exposed in the strong sense John's contemporary Christ-followers had of belonging to a group like this and in basic group beliefs (as discussed by Daniel Bar-Tal) such as the identity and status of Jesus and the reality of resurrection. The emotional dimension appears with considerable force in John 11—12, in the remarkably affective elements of the regard Jesus and this family from Bethany have for one another. But the evangelist is not content merely with the statement that Jesus loved them (11.3, 5), or with extravagant signs of their love for him, such as Mary's anointing of his feet. For John provides the unique notice that when he has been told where they had laid Lazarus, 'Jesus wept', a response which elicited from the Judean onlookers the exclamation, 'Look how he loved him' (11.34–36).

Very often we tell ourselves who we are in belonging to one group by pointing to other groups to which we do not belong. This brings us to the third aspect of social identity, the evaluative one, which addresses how we rate ourselves by belonging to one group rather than to others. For John and, we must assume, for his audience, membership in the Christ-movement entailed loving Jesus and being loved by him. This meant that the identity of such a group was an extremely exalted one. Whatever the members suffered at the hands of outgroups, this mutual love was an abiding feature of membership. As we noted in Chapter 2, a common feature accompanying ingroup/outgroup differentiation is that of stereotyping the outgroup, which means that ingroup members assign to the outgroup attributes that are believed to be characteristic of all its members. Stereotypes are not fixed and immutable but vary according to context. Scanning the whole range of the 27 constituent documents of the New Testament produces a variety of ways in which those who were not members of the Christ-movement were viewed. John provides only one such picture and one that is representative only of how he viewed local outgroups at the time that the final version of the Fourth Gospel was produced. If the document had reached this form at an earlier or later date, the different context may well have led to outsiders being stereotyped quite differently.

Nevertheless, we can only focus on what is before us. The picture that John paints of the nature and impending fate of those who do not come to have faith in Jesus as the Christ and who are steeped in the evil of the world is a remarkably bleak one. The extremely negative way in which they are portrayed creates by the force of the contrast a powerful expression of the privileged and blessed circumstances of the ingroup. Although we are not able within the scope of this volume to dwell upon the status of the outgroup, one of us has been intensively researching this 'dark side' of John and we will now briefly summarize some of his findings to substantiate the point just made, relying on research by one of us into the question of evil in the Fourth Gospel.[30]

However much the Gospel of John may be Christologically oriented, and however much the symbols associated with Jesus focus on images such as 'light', 'darkness' or evil constitute a reality that is essential to the understanding of the Gospel. The Johannine dualisms are indeed two-sided. Thus we can find the author writing, 'And this is the judgement, that the light has come into the world, and people loved darkness rather than light, because their deeds were evil' (John 3.19). Closely associated with this dualism appears to be the contrast between flesh and spirit (John 3.5–6) and between being 'from above' or being 'from the earth' (3.31). It should not be surprising therefore that the Fourth Gospel also has a very developed vocabulary for expressing evil in terms of a supramundane, personalized figure. This figure is variously called 'the Devil', 'Satan', 'the Evil One' and 'the ruler of this world'.

The significance of recognizing clearly the recurrence of such language, and for finding it often expressed in terms of dyadic contrasts or oppositions, is that it supports the perception of an insider/outsider contrast in this Gospel. It is fundamental to the formulation of the identity of the Johannine group(s). Some individual figures in the Fourth Gospel may be full of ambiguities, but the Johannine world-view is structured around sharp contrasts rather than shades of grey. And the decision that individual

30 See Piper 2000 (which sketches the conclusions), and 2007 forthcoming.

figures face is ultimately quite a clear one: whether to believe in Jesus as God's unique Son and agent or not. This Johannine call to decision (a central 'group belief' on which their social identity is based) contrasts with that of the Synoptic Gospels, where the call is more often to respond to the good news of God's coming kingdom. So the 'message' of the Johannine Jesus is quite distinctive in what it emphasizes and what it does not.

We have argued at several points above that the Johannine view of Jesus' saving work is one that particularly is shown to benefit 'his own'. This care for a select group of followers was highlighted in the good shepherd imagery in John 10. Those who know Jesus' voice are a definable 'fold'; boundaries are evident. We have also argued that this is reflected in the passages about Lazarus, Martha and Mary, a context undoubtedly crafted to highlight love and friendship in relation to a 'family'. Yet opposition is also clearly signalled in the Fourth Gospel. The Judeans are labelled as 'of your father the Devil' (John 8.44). The 'world' (*kosmos*), while the object of God's love in John 3.16, is nonetheless a term for opposition to Christ-followers in the Farewell Prayer of Jesus for those whom he is about to leave behind: 'the world has hated them because they are not of the world, even as I am not of the world' (John 17.14). The world is still a dangerous place for them – and probably not just from human opposition: 'I do not pray that thou shouldst take them out of the world, but that thou shouldst keep them from the Evil One (*tou ponērou*)' (17.15).[31] Jesus himself must do battle with the 'ruler of this world' (John 12.31; 16.11). So the dualism over against the 'world' or the Judeans is described as something that Christ-followers face after the departure of Jesus to the Father and is not limited to the time when Jesus carried out his ministry. It appears to be quite fundamental to the Johannine world-view. Whatever Jesus accomplished on the cross, the reality of evil and opposition continues.

If John is realistic about this – as he also is about the real-

31 On the point of the translation 'Evil One' rather than simply 'evil', see (among others) rightly Barrett (1978, p. 510); Brown (1971, p. 761); Schnackenburg (1982, p. 184). All note the clearer suggestions of this translation in 1 John 2.13–14; 3.12; 5.18–19 and the possible link with the reference to the 'ruler of this world' as a *personal adversary* earlier in the Farewell Discourse.

ity of death for Christ-followers, as we maintain – then it is not surprising that outsiders are viewed with a measure of distrust. Boundary maintenance is closely linked to the preservation of their identity. It is far from clear that Christ-followers are ever encouraged to 'love' outsiders, even as a means of winning them over. The love commandment appears to be directed to insiders: 'love *one another* even as I have loved you' (John 13.34). These are words uttered exclusively to the disciples that were with him at the last supper. These are the same ones who are in the world, but not really 'of it' (John 17.14–16). This detachment serves to underline the division drawn between them and the Judeans/ world.

If John realistically assesses that Jesus did not 'clean up' the world during his ministry, then when, if ever, will it be purged of evil? Interestingly, in the Fourth Gospel Jesus never even casts out a demon.[32] And whatever the meaning of John 12.31, evil continues to threaten believers after Jesus' departure to the Father, as we have noted. Moreover, there is no suggestion in the Fourth Gospel that believers will accomplish what Jesus did not achieve, nor is there a great deal of encouragement to try. The division in this Gospel between good and evil in the world is quite persistent. This is a potential problem for scholars who have tried to argue that the understanding of the end-times in the Fourth Gospel is highly realized. John's down-to-earth recognition of the persistence of evil, and the continuation of death even for those loved by Jesus, requires some future resolution. What is interesting is the form that it takes. The resurrection on the last day is of just and unjust alike (John 5.28–29) – the just to life, and the unjust to 'judgement'. But John also presents us with another picture in which Jesus, who has returned to the Father, has gone to prepare a place for those in his care (John 14.1–3). The hope expressed there is that they will join him with the Father. Jesus is not going to return to reside in the world; in the Johannine schema his true place has always been with the Father, from even before creation (John 1.1). So believers will join them in the Father's 'house'. What will happen to the world? There is no record of it ever really being purged of evil, even in this scenario. The unjust, who are not taken to be with the Father, and the Evil One simply seem

32 See Piper 2000.

to remain. Thus the 'world', which is often a label that John uses for all who oppose the followers of Jesus, retains the sense of this label, and even the future perspective of John does not alter the boundary that it depicts.

Having now considered the recognition and fate of the outgroup in the Fourth Gospel, we will consider one other issue related to the identity of the group: the relevance of 'self-categorization' to the family from Bethany.

John Turner's development of social identity theory to embrace the processes of 'self-categorization' finds interesting resonances in the material concerning Lazarus, Martha and Mary. Here we have both personal and social identity, that is, self-definitions based on personal or idiosyncratic attributes and those based on social category memberships. The latter are more prominent but it is necessary to acknowledge the existence of the former. Since Lazarus never speaks and is largely a passive actor, the chief personal attributes in the narrative are those respects in which Martha and Mary differ. As we have noticed in Chapter 3 of this work, Martha comes across as the older and more practical sister. Mary seems to be the younger sister and given to emotional display. The difference in character is quite a prominent feature of John's portrayal. Yet, as Turner has noticed, where social identity becomes more salient than personal identity, people regard themselves less as idiosyncratic individuals and more as similar and prototypical representatives of their ingroup category. In the Johannine narrative the value of this insight is revealed in the fact that the personal characteristics of Lazarus, Martha and Mary are overshadowed by a core feature of their shared ingroup membership – the mutual love existing between them and Jesus. Here we see how definition of people in terms of their membership of a social category – in this case the Johannine version of the Christ-movement – can take precedence over their personal identity.

Lazarus, Martha and Mary as Characters in the Fourth Gospel

At this point we must return to our brief discussion of Johannine characterization in Chapter 1 of this volume. We can say at once that the argument we have mounted in this chapter indicates quite unequivocally how wide of the mark was Franz Overbeck's view that the characters in the Fourth Gospel are but 'a mirror for the manifestation of an alien Being and are of no further significance.'[33] On the other hand, we have done much to confirm Louis Martyn's view that the characters under discussion do speak to the experience of the audience for whom the Gospel was written, even if we have provided a new and socially realistic understanding for how they do have this effect. And yet we need to note just how different is the type of characterization in view in the case of Lazarus, Martha and Mary from that to which we are accustomed in modern literary works.

By and large, those of us who belong to North Atlantic, individualistic cultures and who read the novels (to cite but one literary genre) that have been written in such a context view successful characterization as the process of creating a fully individualized character who engages in relationships with other characters in the work in a realistic way. The more important the character, the more we expect to find a rich understanding of his or her distinctive personality and the inner motivations that drive him or her to act in certain ways. We should not expect this fully realized and individualized characterization in the group-oriented world of the ancient Mediterranean, and we certainly do not find it in the Fourth Gospel.

This does not mean that Lazarus, Martha and Mary are mere ciphers lacking all individuality. As we have seen, John tells us virtually nothing about Lazarus apart from his relationships to his sisters, his place of residence and the probability that he was reasonably well off. Yet, in a world in which honourable men and women lived in accordance with clearly defined social roles, these were significant aspects of someone's identity. John does, however, introduce engaging points of distinctiveness in the characters of Martha and Mary. They do exist as individuals, not just as identical representatives of a group. We also learn something of their inner motivation, in particular their love of their brother and of Jesus, but these are not the subject of any introspective examination such as we regularly find in modern works of literature.

The main point of John's treatment of Lazarus is the fact that Jesus loved him and what this led Jesus to do for him – to raise him from the dead. So it is not anything distinctive or unique about Lazarus as an individual that John highlights, indeed we learn nothing whatever of his individuality. Rather John, while

33 Overbeck 1911, p. 303 (cited in Hakola 1999, p. 223).

situating him in the town of Bethany as a person of some resources whose parents are apparently dead, fixes upon the relationships Lazarus enjoys, both with his sisters and with Jesus. This means that the evangelist presents his character in relation to significant groups in his life, namely, his family and the group of those who have a close and friendly connection of some sort with Jesus. To revert to the theoretical perspective we are employing in this volume, John is not so much interested in the personal identity of Lazarus, but in the social identity he derives from belonging to these groups. In the case of this character then, we see a narrative expression of the situation that John Turner (in developing his self-categorization theory) has described – where social identity becomes more salient than personal identity, people regard themselves and, we might say, are regarded by others less as idiosyncratic individuals and more as representatives of their ingroup category or categories. This may entail a certain 'depersonalization' of Lazarus, but one achieved in the interests of underlining the nature of the group memberships he shares. Thus, in relation to Lazarus, social identity theory therefore provides new insight into the motivation and manner of Johannine characterization. We could mount much the same case for John's characterization of Martha and Mary, even though he does give us some indication of their personal identities.

Group Prototypes, Possible Social Identities and Collective Memory

That John is presenting Lazarus, Martha and Mary, characters from the past of the Christ-movement but clearly relevant to the concerns of his audience as he writes, inevitably foregrounds the question of how this relevance is achieved. We submit that the notions of group prototypes, possible social identities and collective memory that we have explained earlier in this volume allow us a new way to address this issue.

We demonstrated earlier in this chapter that Lazarus, Martha and Mary are exemplars (from the perspective of the original audience who probably regarded these as real figures) or prototypes (if they are actually figures John has constructed for the purpose of his narrative) of Jesus 'own people' (*hoi idioi*), both in the sense of typifying this group and also as being the first in time to have done so. They are the first people whom Jesus loved and the only ones the evangelist names. As such, they provide possible social identities for the Christ-followers who comprised John's original audience. They were Christ-followers from the past who told John's addressees who they were in the present and (which is more relevant to our next chapter) what they might expect to be in the future. They provided personal models of the relationship the believer had to Christ and God by virtue of membership in this new group and the advantages this relationship brought. As a family, they also provided a kinship model for the movement that was adopted as fundamental to its identity and organization, both in the development of house-based communities and in the use of kinship language fictively by its members. The precise means by which John's audience could have appropriated or internalized these group prototypes lies within the field of cognitive psychology, which has only recently begun to make its entry into New Testament scholarship.[34]

John's presentation of these characters also represents an exercise in the creation of a group's collective memory. We have explored this dimension to his work in Chapter 2 of this volume. He is proposing Lazarus, Martha and Mary as maximally representative of the identity of the group and seeking to lodge these figures permanently in its collective memory. Given the importance of ancestors and ancestral values to most of the circum-Mediterranean cultures of the first century CE, the choice of the Gospel genre, with its possibility of working up characters (apparently) contemporaneous with Jesus, the decision to focus on figures who had actually known Jesus made good sense. By his narrative of Lazarus, Martha and Mary John was able to construct and mobilize memory in the service of the community for whom he was writing, both as to its experience and identity in the present and as to its destiny in the future. By writing about the family of Bethany in the way he did, John told his audience where they had come from, who they were and where they were going.

We have seen in Chapter 3, however, just how distinctive was the processing of the past in which the Fourth Evangelist engaged. We have already mentioned that there are signs in this Gospel of tensions with other groups within the wider Christ-movement

---

34 See Esler 2006d for an example focusing on cognitive processes of memory acquisition and construction.

of the late first century CE. There was no one agreed version of the past. Different writers representing different communities presented the past in various ways. While there may have been agreement around certain broad issues, in many respects the past was a field of contestation of which memory constituted an important part. That we have four canonical Gospels, and not one, is a sure sign of how naturally different visions of who Christ was and what he meant for those who believed in him became embedded in the various branches of the movement in his name.[35]

A Theological Reflection

How can results such as these, elicited from the Fourth Gospel by an historical investigation informed with ideas and perspectives from the social sciences, be brought into useful engagement with contemporary Christian life and reflection? One way to answer this is by application of the theological perspective of intercultural communication and communion we have set out in Chapter 2.

Within this perspective, we engage with the narrative as a communication from John and with the aim of taking seriously what he intended by it in the particular context in and into which he wrote it. The Fourth Gospel was not written for us, so we are like those who overhear some momentous communication or discover a document that contained such a message long after it was delivered to its original addressees. Moreover, although its author is dead, we have ways to model communication with John, our ancestor in faith, such as in memory or, if we prefer (and it is not necessary for this purpose that we do), by means of a high theology of the communion of saints where John has a more immediate form of presence. We receive his message in all its historical circumstances, not in spite of them. Although it employs literary techniques, the Fourth Gospel is not primarily a work of literature since it has an expressly didactic purpose: 'but these are written that you may believe that Jesus is the Christ, the Son of God, and that believing you may have life in his name' (20.31; RSV). Such a programmatic statement would cause us to throw down, as noted earlier, a novel if it were to announce such

35 On the process by which the early Church came to rely upon four Gospels, see Piper 2005.

a programme. In addition, this was a work written by someone who had been socialized into a culture very different from ours (especially if we inhabit a Northern European or North American culture or their offshoots in the Southern Hemisphere) and its meaning is deeply implicated in that different setting. This means that as we attempt to understand its meaning we will inevitably need to engage in the processes of intercultural communication, with which we are now reasonably familiar. The cultural difference between John and us also means that not only is his world not ours but that there may well be things about it and his message that we do not like. This reflects the critical dimension of all intercultural dialogue. But communication and even communion can coexist with disagreement; this was a basic insight of Martin Buber's enunciation of the 'I–Thou' relationship.

Somewhat ironically perhaps, the very remoteness of John's work from us allows it to speak to contemporary Christians in fresh and provocative ways. We will concentrate here on one salient aspect of John's presentation of Lazarus, Martha and Mary as prototypical Christ-followers. By and large, modern Christians gather for the purposes of worship in large, tailor-made buildings – the churches that have been a feature of Christian organization since Constantine built the first of them, St John Lateran in Rome[36] – and take part in services conducted by specially trained and full-time functionaries of various kinds. Recent innovations such as the basic communities of Latin America or the house-church movement in Europe and North America represent exceptions of limited significance to this dominant pattern. To this we must add that in most countries Christianity does not suffer from tension with outgroups, while Christian churches are usually open to visitors, even outside the times of regular services. We should never underestimate the significance of these features of contemporary Christian life, especially when we consider the dialectic relationship that exists between architectural structure and the forms of sociality that occur within it.[37]

John and his audience existed within a radically different ecclesial setting. As we have mentioned above, the Johannine

---

36 St John Lateran's Basilica was dedicated on 9 November 318 (Webb 2001, p. 42–3).

37 See Esler 2003, pp. 102–7.

community (just like the others scattered around the Mediterranean littoral in the late first century) met in the houses of the members, where the meetings were presided over by a family member (or perhaps, on occasion, a visiting evangelist). This meant that the Christ-movement was caught up in domestic architectural settings and domestic roles, rituals and relationships. These features are all present in the case of Lazarus, Martha and Mary. We see the complete interpenetration of their love for one another as siblings with their love of Jesus (and his love of them) in the gruelling family circumstance of the death and burial of one of the family members, grounded in a broader context of external opposition to the Christ-movement. We also see them gathered in their house, with Jesus' disciples,[38] for a meal in the presence of Jesus where Mary unleashes her extraordinary show of devotion and where, indeed, there is scope for dissension in the response of Judas.

The model of intercultural communication and communion that we are applying here suggests that modern-day Christians should attend as closely as possible to this thoroughly different vision of the identity of Christ-followers. This means that rather than seeking to strip out of the narrative 'contingent' historical features in the search for 'timeless' truths that can be inserted into some treatise on systematic theology, we should listen with the greatest care to what John has to say on this very subject, deeply embedded in a particular context remote from ours as his communication is. What we learn from this exercise will depend, to a large extent, on the particular modern context in which we attempt it. But it is not too much to say that values of intimacy, of domesticity, of face-to-face encounter with one another and the Lord around a shared meal and, lastly, above all, of realism in the face of the harsh reality of death, will permeate into those who engage in this process.

---

38 Judas alone is mentioned by name (12.4) but it is highly improbable that John intended, or his audience understood, that he was the only disciple present.

5

The Raising of Lazarus from the Dead as Prototypical

A New Approach to the Raising of Lazarus: Its Role in Group Identity

In Chapter 1 of this volume we outlined a spectrum of scholarly views concerning the meaning of the raising of Lazarus from the dead, that extended from the heavily Christological (highlighting the role and status of Christ in the narrative) at one end to the soteriological at the other (highlighting the bearing of the narrative on the destiny of those who believe in Christ). We indicated that the preponderance of interest by scholars lay more with the former dimension than with the latter. The time has now come for us to present an interpretation of the narrative of Lazarus being raised from the dead in John 11 which substantiates our view that, without denying its Christological dimension, the emphasis of the story mainly falls on the status and destiny of those who believe in Christ. To move the discussion from the traditional language of 'soteriology', which is useful although really the product of an approach that has little room for the social aspects of the narrative, we will once again rely upon the social identity theory that we have been employing throughout this volume.

Put simply, our historical interest lies in what answer this narrative gave John's audience to the questions, 'Who, as believers in Christ are we and what is our destiny?' To explore this issue we will need to pay particular attention to that development of social identity theory which deals with group beliefs, but not to the exclusion of other aspects of the theory. We will see that it is not simply a belief in resurrection that John integrates with the social identity to be derived from being a Christ-follower, for he also presents such a belief as part of a much larger web of values and behaviour lying at the heart of what it means to belong to this group.

Having addressed these issues in a process of historical investigation in the current chapter, we will proceed in Chapter 6 to consider how the Lazarus narrative figured in some early Christian art from Rome, most of it in funerary contexts of catacomb frescoes or carved reliefs on sarcophagi. In Chapter 7, the conclusion to this volume, we will reflect on some theological implications of John's communication relating to the raising of Lazarus within the framework of intercultural communication and communion with the evangelist as our ancestor in faith still in some way present to us.

The Raising of Lazarus in John 11: The Problem Addressed in the Narrative

The focal point and dramatic climax of John 11.1–44 is undoubtedly the raising of Lazarus from the dead. On the thesis for which we are arguing in this volume, therefore, we must demonstrate that this is prototypical for members of the ingroup. Such a demonstration will need to show that the narrative took its original audience a long way beyond just a seemingly trite affirmation that believers in Christ can expect to be raised on the last day. Several scholars have come to the recognition that there is indeed a *particular* issue of concern, although there has not always been agreement on precisely what it is. By focusing on the question of group identity in relation to ingroup insecurities we are able to offer a fresh solution.

Ingroup Insecurities, External Danger and the Threat of Death

A brief survey of the context of John 11 confirms that *ingroup insecurities are becoming a focal point* even as the debates with the Judeans are drawing to their end in the first part of the Fourth Gospel. The chapters leading up to chapter 11 increasingly highlight the threats to the Christ-followers. John 9 (the expulsion from the synagogue of the healed blind man who initially does not know Jesus but later confesses him to the authorities)[1] and John 10 (the metaphor of the sheepfold and variety of threats to the sheep) have begun to raise the profile of the question of the identity and security of those cared for by Jesus. The dangers facing believers are developed further in the Farewell Discourses (especially 16.1–4) and the Final Prayer of Jesus (cf. 17.14–15). The two issues of identity and security are closely linked in these chapters, not least because of the anxiety about failing to remain in the group under such pressures.

Indeed the fact of the death of some believers by the time of publication of the final version of the Fourth Gospel must have presented a perplexing concern. A prediction of believers dying is made most explicitly in John 16.2 when the Johannine Jesus announces that 'whoever kills you will think that he is offering service to God'. The warning follows the preceding sayings in John 15.18–20 about the world 'hating' believers and 'persecuting' them. In 16.2, the persecution seems to derive mainly from the synagogue and is associated with their expulsion from it. Even if one must reckon with rhetorical enhancement in the references to 'killing', the example of Jesus and the allusion to Peter's martyrdom in John 21.18–19 mean that there had been historical events to sustain such a perspective. When Jesus prays to the Father for their protection from the Evil One (John 17.15), it is again in the context of the world's 'hate' (17.14).

By highlighting these themes, John reinforces the idea that this is a group that sees itself aligned against society, an 'anti-society' to use the formulation of Bruce Malina and Richard Rohrbaugh to which we have adverted earlier in this work. The descent–ascent motif, which permeates the story of Jesus in this Gospel (as the one who comes from above and who returns to the Father), contributes to the sense of separateness,[2] but it also poses a problem for believers. Jesus eventually left the hostile world. Why should not they who believe in him also be able to do so? Interestingly, the Johannine Jesus explicitly repudiates any suggestion that they be taken out of the world immediately (17.15: 'I do not pray that you should take them out of the world, but that you should

---

1 As further evidence of conscious linkages between John 9 and John 11, note also the parallel of John 9.4–5 with John 11.9–10.

2 See Meeks 1972 for a magnificent explication of this theme in the Fourth Gospel.

keep them from the Evil One'). In other words, the Johannine Jesus announces that there is no *immediate* form of escape that might remove them from the world's hostility and presumably even from martyrdom. Whether or not escape was ever a realistic option, the explicit rejection of it – as though it were a possibility – is significant. After all, even Jesus went to a cross.

In their present circumstances, therefore, there is no escape for them from external opposition and even the possibility of death at the hands of outsiders. The kind of protection that is sought for believers is aimed at keeping them loyal under pressure, rather than encouraging them to believe that they can escape from the pressures themselves. Wavering ingroup loyalty ('apostasy') may well have been the reality underlying such statements, as well as lying behind other calls for believers to 'abide' or 'remain' in him (especially John 15.1–11).

One also finds such concerns addressed before the Farewell Discourses, strikingly in what may be an addition to the Lazarus story, in John 11.7–16. Here the evangelist displays not only the resolve of Jesus to go to Jerusalem despite the awareness that they are seeking to kill him (11.8), but also the implicit threat to the disciples too, which Thomas at least seems willingly to face (11.16). Disciples are encouraged here to follow Jesus and not waver even in the face of threats to life.

Group Insecurities Caused by Death from Natural Causes

Not all anxieties about death, however, need be concerned with external threats. The story of Lazarus involves death through illness, and this is the immediate concern of the 'family'. The Lazarus situation, accordingly, seems to address a concern about believers dying from a natural cause. He is quite literally '*the brother* who dies'.[3] Is this a credible line of interpretation?

It is certainly a credible concern within early communities of Christ-followers. We find it expressed perhaps most explicitly by Paul in 1 Thessalonians 4.13–18, where Paul reminds his audience that they should not, like people who have no hope, be grieving for Christ-followers who have died, for when the Lord

3 On the significance of 'brother' here as being representative of 'any Christian', see Koester 2003, pp. 67–8.

returns those who have died in Christ will rise first, followed by those who are still alive.[4] Paul needs to paint an evocative picture of the End to allay anxieties clearly present in Thessalonika regarding those believers who had died prior to the 'coming of the Lord'. In a Johannine context where *parousia* concepts seem even more muted (an issue to which we will return shortly) and when 'life' is so strongly presented as 'realized', the confusion occasioned by the death of believers would have been even greater. In what sense did they have eternal life in the present? The Gospel frequently promises to believers that they will not perish (3.16; 10.28) or will never taste death (8.51), or will receive eternal life (3.15, 36; 4.14, 36; 5.24; 6.27, 40, 47, 54; 10.28; 12.25; 17.2; cf. 20.31). Because eternal life can be understood in more than one way, such promises can generate misunderstanding. How does one reconcile the theology of eternal life with the realities of death and an absent Jesus? And if one interpretation of Jesus' death is laying down his life for his friends/his sheep (15.13, cf. 10.11, 15, 18), then why should it be necessary for these sheep/friends to experience death at all?

The Lazarus Narrative as a Response to the Problem of Group Insecurities Concerning Death

Confronting the Reality of Death

The Lazarus episode directly addresses such concerns in a number of respects. One notable and perhaps surprising feature of the narrative is its uncompromising acceptance of the reality of death. This story, more than any other prior to John 21, indicates how, despite the life that Jesus brings, no member of the ingroup should expect to be able to escape death. This is dramatically presented in terms of those who might have the greatest expectation of being exceptions, those to whom Jesus was closest. There are three such male figures described in the Gospel – Lazarus, whom Jesus loves (11.3, 5, 36; cf. 11.11); Peter (21.18–19), the one to whom Jesus commits his sheep after a relationship of love

4 With regard to issues of overly realized end-time interpretation, Neyrey (1988, p. 238 n.10) also rightly draws attention to 2 Tim. 2.17–18 and 1 Cor. 4.8. Also see Rev. 14.13.

is confirmed; and the Beloved Disciple (21.21–23), to whom Jesus commits his mother.[5] This provides a further explanation for why the love relationship is more important than discipleship or a solely confessional relationship in the portrayal of Lazarus. It is those to whom Jesus is particularly close who might, if anyone, expect favourable treatment. It is precisely these whose death is explicitly 'permitted' or predicted by Jesus.

With respect to Lazarus, the writer makes crystal clear that Jesus allows Lazarus, who is reported to be ill, to *die without intervention* (John 11.6, 13–14, 21, 32). While John might easily have written the Lazarus story in such a way that it was reported to Jesus that his friend Lazarus had suddenly died, and thereby avoided the seeming embarrassment of Jesus deliberately allowing his friend to die, in fact John went out of his way to show that Jesus let Lazarus die (cf. 11.37). Jesus refused to intervene. This deliberate delay in responding to the plea of Lazarus' sisters has sometimes been interpreted by scholars as a Johannine recognition of the problem of the delay in the *parousia*. In other words, in view of some Jesus traditions in the Synoptic Gospels (see Mark 8.38—9.1; 13.26–27; also see 1 Thess. 4.13–18) anticipating the imminent return (*parousia*) of Jesus, the passage of time during which this was not realized increasingly posed a difficulty for those with this expectation and this is known as the problem of the delay of the *parousia*. James Martin, for example, suggests that this is not only an implication of Jesus' delayed response in the Lazarus narrative (meaning that Jesus would come but at a time later than we expect). He also finds other clues to an endtime, *parousia* context, in the statement of Jesus 'I am the resurrection and the life' which he believes points to such a context.[6] Yet it is far from clear that such a resurrection reference is intended to draw attention specifically to the *parousia* here in the Fourth Gospel. There is no reference in John 11 to a future 'coming' of Jesus (in contrast to 14.3).[7] Furthermore, there are substantial

---

5 The other 'friend' of Jesus in the Gospel is John (the Baptizer), another well-known martyr (cf. John 3.29).

6 Martin 1964.

7 As we have noted in Chapter 4 above, we regard the reference in 11.27 to Jesus as the one coming into the world to be linked to the statements about the coming of Jesus in John 6.14 and 12.13 and not to any future endtime coming; on this also see Schnackenburg 1980, pp. 332–3.

differences between John's understanding of the future coming of Jesus and those expressed in heavily mythological language in sayings about the Son of Man coming in clouds.

Thus Schneiders states that the delay of the *parousia* is a 'misfocusing of the Johannine perspective' and 'perhaps a subordinate theme'. She rightly objects to the 'delay of the *parousia*' as a description of the main problem, preferring (more accurately) to highlight the problems of the *absence* of Jesus and the experience of death in the community of eternal life.[8] Indeed we would stress this point even more firmly than Schneiders, because we cannot agree with her other view that Jesus' delay in the Lazarus narrative is comparable to Jesus' refusals to act in John 2 (in response, initially, to his mother's request at the wedding feast in Cana) and in John 4 (in response to the royal official's request to attend to his ill child in person).[9] In these two accounts – both designated formally as 'signs' – there was in fact no significant delay in narrative terms and not even clear refusals. The repeated attention given to the delay in John 11 is much more prominent a theme and quite different in kind to these previous incidents.

We must also reject the view of T. E. Pollard that Jesus' delay in John 11 revealed Jesus adhering to a divine timetable, pursuant to which he was waiting for some guiding signal, but from which he diverged because of his concern with Mary's disbelief.[10] Brendan Byrne has expressed a similar view.[11] But Pollard's view has attracted criticism from C. F. D. Moule. Moule concedes that John 'habitually represents Jesus as dependent on the divine hour', but considers it unlikely that the evangelist would show Jesus as diverted to a course of action that he had not originally intended to follow. Pollard's view also leaves unexplained Jesus' statements in John 11.4 and 15.[12]

At face value, this delay by Jesus before responding to the message from Martha and Mary might seem to be a problem for the thesis we have developed in Chapter 4 of this volume, that Lazarus is prototypical in the sense that he shows Jesus' love for

8 Schneiders 1987, p. 47.

9 Schneiders 1987, p. 47.

10 Pollard 1973.

11 Byrne 1991, 51: Jesus 'has his own divine timetable and will not be imprisoned in any other'.

12 Moule 1975, pp. 118–19.

group members, in ways similar to Jesus' care for his sheep in John 10. There Jesus tries to protect them from 'the wolf', while in John 11 he sits around and lets Lazarus die. Given the notice that Jesus had been given of Lazarus' illness, Martha and Mary affirm the belief that Jesus had the power to prevent Lazarus' death (11.21–22, 32), if he had chosen to do so. So how can Jesus' lack of response be reconciled with the earlier message of his care for his own? In our view, the explanation for the delay lies in John's insistence on the reality of death. As suggested above, there is an awareness of, and concern about, Christ-followers dying. Death by natural causes and persecution are certainly on the agenda of the evangelist, and even the very closest followers of Jesus are not exempt.

The Presentation of Jesus' Care for the Ingroup in John 11: Life, But After Death

Since John is avowing that ingroup members must die, how then does he display Jesus' care for his flock? In essence, he indicates that Jesus' concern lies ultimately in the power to give life – even after physical death, if it comes to that. It is important that believers should recognize this and not desert in the face of opposition and hostility, even death, wondering what has become of their protector. On this understanding, the story of the raising of Lazarus is not primarily intended to prefigure the resurrection of Jesus – which is a different kind of raising in any case. It primarily depicts exactly what it purports to depict, the giving of life to a 'beloved' one who has died. This may be taken as metaphorical for the imparting of spiritual or eternal life, *but the main function of the account of the raising of Lazarus is to serve as a prototype of the destiny awaiting group members who have died.*

The evangelist actually prepares his audience for the importance of resurrection by a promise Jesus makes earlier in the Gospel:

> Do not marvel at this; for the hour is coming when all who are in the tombs will hear his voice and come forth, those who have done good, to the resurrection (*anastasis*) of life, and those who have done evil, to the resurrection (*anastasis*) of judgment (5.28–29; RSV).

Lazarus is the tangible proof of that promise, albeit presented as an anticipatory prototype of the general resurrection to come later. He hears Jesus' voice and comes forth. Since he is good (which must surely be the presumption of the narrative), he enjoys a prelude of the resurrection of life in the form of table-fellowship with Jesus, his sisters and other people as well (12.2). Lazarus makes visible what will eventually happen to all the 'good' members of the group. His return to life typifies what they will experience.

For this reason, the evangelist is able to link the raising of Lazarus to his views on the inevitability of death and the need to accept it, which we have already discussed. For in John 11 the author draws attention to Jesus' own lack of effort to avoid death, by his decision to return to the threatening environment of Judea (11.7–8). This becomes a point of exhortation to the disciples themselves (11.9–10), leading to the striking conclusion to the entire conversation with the disciples in 11.7–16 with the resigned and ironic statement of Thomas to his fellow disciples 'Let us also go, that we may die with him' (11.16).

This statement of Thomas follows an important set of 'misunderstandings' by the disciples about Lazarus 'falling asleep',[13] which, as Schneiders has pointed out, serves the purpose of rejecting one possible interpretation of death amongst Christ-followers – that death for those with eternal life is illusory. Schneiders also observes that in John there is no distinction in vocabulary between natural death and spiritual death, which accentuates the ambiguity concerning these two types of death. Both use *thanatos* for death, which is significant in view of the distinction that is drawn between two words for life: *zōē* and *psychē*.

Yet Rochais draws attention to a contrast between Mark 5.39 where Jesus contrasts death and sleep ('the child is not dead but sleeping') and John 11.11–14 where Jesus seems to identify sleeping and death (to the confusion of his disciples). He notes the antiquity of the metaphor of sleep for death, and asks whether 'sleep' is an adequate way of referring to the intermediate state between death and resurrection (as suggested by Cullmann and

13 More generally, Stibbe (1994, pp. 45–6) observes that in John 5—10 the device of misunderstandings is mainly applied to Judean opponents. Thus John 11.1–16 marks a change that prepares for the disciples' 'otiose reactions in the farewell discourses'.

Michel).[14] Ephesians 5.14 also contains an interesting combination of similar images as in John 11, but here scholars have often seen sleep and death as metaphors used to express the pre-Christian life or a pre-baptismal state prior to being awakened and made fully alive by Christ.[15] The pre-existing friendship of Jesus with Lazarus seems to exclude this latter interpretation for John 11, but John does seem to be both (a) affirming the reality of death, even when using the metaphor of sleeping, and (b) possibly suggesting a 'comforting' understanding of the nature of the post-mortem, pre-resurrection state of the believer as 'sleep'. Thus the two ideas are related in John without compromising the fact that Lazarus, whom Jesus will go on to raise, has indeed died.

Accordingly, the discussion presented in John 11.7–16 mentioned above, which might otherwise seem to intrude into the Lazarus story, is therefore a crucial part of John's formulation of the story – the apparent acceptance by Thomas and Jesus' disciples that they should go forward to Judea with Jesus *and die if necessary*.[16] It seems an ironic statement in the context, but it points to a recurring interest of the evangelist. This concern becomes more explicit later with respect to Peter and the Beloved Disciple in chapter 21, which is a further indication of its particular importance for the later editorial activity responsible for this appendix. For both of these prominent disciples, the idea that death might be evaded by those whom Jesus especially loves is countered. C. R. Koester argues that the story of Lazarus may have been composed before the death of the Beloved Disciple.[17] Thus he sees John 21 (which is probably a later addition to the Gospel) stemming from the crisis caused for the community by the Beloved Disciple's death, whereas the Lazarus episode (being earlier) relates to the general issue of the death of believers. Yet the issues are closely related, and it is far from certain that John 11 (esp. vv. 7–16) and John 21 reflect markedly different perspectives. John 21, after all, is not only curious about the death of the Beloved Disciple; it is also interested in the death of

---

14 Rochais 1981, pp. 192–9.   15 Muddiman 2001, pp. 242–3.

16 The highlighting of Thomas is interesting. In John 11 he is apparently a witness to the raising of Lazarus. This makes his later hesitation at belief in Jesus' resurrection (20.24–25) all the more poignant. There would appear to be an indication that Thomas, like other disciples, has to be led somewhat painstakingly towards faith.

17 Koester 2003, pp. 65–6.

another disciple, Peter. The link between concerns about death among the wider circle of disciples in John 11 and the interest in the deaths of the Beloved Disciple *and Peter* in John 21 is worthy of serious attention. Wuellner also finds common ground in that 'the story of the disciples' death, equally unheroic, gets only fore-"told" (as in John 21.18–19), but is not "shown"'.[18] A recurrent concern about death seems to take priority over interest in the story of individual disciples; nor is martyrdom the only kind of death that is of interest.

Contrary to the view of some of the Jesus-followers *who thought the Beloved Disciple had been promised some alternative to death*, this rumour that had 'spread abroad' (21.23) is decisively, even if gently, quashed. In the Johannine view, the vindication offered to believers is not escape from death, but subsequent resurrection, of which the raising of Lazarus is prototypical.

Indeed, the evangelist explicitly refutes any notion that the model of the *revivified* Lazarus might offer some subsequent immunity on earth from threats, since Lazarus himself becomes an example of the Jesus-follower whom the authorities seek to put to death – after his revivification, on account of the testimony to Jesus that his raising had provoked (John 12.10–11).

Jesus' Anger and the Judeans

There is one particular aspect of Jesus' response to Lazarus and care for his followers that is worth noting for the manner in which it embodies important group-oriented aspects of this narrative and for other issues connected with the attitudes of the Judeans. It is the description of his emotional agitation in 11.33–35:

> [33] When Jesus saw her weeping, and the Judeans who came with her also weeping, he was deeply moved (*embrimōmenos*) in spirit and troubled;
> [34] and he said, 'Where have you laid him?' They said to him, 'Lord, come and see.'
> [35] Jesus wept.[19]

A key point in the interpretation of this passage is the translation of *embrimōmenos* in verse 33, which typically is an expression of

---

18 Wuellner 1991, p. 118.

19 The translation is from the RSV, but substituting 'Judeans' for 'Jews'.

anger despite the somewhat ambiguous RSV translation 'deeply moved'. John initially introduces the Judeans as consoling Mary (11.31) and as fellow mourners who expect to follow her to the tomb (11.33). Yet in 11.36–37 there is a typical Johannine division in responses to Jesus between some who remark on Jesus' love for Lazarus and others who voice the question about whether Jesus could not have prevented Lazarus' death. The assessment of the Judeans here, and in relation to Mary, is caught up with the apparent expression of 'anger' (*embrimōmenos*) on the part of Jesus in 11.33. Why exactly might Jesus have been angry?

Commentators have speculated about the cause. C. Story interprets the term *embrimōmenos* as a rebuke of Jesus as against himself for the delay in his arrival;[20] yet this is surely an unlikely Johannine perspective and completely at odds with John 11.7–16. Alternatively, should we regard Jesus' anger as directed at the lack of faith indicated by the mourning of Mary and the Judeans? Does their mourning imply their belief that Jesus can do nothing? Weighing against this view is that Jesus himself begins to weep in 11.35. Other scholars, such as Brown,[21] see the anger directed at the realm of death or Satan, or see the emotion as distress at Jesus' own approaching hour, which is perhaps sparked by the presence of the Judeans and the danger they represent to Jesus.[22] Sproston North contains a full discussion of the 'anger' reference. She rejects Lindars' theory that it represents a reminiscence of an exorcism account. Instead, she suggests that it is a term taken from Mark 14.5 (where there is criticism by the leaders of the Judeans at the extravagance of the anointing of Jesus by the unnamed woman!) and internalized by the evangelist to express Jesus' anguish at the thought of his own impending death.[23] Still others suggest the anger is Jesus' response to the challenge by Mary and the Judeans that Jesus was not present to prevent Lazarus' death; but then it is necessary to be able to explain the sudden change of mood of Jesus, from anger to grief. It is clear that scholars have struggled to provide a plausible explanation for Jesus' anger.

The apparent change in mood, however, may be most easily understood in terms of the Johannine portrayal of the Judeans. At face value, it is possible to argue that in this narrative the

20 Story 1991. 21 Brown 1966, p. 435.

22 So Lee 1994, pp. 208–12 and Kremer 1985, pp. 72–3.

23 Sproston North 2001, pp. 146–54.

Judeans were acting in a perfectly proper way, demonstrating commendable solidarity with the sisters and compassion in grief. Yet the Johannine construction of the narrative will soon show that everything is not as it initially seems. First, in John 11.36–37 the narrator records a division among the Judeans. They are not a homogeneous group. Some remark on Jesus' love; others criticize his lack of action earlier. It is true that even this public challenge[24] may not seem far removed from Mary's anguish earlier in 11.32, declaring 'Lord (*Kurie*), if you had been here, my brother would not have died.' But there are important subtle differences in Mary's expression of anguish, using a title (*Kurie*) that Martha in verse 27 associates with an expression of faith, and the Judean response. The Judean response in verse 37 ('Could not he who opened the eyes of the blind man have kept this man from dying?') recalls the healing of the blind man in John 9. It is precisely in this episode that opposition to Jesus by the Pharisees (9.13, 15, 16, 40) or Judeans (9.18, 22) emerges to the point of John's stating that 'the Judeans had already agreed that if anyone should confess him to be the Christ, he was to be put out of the synagogue'. The narrator thus draws a connection with opposition to Jesus that he is going immediately to develop. In typical Johannine fashion, the narrator describes in 11.45–46 how a division occurs among the Judeans, with 'some' going to report to the Pharisees, effectively reconstituting an alliance of opposition found in John 9. Next the narrator records the crucial decision by the chief priests and Pharisees 'gathered in council' to put Jesus to death (11.47). The author inserts this episode between the raising of Lazarus (11.1–44) and the anointing meal with the Bethany family (12.1–8). There is no doubt that in this context the author seeks to present the leaders of the Judeans as a threat. Thus while it may be attractive, with R. E. Brown, to argue that Jesus' surprising anger in 11.33 is simply at 'death' in a general sense, a wider appreciation of the narrative development suggests that the anger may be more specifically aimed at the Judeans, however compassionate they may seem.[25] Indeed 11.33 is the

24 Malina and Rohrbaugh 1998, p. 200.

25 The role of deception in care for the sheep was also a theme in John 10. With regard to the division between the Judeans, it may be significant that Koester cites the example of Dio Chrysostom as one who directed his readers by use of contrasting positive and negative examples; see Koester 2003, p. 37.

first confrontation between Jesus and Judeans in the Lazarus narrative. Is it coincidental that his anger appears exactly at this moment?[26]

The Raising of Lazarus as Prototypical

Prototypicality of Lazarus

Let us now turn our attention to some of the prototypical dimensions of the 'revivified' state of Lazarus for the identity of this group. In Jesus' final prayer in John 17, those who belong to (or who are given to) Jesus are described as in the world but not 'of the world' (17.14–16). Lazarus effectively depicts this is in what happens to him. He is back in the world, but is 'revivified' in a way that makes him not of it in the same way as before. He lives anew. Earlier followers are described as 'born of God' (1.13) or 'born anew' (3.3) or 'born of water and spirit' (3.5, cf. 3.6, 8). They can also be described as 'sons of light' (12.36). The evangelist uses a wide range of metaphors to depict the existence of Jesus-followers in the world. Lazarus becomes one who quite 'literally' has passed from death to life, not as a prototype of conversion (since there is no use here of baptismal imagery) but as a prototype of one 'literally' raised from the dead. This metaphor of passing from death to life was used for followers previously in John 5.24 in close conjunction to the description of resurrection on the last day (5.28–29). Lazarus' story typifies the anticipated experience of the follower of Jesus. As such, he becomes an especially suitable Johannine 'prototype'.

The seeming passivity of Lazarus in the passages in which he appears in the Fourth Gospel is not to be understood as an obstacle to the prototypicality of Lazarus but as a feature of it. Quast has suggested that even the contrast between the Beloved Disciple and Peter can be portrayed as between passive and active types of

---

26 On the importance of the seemingly tangential references to 'the Judeans' to maintain the main plot through John's rearrangement of existing material in John 11—12, see also Sproston North 2001, pp. 124–7.

discipleship.[27] For example, the Beloved Disciple 'does' very little in the Fourth Gospel, although he is said to 'believe' at the empty tomb in John 20.8. Yet he is undoubtedly given high reverence in view of his witness being the basis for this Gospel. The testimony preserved by the Beloved Disciple surpasses any obvious activity by him. There is never any other explanation for why he is 'beloved' by Jesus; in narrative terms, this is simply presented as his initial state.

When one turns to the blind man in John 9 a further interesting parallel is suggested. This figure has achieved particular scholarly interest since J. L. Martyn's seminal study.[28] Martyn notes that the blind man is the first example in the Johannine narrative of a believer who is expelled from the synagogue, representing on a 'second level' the situation of the Johannine believers in the author's day. This character, too, is initially a recipient of mercy *prior* to his confession of belief. If the blind man in John 9 serves as a figure indicative of later believers in this respect, it is even more strongly the case for Lazarus. *The group member is the one who receives God's mercy and becomes a testimony to it.*

The testimony associated with the mercy shown to Lazarus is not described in terms of a personal confession of belief in Jesus, but the presence of a 'testimony' associated with Lazarus is nonetheless specifically noted by the evangelist. First, belief is the explicit test for his sisters Mary and Martha linked to his raising (11.21, 25–27). Second, and perhaps more importantly, what happens to Lazarus causes others to believe in Jesus (disciples in 11.15, and many Judeans in 11.45 and 12.9–11). The raising of Lazarus is noted in John 12.17–18 as being responsible for the crowd coming to greet Jesus as the one who comes in the name of the Lord and for the statement in 12.19 by the Pharisees 'Look, the world has gone after him'. Indeed the testimony associated with Lazarus is more clearly demonstrated by the evangelist to have been 'bearing fruit' (cf. John 15.1ff.), stimulating belief among others, than that of the blind man in John 9.

---

27 Quast 1989, pp. 164–70. Quast judges that the Beloved Disciple is noted for his faithful witness and insight, while Peter is noted for his leadership.

28 Martyn 1979.

Prototypicality of Martha in Relation to the Raising of Lazarus

While Lazarus provides a 'testimony' to Jesus without a confession, Martha is associated with a series of confessional statements related to her brother's being raised from the dead. As noted earlier, what Martha testifies is not to be relegated simply to a set of misunderstandings. Starting from an immediate recognition of Jesus' brokerage with the Father (11.22), Martha accepts Jesus' promise that Lazarus will rise in terms of resurrection at the last day. This recalls the earlier teaching attributed to Jesus himself in John 5.25–29, as most scholars note. Jesus' response (11.25–26), which has been examined above, makes the offer of resurrection less distant, both temporally and in terms of his own role. The question that he puts to Martha is whether she 'believes this' (*pisteueis touto*; 11.26). She is not asked to believe in him as such (contrast the general propositions in 11:25, 26a: 'the one believing in me' [*pisteuōn eis eme*]).

Yet Martha's reply in 11.27 is the crux for understanding her role here: 'She said to him, "Yes, Lord; I believe that you are the Christ, the Son of God, he who is coming into the world"'; RSV). Even though Martha still seems unaware of the implications of what Jesus is saying with regard to what will happen to Lazarus, Barrett is certainly correct that Martha's reply comes in 'creed-like form', represents true belief and takes the discourse a step forward.[29] As noted earlier, the titles 'Christ' and 'Son of God' closely represent the evangelist's own credal conclusion in John 20.31 ('but these words are written that you may believe that Jesus is the Christ, the Son of God, and that believing you may have life in his name'; RSV).[30] 'He who comes into the world' appears to be

29 Barrett 1978, p. 330.

30 Neyrey (1988, pp. 86–7) considers that these titles, however, still represent a 'low' Christology and even that John 20.31 is to be seen as the low Christology of the Signs Source. In particular, he considers that the titles here (1) do not go beyond what Nathanael confessed at the outset, and (2) do not equate Jesus with God. It is arguable, however, that Neyrey underplays the significance of the third clause 'he who is coming into the world'. This clearly goes beyond Nathanael's 'King of Israel' and takes even the title 'Son of God' into the realm of Johannine descent–ascent concepts (cf. John 1.9). It also prefigures the prayer attributed to Jesus himself in 11.42 about what witnesses of Lazarus' raising will understand, namely 'that they may believe that *you did send me*'; see Schneiders 1987, p. 53.

a third significant description, alluding to the descent motif – one of the Johannine fundamental perceptions about Jesus' origin and mission – as well as prefiguring the crowd's exclamation in 12.13: 'Hosanna! Blessed is he who comes in the name of the Lord, even the King of Israel' (cf. 6.14).[31]

Based on John 11.39 – where Martha seems to resist Jesus' instruction to remove the stone from Lazarus' tomb and seems to have no expectation of what Jesus is about to do – some scholars have argued that, despite the lofty titles she used in 11.27 ('you are the Christ, the Son of God, he who is coming into the world'), Martha still lacks adequate belief in Jesus.[32] It is certainly true that 11.39 shows that Martha is unaware that Jesus intends to raise Lazarus now, but Jesus has not previously indicated this intention to her. Only obliquely has Jesus indicated this to the disciples in John 11.11, where their understanding seems considerably more limited than that of Martha. Belief in Jesus does not mean full knowledge of his intentions prior to his revelation of those intentions. Moreover the response of both sisters in 11.41a (on the reasonable assumption that it is they who took away the stone,[33] or at least permit it) is obedience to what Jesus instructs.[34] The confession of Martha is surely the confession of the true Johannine believer, and her actions in a challenging and perplexing situation depict obedience to the one whom she calls *Kurie*, 'Lord'. Accordingly, although Lazarus is (just as the narrative requires) not a party to the discussion taking place outside his tomb, the confessional statements and obedient actions of Martha and Mary are prototypical of the values and identity of the group toward raising from the dead and the status of the Lord through whom it occurs.

---

31 Barrett 1978, p. 330.

32 For example, see Brown 1966, p. 433; but differently in Brown 1979, pp. 190–2. For a fuller discussion of this point see Sproston North 2001, pp. 143–4.

33 Note that it is 'taken' away, not rolled. The same verb is used in 20.1 with respect to Jesus' tomb. In contrast to the Synoptics, John seems to envisage tombs sealed with stones small enough to be lifted, perhaps indicating tombs that are below surface level (cf. 20.5).

34 Martha's lack of understanding of what Jesus intends also serves another purpose, namely, to underline again that Lazarus is truly dead. It is unnecessary to attribute two pictures of Martha's faith to different accounts of the Lazarus story, *contra* Burkett 1994, pp. 219–20.

Family Life, Group Identity and the Raising of Lazarus

The role of Martha and Mary in bringing out the significance of the raising of their brother indicates the extent to which identifying a prototype for members of the Jesus-group also involves the dimension of 'community', some awareness of the nature and identifying features of the group and their relationships. This is difficult to portray in a single individual. An individual character may represent 'a group', but it is more difficult for a single figure to represent the diversity and dynamics of a group. The group of disciples is a very fluid feature of the Fourth Gospel, and even 'the Twelve' are mentioned in only two contexts in the Gospel (John 6.67–71 and 20.24). Disciples are recipients of instruction, particularly in John 13—17, but rarely are exemplary.

It is all the more striking therefore that the 'family' depicted in the Lazarus episode and its sequel in John 12 prefigure many of the features about which disciples are later instructed in John 13—17, not simply to the extent that they are loved, but in relation to basic beliefs concerning resurrection and eternal life. Scholarship has sometimes looked to the figure of Lazarus and what he may represent with respect to concerns about death among followers, and some feminist scholars have tried to highlight the women's roles in the episodes. Nevertheless, an understanding of how the three 'beloved' characters function together has seldom been approached,[35] yet becomes extremely significant when a model of prototypicality and social identity is applied to the text. The prototypicality of Lazarus with respect to his raising probably addresses an issue of real concern among early Christ-followers regarding those who are dying, but the prototypicality of the Bethany family sets this theme in a larger context of how believers should relate to one another and to Jesus. In other words, the care shown for believers who die is but one part of the care that should permeate the community of Christ-followers and the mutual expressions of trust and care between believers and Jesus.

---

35 C. R. Koester, it is worth noting, does argue that 'together . . . they are portrayed in a way that reflects the experience of Christians living at a later time'. His thesis is, however, that the women depict above all different responses to the death of their 'brother', even though he regards them as positively assessed (2003, pp. 65–8).

The Raising of Lazarus and Group Beliefs

It is worth connecting this portrayal of the event of raising from the dead, its consequences and attitudes taken by Martha and Mary to it with the discussion set out in Chapter 2 of the relationship between social identity and beliefs. Bar-Tal has suggested, it will be recalled, that central group beliefs are prototypical for ingroup characterization. Beliefs of this sort, first, are functional for group formation and maintenance, especially by differentiating between ingroup and outgroup; second, they hold the attention of group members because of their prominence and distinctiveness; and, third, they are treated as group beliefs by the 'epistemic authorities' of the group and are supported by them. The first requirement (ingroup/outgroup differentiation) is directly satisfied by John 5.29 (those who have done good enjoy the resurrection of life / those who have done evil suffer the resurrection of judgement). This and other data in the text substantiate the second requirement, namely, prominence (as in being loved by Jesus) and distinctiveness (as in the nature of the miracle and its position before the Passion). We must linger a while here on the third condition, the support of epistemic authorities.

Jesus plainly qualifies as an epistemic authority of the sort described by Bar-Tal. Not just a leader of the group, he was its very founder. Even more, not only does he endorse the belief, he actually embodies it. For the Johannine audience, Jesus has already experienced the resurrection to life that awaits the just. That is why there is particular power and poignancy to his statement in John 11.25: 'I am the resurrection and the life; the one who believes in me, even though that one dies, will live'. It is difficult to imagine how a group belief could be invested with more epistemic warrant than happens in relation to the evidence Jesus provides for the coming resurrection of those who believe in him. This consideration of how the group's principal epistemic authority has thrown his weight behind the belief in resurrection raises important questions over the place of Christology in the Lazarus narrative.

The reality of the threat of death is explicitly addressed in the Lazarus episode in the key 'Christological' statement of John 11.25 about Jesus being the resurrection and the life, which we have just quoted. Earlier in the Fourth Gospel, the reality of dying has implicitly been a feature of the sayings about resurrection on the last day, found especially in chapters 5 and 6 (5.29; 6.40,

54). Even the promise that the one who keeps Jesus' words will never see death (in John 8.51) is followed by a typical Johannine misunderstanding on the part of opponents who think Jesus refers to not dying physically (8.52–3). Schnackenburg argues that these sayings might draw upon some contemporary 'Jewish' ideas about the ascension of Enoch and Elijah or possibly a measure of protection offered to the just against 'the angel of death'.[36]

From whatever source ideas about escaping death might be derived, however, within the Lazarus episode in John 11 a determined effort is made to counter them. Apart from what is noted above with respect to the deliberate point of letting Lazarus die within the narrative itself, a number of other clues can be found in other seemingly redactional material attached to the narrative. The discussion of Jesus with his disciples in John 11.7–16 is one such diversion from the narrative that underscores this point (see above). Yet particularly important is the saying in John 11.25, in which the Johannine Jesus states 'I am the resurrection and the life; the one who believes in me, *even though that one dies*, will live.' The italicized clause *(kan apothanē)* is the one that underscores the point and could easily be a redactional modification of the simpler and more typical Johannine statement that the one who believes in Jesus will have life (cf. John 3.15, 36; 5.24; 6.47; 20.31).[37] It is all the more striking because of the conjunction with 11.26 ('everyone who lives and believes in me will never die').[38] Without the *kan apothanē* clause in 11.25, the entire tenor of the sayings would be different. This short clause alone makes the point that the life that Jesus offered does not exclude physical death, so that the promise that they 'will never die' in 11.26

36 Schnackenburg 1980, p. 220.

37 In addition to John 21 clearly showing signs of late editorial influences, the sayings about raising up on the Last Day have of course also been much discussed in this regard. Moreover the clearest reference to the death of disciples in the Farewell Discourses, John 16.2 (cf. also 15.18–20), is attributed by many to a later extension of the first version (14.1–31) of the Farewell Discourse. John 3.16 interestingly refers to not 'being destroyed' rather than not 'dying'.

38 Brown suggests (1966, p. 425) that the prepositional phrase 'in me' is governed by both 'believe' and 'live', rather than just by 'believe'. This may shift the focus slightly towards the receipt of life by believers.

must mean life of some other kind. Yet at the same time, this life which is being offered is given warrant by Jesus' statement about his own status: 'I am the resurrection and the life.' In context, this functions to give the life on offer to members of the group an epistemic warrant of a particularly exalted kind. That is to say, Jesus' assertion of who he is tells the audience of this Gospel much more about the extraordinary foundation for the central group belief about final resurrection and eternal life for group members than it does about him.

It is worth noting with respect to the 'I am' statement in John 11.25 that a further modification may have been introduced at the stage where concerns about the death of believers arose. There is a text-critical point to note. The presence of 'and the life' with 'I am the resurrection' is disputed textually: P45 appears to lack the words, while P66 and P75 include them. The strength of the external evidence is certainly in favour of inclusion, but the early absence from P45 raises the possibility of variant traditions that may go back much earlier than these papyri. It is not our intention to oppose the consensus view that the words 'and the life' are to be found at least in the stage of the Gospel text represented by the other redactional elements that have been discussed. Yet the discussion raises the question of the significance of the words. The words 'and the life' are more important than they might initially seem because they introduce another nuance into the argument.

When Martha declares that she knows that her brother Lazarus will rise again on the last day (11.23), this is typical Judean belief for the period. Yet for the evangelist, the issue back in John 5.28–29 is not whether one will rise on the last day, but whether the resurrection will be to *life* or to judgement. Everyone will rise; resurrection is not just for believers! That is why this passage is fundamental for ingroup/outgroup differentiation. So the link between rising *and life* is essential to 11.25–6 (and may not all be in 'realized' terms). Those who believe in Jesus will rise *to life*. It is arguable that in narrative terms this is also the point about *unbinding* Lazarus after he has emerged (somehow walking!) from the tomb.[39] Throwing off all the coils of death is therefore

39 Surely the comment of Wuellner (1991, p. 120) that the 'unfinished task of untying Lazarus becomes the readers' task of untying the text' imports a rather modern significance into the unbinding.

as important as coming forth from the tomb. Only believers, like Lazarus, have the hope of both resurrection and life. In effect, Jesus the judge calls forth the dead from their tombs and determines whom among these to unbind. So in the context of the Lazarus narrative the phrasing 'I am the resurrection *and the life*' is not just saying something about Jesus. Its main point is to say something remarkably specific relating to the fears about believers who have died. Sproston North emphasizes the contrast here with the resurrection of Jesus. Lazarus needs to be unbound, but Jesus does not.[40] This is indeed one of several contrasts between Jesus' resurrection and Lazarus' revivification, but such comparisons all too frequently rest on the assumption that the *main* concern of the passage is to prefigure in some way Jesus' own resurrection, an assumption that our analysis challenges.

Our interpretation, therefore, involves some reassessment of the Christological dimensions of the Lazarus narrative. One can hardly deny that the first half of the Fourth Gospel is occupied with debates about the identity of Jesus as God's son. The miraculous signs in this part of the Gospel have often been considered to serve primarily to reveal truths about who Jesus is. In this sense, the signs are interpreted to be 'Christological'. In the case of the Lazarus story, Jesus is certainly the 'Life-giver' par excellence. Nevertheless, our discussion of how Jesus serves as epistemic authority in the Lazarus narrative shows how affirmations of Jesus' authority are not simply directed at evaluating who Jesus is.

This can be seen by an analysis of the three important statements from Jesus' lips in John 11 about 'belief'. The first is in John 11.15, where Jesus indicates the sign is so that disciples 'may believe'. The second appears in John 11.25–26, where Jesus promises that the one who believes in him shall live, even if that one should die. The third is in John 11.42, where Jesus explains that the Father has heard him for the sake of the onlookers so that they might believe that God sent Jesus. In John 11.15 the object of belief is unstated, and the context is one that links the death of Lazarus (11.14) and the death of disciples (11.16). The object of belief may well be the reality of resurrection. In John 11.25–26 belief is 'in me', but the belief is tied to its consequence, namely

40 See Sproston North 2001, pp. 159–60. See earlier, Reiser 1973.

resurrection and life for believers. Interestingly, Jesus confirms this wider reference for belief at the end of verse 26 by asking, 'Do you believe this?' It is left to Martha to convert this to a more explicit confession of Jesus as 'the Christ, the Son of God, he who is coming into the world'. In any event, the thrust of the exchange is soteriological. This brings us, third, to John 11.42. Jesus' statement to Martha in John 11.40: 'Did I not tell you that if you would believe you would see the glory of God?' serves in part to link 11.25–26 and 11.42 (with reminiscences of 11.4). Yet it also suggests that John 11.42 is not solely concerned with belief in Jesus as God's chosen agent or broker; there is some further recognition that derives from Jesus' agency in the raising of Lazarus (described as seeing God's glory). In John 11.42, Jesus himself expresses the object of belief in terms of 'that thou [God] didst send me'. In this context, Jesus thanks the Father for hearing his prayer, presumably to raise Lazarus (11.41). By making the Father (at Jesus' behest) rather than Jesus himself directly responsible for the raising of Lazarus, some tension is set up with the earlier claim that *Jesus* is the resurrection and the life (11.25). The authority *behind* Jesus is emphasized. Why this should happen at the end of the raising narrative is significant. The implied presentation of a petition by Jesus to the Father, and the statement in 11.42 that 'I have known that you hear me always' can easily be understood to be an *example for the Jesus-group* to present their petitions to the Father, a point also encouraged in the Farewell Discourses in John 16.23–28 (perhaps modifying the earlier parallel in 14.12–14 in which Jesus seems to be the one who answers petitions from followers).[41] Thus the situation and concerns of Jesus' followers are integrally tied to the three statements of Jesus about belief. This reinforces our argument that Jesus serves as an epistemic authority. Certainly the author is concerned to acknowledge the authority of Jesus. This is not just an end in itself, however, but rather a means of commending trust among followers in relation to their concerns about death.

41 See Sproston North 2001, pp. 102–17.

Belief in Resurrection among Other Christ-Followers in the First Century CE

Before concluding this section, we should address a significant issue Richard Rohrbaugh raised when responding to a paper that outlined our original formulation of the thesis in this volume.[42] Rohrbaugh asked how raising from the dead can be prototypical for the Johannine community when it was common to other groups in the Christ-movement and even among Judeans. How could such a belief serve to establish and maintain the boundaries of the Johannine group?

One answer to the problem is that even if a belief in resurrection was widely shared among the Christ-movement and did not help to establish a particular boundary for the Johannine group in relation to other Christ-following groups, it does not follow that it could not have been prototypical for John's audience. This is because the Johannine community could have acquired distinctiveness in other respects, even while having a belief in resurrection in common with other groups in the Christ-movement.

In relation to the Judeans, what is distinctive is that Jesus is the agent (or exclusive broker; cf. 11.41–42) in the raising of Lazarus. The problem that John attributes to the Judeans is their rejection of the agency of Jesus in relation to divine–human relations, as in chapter 6 where Jesus' repeated 'I will raise them/him up at the last day' (6.39, 40, 44 and 54) sounds in a broad context of Judean rejection of his personal role in salvation.

Yet, in fact, even with respect to other Christ-following groups it cannot be assumed that a common set of beliefs about death and resurrection existed. Whereas in the Fourth Gospel, there is, as we have argued, a strong emphasis on the reality of death, in some other groups there seems to have been an interest in death as metaphorical. This is part of a gnosticizing tendency, where there is less interest even in the reality of the body. There is evidence, even within the New Testament, for a variety of beliefs about death and what followed. In Thessalonika, for example, we know from Paul's letter that some Christ-followers had despaired of a future life for those of their number who had already died before the Lord had returned (1 Thess. 4.13). In Corinth, Paul finds

42 This was when we jointly presented a paper to the Meeting of the Context Group in Aston, Pennsylvania on 14 March 2003.

it necessary to confront some Christ-followers who are simply denying the reality of resurrection (1 Cor. 15.12). He must also insist on bodily resurrection (1 Cor. 15.35), facing scepticism on this score that was probably entertained by those with a more spiritual interpretation of life after death. Yet his own formulation of the resurrected entity as a 'spiritual body' (*sōma pneumatikon*; 1 Cor. 15.44) seems itself to push the concept in a spiritual direction. In 2 Thessalonians 1.1–2 there is evidence for the fact that some early Christ-followers were alleging that the Day of the Lord had already come, which suggests that such people believed in a physical resurrection. In Revelation 20.4–6 the author states that there will be a 'first resurrection' for those who have been martyred by beheading for their testimony to Jesus. Among early Christ-followers there was also a variety of beliefs about post-mortem existence by those who had died before the arrival of Christ, that is before any resurrection. These beliefs outcrop in Hebrews 11 and 12 and in 1 Peter 3.18 and 4.6.

If we turn to early Christian texts outside the New Testament we find evidence of still other possibilities. *The Gospel of Thomas* opens with the saying 'Whoever finds the interpretation of these sayings will not experience death.' This suggests a model for eternal life that is not based on resurrection, which is utterly different from the Johannnine picture. Furthermore, in the *Acts of John* we find the apostle himself effecting revivifications of deceased persons;[43] this diverges radically from the Johannine picture where Jesus is the agent of resurrection of his followers.

The distinctiveness of John's view in the light of this diversity of opinion on death and its aftermath is clear in several respects. First, he affirms the stark reality of physical death, to be accompanied by the usual rituals of mourning by the bereaved, even for those who believe that they have eternal life. Second, in a fairly distinctive manner, he insists that both the just and the unjust will be raised, with the former to the resurrection of life and the latter to the resurrection of judgement. This view, which also occurs in Acts 24.15 (and cf. Rev. 20.12–15) does have precedents among ancient Israelites (see Dan. 12.2, 2 *Baruch* 50.2–4, 4 *Ezra* 7.32 and *1 Enoch* 51.1f.). But elsewhere in the New Testament we find other references to resurrection of the righteous. This is

43 Cf. Paul in Acts 20.9–12.

the view of Paul (in Romans, 1 and 2 Corinthians, Philippians and 1 Thessalonians) and of Christian writers after him (such as *Didache* 16.7 and Ignatius, *Letter to the Trallians* 9.2) and lying behind it are Israelite traditions such as 2 Maccabees 7.9, Psalm of Solomon 3.12.[44] Third, he focuses on resurrection to life as a very personal process, in which the context of being raised to life is an expression of Jesus' love for those who are his own. This latter dimension is reinforced by imagery of the meal in John 12 where there is a restoration of friendship among believers with Christ in the midst of them, which gives the Johannine picture of the final state an air of intimacy and domesticity that is not evident in some other parts of the New Testament, such as the picture of the Holy City in Revelation 21 where the thrust is rather political and monumental.

Conclusion

The result of our discussion in this chapter is not to deny all Christological interest in the Lazarus episode. The general context of the Fourth Gospel makes this hardly plausible. Even our analysis has suggested that Lazarus also has a 'testimony' to Jesus, in so far as his raising stimulates belief in Jesus. This is why it would be unwise to set up a polarity between prototypicality and Christological significance.[45] The problem has been that the latter has tended to receive centre stage, whereas our analysis finds here support for Bar-Tal's idea of central group beliefs needing to be supported by the group's epistemic authorities. Moreover, there is evidence that the sign itself has been partly shifted in the course of later composition towards the direction of believers' concerns

44 See Wright 2003, p. 442, especially footnote 126 for this information.

45 As noted above, Neyrey adopts a redactional solution to the dual emphases. The first redaction addressed the community's crisis in doctrine regarding why believers with 'eternal life' should die; the second relates this to the end-time power credited to Jesus in John 5.21–29 whereby he is 'equal to God', a Christological development. See Neyrey 1988, pp. 81–93. Yet we find a diachronic distinction between the two themes difficult to maintain. Interestingly, Neyrey only identifies the later redaction in 11.4 and 25a.

about dying – for example, by 11.7–16. Even the unusual description of Lazarus as 'loved by Jesus' and the emphasis on Jesus' delay in responding to his friend's need might easily be touches to emphasize the features of prototypicality – that even someone so loved may have to reckon with death but can be assured nonetheless of life. Already this sphere of interest has been signalled in John 9 and 10, and the potentially dangerous situation of Jesus' followers will become uppermost in John 14—17. John 11.1–44 therefore is located at a point of transition in this Gospel. The application of the model of prototypes demonstrates in how many ways the Lazarus story fulfils the function of addressing the social identity of Christ-followers.

6

The Raising of Lazarus in Early Christian Art

In the previous chapter we argued that the raising of Lazarus from the dead in John 11 was meant to be taken as prototypical of the destiny of Christ-believers. To this extent we diverged from other commentators who see in the raising of Lazarus a prefiguring of the resurrection of Jesus. We are in the unusual position of being able to cite empirical support for our position in the manner in which the raising of Lazarus is regularly presented in the earliest Christian art that we possess – from the frescoes in the catacombs in Rome and from other sources, such as Christian sarcophagi.[1] These artistic representations constitute a very early moment in the reception-history of the Fourth Gospel. Very importantly, they appear to represent the views of ordinary Christians, not those of theologians whose writings are normally the source of information about the early Christian world. The Roman catacomb frescoes and sarcophagi sculptures thus provide us with the unusual opportunity to test our views on the meaning John's presentation of the raising of Lazarus would have conveyed to his addressees against pictorial representations of the scene created less than two centuries after he wrote this Gospel. In this chapter our aim is to demonstrate that these representations (and we

---

1 See, for example, the discussions in Kremer 1985, pp. 111ff.; Puchner 1991, vol. 1, pp. 17–59; Hakola 1999, pp. 247–55. A useful source for the catacomb paintings is Giuseppe Wilpert's *Roma Soterranea: Le Pitture delle Catacombe Romane*, published in 1903, which contains splendid colour reproductions, although Wilpert tended to date the paintings too early (by a half century or more in many cases). Note the review of Kremer 1985 by Forestell 1987.

will concentrate on the frescoes) portray Lazarus as prototypical of Christ-believers in respect of their ultimate destiny and thus provide interesting corroboration for part of the thesis we are maintaining in this volume. A closer investigation of this evidence is therefore pertinent to this study. A full study of this subject is beyond the scope of this volume, so we will concentrate on a sample of the available material.[2]

We should mention at the outset that we are dealing with art produced for Roman Christians who were probably members of the non-elite in most cases; that is, they probably did not belong to the aristocratic and administrative elite who ruled the city. This is especially the case for the period with which we will mainly be dealing – before 313 CE and the Edict of Milan, by which Constantine and his co-emperor Licinius guaranteed religious freedom to Christians (the so-called 'Peace of the Church'). In choosing to decorate their tombs with paintings, or their sarcophagi with sculptures, these Roman Christians were following in a long tradition at Rome, that John Clarke has recently subjected to impressive scrutiny (although without mention of the Christian materials).[3]

The Lazarus Frescoes in the Roman Catacombs

Aldo Nestori's definitive repertory of the paintings of the Roman catacombs lists 66 that feature Lazarus, although 3 of them are doubtful.[4] Nestori's repertory also reveals that the most popular New Testament subject in the catacomb frescoes is the Good Shepherd, with 85 instances, with Lazarus coming second. The next most popular figure is Jonah (usually as he is ejected from the mouth of a large fish), with 65 representations. Many of the catacomb frescoes of Lazarus date to the pre-Constantinian period.[5]

The popularity of the Lazarus theme is significant, given that

---

2 For a recent treatment of the raising of Lazarus in early Christian art, see Jensen 1995.

3 Clarke 2003.

4 Nestori 1993, p. 205. Schiller (1971, p. 181) erroneously says there are approximately 40.

5 So Jensen 2000, p. 65.

Old Testament themes are about four times more popular than themes from the New Testament in the early period (second to fourth centuries CE) and some New Testament scenes from Jesus' life are never depicted, while others only appear quite late (for example, his nativity, transfiguration, last supper, Passion and resurrection).[6] Yet the Lazarus motif was so popular that it also appears on sarcophagus reliefs, mosaics, and in ivory carvings on diptychs, reliquaries and pyxides.[7]

Robert Darmstaedter has provided a detailed account of the iconographical development of the raising of Lazarus in early Christian and Byzantine art. He has outlined a number of phases in the development of the motif in the frescoes and on sarcophagi from early Christian Rome.[8] We need only concern ourselves with the first two of these: (1) the 'magician type', where Jesus is holding a wand or staff of some sort, so that Darmstaedter argues Jesus is depicted as a magician;[9] and (2) the 'mummy type', in which Lazarus is depicted wrapped in bandaging from head to foot.[10]

Darmstaedter's 'magician type' contains what are generally agreed to be the earliest surviving representations of the raising of Lazarus: those from rooms A2 and A6 of the Chapel of the Sacraments in the Catacomb of Callixtus ('San Callisto'), probably to be dated to 240–70 CE, with the fresco in room A2 being the oldest.[11] The Catacomb of Callixtus is very old. A literary source states that Pope Zephyrinus (199–217) appointed the presbyter Callixtus (who himself became Pope in 217) as its administrator and later, when he himself had become Pope in 217, extended the pre-existing set of underground chambers and galleries.[12] Pope Sixtus II was martyred in this catacomb in 258 CE. Thus we are

6 Jensen 2000, pp. 64–5, 68–9. Lowrie makes a similar point (1969, p. 40). For a fine account, with illustrations, of the Christian artistic and archaelogical remains before Constantine, see Snyder 2003.

7 Jensen 2000, p. 169.

8 Darmstaedter 1955, pp. 7–14.

9 Darmstaedter 1955, pp. 8–9.

10 Darmstaedter 1955, pp. 9–11.

11 For the dating and other details, see Schiller 1971, p. 182 and Fig. 559, and Albertson 1995, p. 124.

12 The literary source is the *Philosophumena* of St Hippolytus (died *c.* 235): see Webb 2001, p. 229 for these details. She discusses these catacombs on pp. 229–31.

dealing with what had been a Christian cemetery, one vital to the life of the Church in Rome, since at least a century before the Edict of Milan in 313 CE.

We must now consider some of the examples of the 'magician' and 'mummy' types of Lazarus representation. First, we will describe these representations and then assess the nature of, and reasons for, their assimilation to the Roman context, for this will bear directly upon how the images should be interpreted.

The Distinctive Portrayals of Lazarus in the Roman Context

We will first consider one of the frescoes from Chapel A6 of the Catacomb of Callixtus which, as already noted, may be among the oldest representations of Lazarus (see Figure 1).[13] A large Christ stands towards the centre of the fresco, facing the viewer. He is clad in what appears to be a toga, his right hand is outstretched in the direction of Lazarus on his right, with fingers extended. In his left hand he holds a staff or wand. On the left appears Lazarus, having just emerged from a tomb. He is also facing the viewer and appears to be lightly draped in a mantle, that leaves his lower legs bare. There is no one else in the picture.

Our second fresco is of the 'mummy' type, from the Catacomb of Peter and Marcellinus (Figure 2). This catacomb was established on an imperial property in the second half of the third century CE.[14] It is large and richly illuminated.[15] The dating of the Lazarus frescoes in this catacomb is not very clear, but they are probably pre-Constantinian, and there is evidence to suggest that the 'mummy' type originated around or after 270–80 CE.[16] Accordingly, this too is an early representation of the Lazarus miracle, given that fresco painting continued in the catacombs until the fifth century CE. The broad arrangement of this scene is much the same as for Figure 1, but there are very significant differences of detail. Jesus occupies most of the right half of the

---

13 See Wilpert, 1903, Plate 46b (who misdates it to the end of the second century CE).

14 Webb 2001, p. 279.

15 Webb 2001, p. 281.

16 See the arguments in Albertson 1995, pp. 124–7.

picture. He faces the viewer. His left arm is covered by his toga, while he holds a staff in his right hand which he has stretched out so that it touches the top of Lazarus' head. A diminutive Lazarus is emerging from the door of the tomb, completely wrapped in bandages. Access to the door of the tomb is by means of a flight of stairs. There is no one else in the picture.

This last aspect, the restriction of the scene to Jesus and Lazarus which is common to both 'magician' and 'mummy' types, provides a good point of entry to a comparison with the Johannine representation of the scene. Whoever painted the fresco, either of his own volition or at the prompting of whoever paid for it,[17] has demonstrated great freedom in relation to the details in John 11 and we must note these details and consider their significance.

First, as Darmstaedter has observed, the large cast of characters that was present in John 11 is missing.[18] The artist has omitted to include Martha and Mary, the Judeans who followed Mary to the tomb (John 11.31) and saw what Jesus did (John 11.45), and the disciples of Jesus who accompanied him to Bethany (John 11.14–16) and were presumably also understood to be present. Instead, the artist depicted only Jesus and Lazarus. This has the effect of stripping the narrative down to its very bare essentials: what Jesus did for Lazarus.

The tomb is also different. In the Johannine narrative (11.38) Lazarus has been laid in a tomb in the form of a cave (*spēlaion*); in other words, John has his readers/listeners imagine Lazarus as laid in a hole that has been cut (or, less probably, that naturally occurs) in a hillside, a very common practice in Palestine. The tomb entrance had been covered by a stone (*lithos*). In the two frescoes, however, Lazarus appears at the opening of what is very evidently a Roman tomb, with doors not a stone. There was a great variety of Roman tombs. In the second fresco, the tomb from which Lazarus is emerging is clearly of the 'temple' type, in a fairly simple form, with a windowed *cella* on a raised podium, up to which steps lead, with two columns holding up the

17 Note Clarke 2003, pp. 9–13, for a very helpful discussion of the different roles of patron, artist and viewer in relation to non-elite Roman art.

18 Darmstaedter 1955, p. 8.

pediment.[19] Probably, the tomb in the first fresco is also of this type, although it is even simpler in form, in that it lacks pillars. This style of constructed tomb probably suited Romans of some, but modest, means.

We should not miss the significance of this type of tomb. Whereas in the case of those present, the artist has simply failed to portray some of the characters in the Johannine narrative, here he has provided a representation that directly contradicts a detail in the Johannine narrative: a temple-tomb is not a cave. Thus the artist has radically assimilated the biblical picture to the Roman context. As John Clarke has noted: 'Only if we consider non-elite art as a system of communication embedded within a specific culture can Roman individuals emerge with any distinction . . . Context is everything.'[20] And yet perhaps the Johannine framework imposed some restraints after all. For the Lazarus of these two frescoes is emerging from the type of tomb used by non-Christian Romans of the sort to be seen along the roads leading out of Rome; he is not appearing from any sort of catacomb burial place, such as an *arcosolium* (an arched recess built into a catacomb wall and used for burials). Perhaps such a representation, which would have aligned the depiction of Lazarus much more closely to the deceased buried in the chamber illustrated in this way, was simply too far from the Johannine description to be acceptable and the artist (or whoever commissioned the work) has opted for a tomb in use among non-Christians.

The way Lazarus is portrayed in both frescoes also diverges from the John 11 account. John says that the hands and feet of Lazarus were bound with bandages and his face was wrapped in a cloth (11.44).[21] In the San Callisto fresco the face, legs and feet of Lazarus are uncovered, while in the one from the Catacomb of Peter and Marcellinus he is completely wrapped up in bandages, like a mummy.

---

19 See the discussion of temple-tombs in Toynbee 1971, pp. 130–2. Plates 36 and 37 in Toynbee 1971 are scenes from a sarcophagus in which Jesus (wand in right hand) is raising Lazarus who is coming out of such a two-columned temple-tomb and of a Roman tomb of similar style, which is much more imposing with four columns at the front.

20 Clarke 2003.

21 A description that accords with first-century Palestinian burial practices as known from recent archaeological discoveries, as shown by Zangenberg 2006 forthcoming.

Jesus as Wand-Bearer

In the portrayal of Jesus this tendency to assimilate the imagery to the Roman setting reaches new heights: Jesus is holding a wand. This does not represent an alteration to the biblical narrative as was the case with the substitution of temple-tomb for cave, but it is certainly a remarkable addition. Darmstaedter took the view that the wand was an attribute of a magician,[22] and in this he was largely correct. In relation to the first fresco, from San Callisto, where the staff or wand lies in Jesus' left hand and plays no part in the miracle, Albertson has argued against Darmstaedter's interpretation, suggesting instead that it is merely a symbol of religious authority, similar to those held by Roman magistrates when they were taking part in a sacrifice. Whether Albertson is right or wrong with respect to this image (and perhaps the viewer was meant to understand that Jesus has just used the wand that he now holds at his side), even he agrees that in relation to the 'mummy' type the 'staff is now clearly denoted as the instrument through which the miracle is performed'.[23] There are numerous other illustrations, many of them sarcophagus carvings (which generally have fourth- or fifth-century CE provenance), where Jesus holds a staff in his right (or left) hand and touches Lazarus at the front of the tomb.[24] There is even a sarcophagus relief where Jesus is shown using a staff or wand carried in his left hand to bring back to life the daughter of Jairus (see Figure 3).[25]

Although Morton Smith argued that the historical Jesus should be understood under the guise of magician,[26] his thesis has not won wide scholarly acceptance. There seems to be too little evidence of Jesus of Galilee having acted as a magician for Smith's hypothesis to carry conviction among modern critics. The evidence from early Christian art, however, clearly indicates that among the Christians of Rome in the third, fourth and fifth centuries CE Jesus was regularly depicted as something very like a

22 Darmstaedter 1955, p. 8 ('Der Stab, den Christus in Händen hält, ist das Attribut des Magiers').

23 Albertson 1995, p. 124.

24 See Jensen 2000, p. 169 (figure 62) for Jesus using a staff or wand in his left hand to raise Lazarus.

25 See the representation in Jensen 2000, p. 96 (figure 30).

26 Smith 1985.

magician. Robin Jensen has observed that although Jesus 'commonly holds a wand in scenes of raising people from the dead or working certain wonders, he rarely holds the wand in contemporaneous images of healing'. In the latter case he tends simply to lay on his hands.[27] Jensen's notion that Jesus' activities were seen as differentiated into a thaumaturgical type (revivifier and wonder-worker), where he used a wand, and a healing type, where he laid on his hands, is worth pursuing.

In 1927 Ferdinand de Waele published an important work entitled *The Magic Staff or Rod in Graeco-Italian Antiquity*, which has, surprisingly, attracted insufficient attention hitherto among those researching these catacomb frescoes.[28] Of particular interest is Waele's discussion of the magic staff or rod used by the god Hermes/Mercury. As early as the *Odyssey*, Hermes, with his staff (*rhabdos*), had acquired the function of leading deceased persons to Hades (24.1ff.). This chthonic function developed and he came to be viewed as a *psychopompus* ('guide of souls') or *psychagōgos* (a leader of souls to or from the lower world) who could lead souls out of the underworld.[29] He also came to be regarded as the messenger of the gods.[30] In time Mercury acquired two staffs, the first his characteristically shaped *kerukeion* (his staff having an end of two intertwined snakes; *caduceus* in Latin) which eventually came to have little more than symbolical significance, and a second, more powerful staff, that was used in raising souls from the dead.[31] Having considered a spread of evidence from Roman tomb reliefs and monuments, Waele observes:

> From all these representations we may draw the conclusion that in the Roman period, at least in certain parts of the empire, possibly as a result of a mere local tradition or individual opinion, Mercurius was represented with a caduceus and a second rhabdos or virga, this being an indispensable instrument in raising the dead.[32]

A good example is the picture on a *leucythos* (vase) from the

27 Jensen 2000, pp. 121–2.

28 Thus, it does not appear in Darmstaedter's bibliography (1955). But Waele's work is mentioned by Albertson 1995, p. 128.

29 Waele 1927, pp. 31, 38.

30 Waele 1927, p. 32.

31 Waele 1927, pp. 55–61.

32 Waele 1927, p. 59.

Figure 1: The Raising of Lazarus in Chapel A6 of the Catacomb of Callixtus; reproduced from Wilpert 1903.

Figure 2: The Raising of Lazarus, from the Catacomb of Peter and Marcellinus; reproduced from Wilpert 1903.

Figure 3: Sarcophagus relief showing the raising of Jairus' daughter; photo copyright Robin Jensen.

Figure 4: Hermes raising souls from the dead; photo copyright the University of Jena.

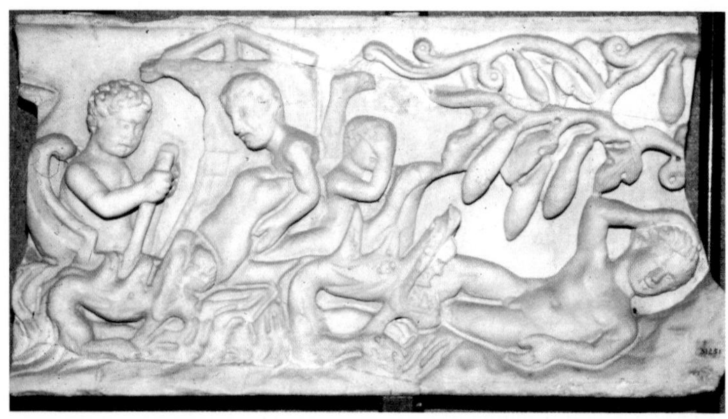

Figure 5: Sarcophagus relief showing Jonah being expelled from the fish; photo copyright Robin Jensen.

Figure 6: Detail of sarcophagus relief showing Jesus with Lazarus and Mary; photo copyright Robin Jensen.

museum in Jena (see Figure 4). Here we see Mercury standing next to a *pithos*, a storage-jar, holding his characteristically shaped *kerukeion* in his left hand and a little staff in his right that he is using to summon winged souls from the *pithos*. We consider that this role of Hermes as mentioned by Waele underlies the catacomb presentation of Jesus with a plain staff or wand raising Lazarus. Jesus adopts a role similar to that of Mercury and uses the same type of staff for this purpose. We have subsequently learned that Darmstaedter also had this idea.[33] Albertson knows of Waele's work but notes that the Hermes *Psychopompos* motif explains the staff but not the mummy.[34] Albertson favours a derivation for wand plus mummy from imagery connected with the cult of Isis.[35] As already noted, however, Jesus has a wand in the first catacomb fresco we discuss above, where Lazarus is not wrapped like a mummy. Yet even if Albertson is correct, on his view the figure with the wand is still Hermes Psychopompos, even if the mummy wrappings are explicable as influenced by the cult of Isis. This result is significant for the argument we are about to advance as to the prototypicality of the raising of Lazarus for the resurrection of Christians.

We should not be surprised by the possibility that artists working for Christian patrons in the catacombs relied upon imagery drawn from the pagan world. We have already noted that the image of the very tomb from which Lazarus appears is often derived from the form of the temple-tomb of pagan Romans. In addition, C. Murray has persuasively shown that a large number of motifs from pagan religious beliefs have found their way into Christian funerary art in Rome, albeit in a transmuted form.[36] One example is the representation of Jesus in the (transmuted) guise of Orpheus.[37] To draw upon Greco-Roman traditions of

33 Speaking of the staff in Jesus' hand he says: 'Ursprünglich war es der Stab des Hermes, mit dem dieser die Seelen aus dem Hades heraufholte, wie es der Vorstellung der Orphiker und Pythagoreer entspricht. Die Vorstellungen, die mit der Lazarusszene verknüpft werden, wären also folgende: Christus ist der Magier, der die Seelen der Verstorbenen aus dem Hades erlöst' (1955, p. 8). He was unaware of Waele's book, but came upon representations of Mercury in this guise in Fritz Wirth, *Römische Wandmalerei*, 1934 (*non vidimus*).

34 Albertson 1995, p. 128.

35 Albertson 1995, pp. 129–32.

36 Murray 1981.

37 Murray 1981, pp. 37–63.

Hermes/Mercury represents another form of this process, though the space available to this subject in the present volume does not permit a detailed presentation of the type Murray has provided with such erudition. We might, however, ask whether it is better to refer to Jesus as assimilated to a magician or a god? This is an interesting question, which need not detain us here on account of the position we must now express.

The use by Jesus of what looks like a magician's wand carries important implications for the thesis we are maintaining in this volume. Before proceeding to consider them, however, we should consider some existing interpretations of the purpose of the Lazarus representations.

Some Existing Interpretations of the Lazarus Imagery in Rome

The Comparison with Jonah

We will begin with the Christian sepulchral imagery of Jonah's expulsion from the great fish, since at first sight it may not seem to help the thesis of the prototypicality of the resurrection of Lazarus. We have noted above how popular in catacomb art was the representation of Jonah being expelled from the mouth of a large fish (see Figure 5). Murray has observed that the 'story of Jonah is reproduced in profusion on Christian monuments of all sorts, lamps, glasses, sculptures and frescoes, and is one of the earliest subjects to be found represented in the pre-Constantinian period'.[38] Why is Jonah so often depicted in catacomb frescoes? On its face, the image does not seem appropriate, since Jonah did not die, but merely spent three (no doubt uncomfortable) days and three nights in the stomach of a great fish (Jonah 1.17) before, at God's command, it vomited Jonah out on dry land (Jonah 3.10). Part of the reason may be that Jonah himself, in his prayer to God from inside the fish, states that 'out of the belly of Sheol I cried' (Jonah 2.2); that is, Jonah himself draws an analogy between his piscine enclosure and death. Yet it is also probable, as scholars

38 Murray 1981, p. 76.

have suggested,[39] that inspiration for the Jonah imagery actually comes from Matthew 12.40: 'For as Jonah was three days and three nights in the belly of the whale, so will the Son of man be three days and three nights in the heart of the earth' (RSV). On this view, the Jonah imagery is connected with the resurrection of Christ.

So why is Jonah imagery thought appropriate for Christian sepulchral art? C. Murray states that in the first three centuries the Church appears to have adopted the Matthean interpretation of Jonah and regarded him as the 'chief image of the death and resurrection of Christ'.[40] But she then cites references to Justin (*Dialogue* 107–8), Irenaeus (*Adversus Haereses* 3.21.1) and Tertullian (*De Carnis Resurrectione* 32) that indicate that it is not so much the resurrection of Christ itself that is in view, but the power that God has to raise the dead generally. Surely this is a necessary dimension to this imagery. For while it is not impossible that an early Christian would decorate the grave of a deceased relative or friend with an image referring to the nature of Christ, it is far more likely that he or she would seek a representation that spoke of his or her hope for the deceased. Murray comes close to this when she adds, soon after the quotation just given, that an earlier scholar was correct in 'interpreting the scene of Jonah as symbolic of the death and resurrection of Christ *and that of the Christian*'. Christ, by his own death and resurrection, '*will ensure the resurrection of the faithful*'.[41] But if it is necessary (as indeed it is) to interpret the Jonah imagery, which Matthew 12.40 had directly linked to the death and resurrection of Jesus, with respect to the fate of the ordinary Christian buried in a catacomb *loculus*, how much more likely is it that representations of Lazarus will have the destiny of the deceased in view?

---

39 Lowrie 1969, p. 65 and Murray 1981, pp. 76 and 77, where she notes that the Jonah scene in a particular tomb 'is reflecting an attempt to illustrate the New Testament text rather than the Old Testament story and the biblical basis for this particular composition is the Gospel of S. Matthew' (namely Matt. 12.40).

40 Murray 1981, p. 93.

41 Murray 1981, p. 94 (emphasis added in both places).

The Significance of Jesus as Wand-Bearer for Interpreting the Lazarus Imagery

Whether Jesus with his wand raising Lazarus is viewed as a magician or as having a role more like the god Mercury himself, the crucial point is the dominant role attributed to Jesus in relation to Lazarus. Jesus, armed with his staff, is bringing life to Lazarus. There seems no room in this style of representation for the possibility that the resurrection of Jesus himself is in view, since Jesus is depicted in a dramatically non-biblical way as an agent who effects revivifications of the dead with a wand, a role which has nothing to do with his own resurrection through the agency of the Father. On this occasion, we must accordingly diverge from Robin Jensen's view that the raising of Lazarus was a prefigurement of Christ's own death and resurrection, as well as that of Christians.[42] The imagery of Christ with a wand raising Lazarus certainly corroborates his prototypical role for those with faith in Christ, but it is quite inconsistent with the former alternative.

The Lazarus Imagery in Rome and the Prototypicality of his Raising from the Dead for Christians

From these considerations we are led to suggest that such an image of Jesus is closely in accord with our understanding of the prototypical function for Christ-followers of the raising of Lazarus in the Fourth Gospel. We submit that when the early Christians of Rome, who had interred their loved ones in the catacombs, commissioned artists to paint scenes of Lazarus and Jesus with a wand effecting his revivification in close proximity to their dead, they did so because they saw in this image the future destiny of the deceased person whom they memorialized in this way and, indeed, of all the faithful in Christ. What had happened to Lazarus, being raised from the dead, would happen to the relative or friend they had buried, and to themselves, at the last day. For loyal Christians, Lazarus was thus prototypical of their fate.

Our views coincide quite closely with the particular interpretation that Jensen proposes for the frescoes depicting Lazarus:

---

42 Jensen 2000, p. 167.

> The sepulchral location of most of these Lazarus compositions suggests that the scene conveys a message of reassurance of resurrection, or life beyond death. *Lazarus, returned to life, is a prototypical figure symbolizing the recently dead one's resurrection to the next life.* Although Lazarus will one day die again, his first raising is the proof that God can bring the dead back to life, either here or in paradise.[43]

To much the same effect, Schiller comments that 'For the persecuted Christians it (sc. the resurrection of Lazarus) was the embodiment of their hopes of resurrection and eternal life.'[44]

Jensen notes that the Lazarus narrative also functions within the Fourth Gospel as a link between the ministry of Jesus and his Passion and, indeed, to foreshadow his entombment and resurrection. This latter connection is picked up occasionally in art, as with a fifth-century ivory diptych that shows in one section the women outside the empty tomb of Jesus which has on its doors (no stone here!) a carving of the resurrection of Lazarus.[45] Yet a composite image such as this should not distract us from the fundamental fact that a catacomb fresco of Lazarus emerging from the tomb is primarily a reference to the glorious fate of the person buried there, not to the resurrection of Jesus. For while it is perhaps impossible entirely to separate the resurrection of Lazarus from that of Jesus, frescoes of Lazarus emerging from a very Roman looking tomb at the bidding of Jesus wielding a wand directly address what will happen to the person buried in a Roman catacomb, and only very indirectly, if at all, evoke what has already happened to Jesus. Such images represent visual proof that the resurrection of Lazarus was taken as prototypical of the destiny of Christians from at least as early as the mid third century CE and, we can surmise, surely much earlier.

To assist in interpreting this scene, Robin Jensen turns to some literary texts (in line with her methodology of allowing text and image, which has a life of its own, to interpret one another, not to see the image simply as an illustration of a text). Of particular importance is the treatise by Gregory of Nyssa (*c.* 334–385/6 CE) entitled *On the Soul and the Resurrection*, which recounts

43 Jensen 2000, p. 170 (emphasis added).

44 Schiller 1971, p. 181.

45 This is Fig. 59 in Jensen 2000, p. 163.

his conversation with his sister Macrina, after the death of their brother Basil. The text covers both the immortality of the soul and the resurrection of the body.[46] Here Macrina is the teacher, offering Gregory explanation and consolation. Part of her explanation involves proof texts from scripture, including the dry bones of Ezekiel 37, Jesus' raising of Jairus' daughter and the widow's son and Lazarus, and Jesus' own resurrection on Easter morning.[47] These New Testament examples, all offered by Macrina in the cause of consoling Gregory of the eternal destiny of their brother Basil, are preceded by the following general remark:

> The expressions in the Gospels also I will pass over; for their meaning is quite clear to every one; and our Lord does not declare in word alone that the bodies of the dead shall be raised up again; but He shows in action the Resurrection itself, making a beginning of this work of wonder from things more within our reach and less capable of being doubted.[48]

We should note, however, that although Gregory of Nyssa quite rightly saw in Jesus' resurrection a demonstration of what the resurrection of the faithful would be like, he is not here suggesting that the raising of Lazarus prefigures the resurrection of Jesus. Rather, both substantiate the reality of the coming resurrection of the faithful.

Mary and Martha in Roman Frescoes and Sarcophagus Reliefs

In this chapter we have reflected upon the earliest known images of the Lazarus scene, which restrict the figures portrayed to Jesus and Lazarus. But as we noted above, many of the extant representations of the raising of Lazarus in painted plaster and

46 Gregory of Nyssa, *On the Soul and the Resurrection, Patrologia Graeca*, Volume 46, 11–160. This translation is from the *New Advent Website* (http://www.newadvent.org/fathers/2915.htm), an online version of the Catholic Encyclopedia. There is a German translation in Bardenhewer, Weyman and Zellinger 1927, pp. 243–334.

47 Gregory of Nyssa, *On the Soul and the Resurrection*, §16.

48 From the *New Advent Website* (http://www.newadvent.org/fathers/2915.htm).

carved stone from early Christian Rome depict other characters from the Johannine narrative, especially Martha and Mary (as in Figure 6). Versions of the raising of Lazarus such as this bring out many aspects of the narrative that we have argued in earlier chapters of this volume fulfil a prototypical function for John's addressees. These include the familial love and intimacy among Jesus and his followers, Mary's devotion to Jesus, and Martha's confession of faith and service to the other members of the group. Although it is not possible within the scope of this volume, a detailed consideration of early Christian Lazarus representations from this angle would be very worthwhile.

Conclusion

The existence of visual representations of the raising of Lazarus from the early Christian art of Rome, some of them created less than two centuries after the Fourth Gospel appeared, provides an unusual control against which we have been able to test our theory that John presented the raising of Lazarus as prototypical of the coming resurrection to eternal life of those who believe in Christ. While we have not been able to consider more than a sample of the evidence, we submit that the frescoes and sarcophagus reliefs portraying Lazarus being raised by Jesus wielding a wand clearly carry this meaning.

In addition to providing corroborating evidence for our thesis, however, the sepulchral imagery of Lazarus from Rome also testifies to the power of the Johannine narrative to inspire Christian imagination in relation to the fundamental questions of death and rebirth to eternal life. The context-shaped interaction of the ordinary Christians of Rome in the face of death with John's message of how Lazarus was raised to life also parallels our approach to accessing the Johannine narrative theologically through intercultural engagement with the evangelist's meaning. Although one area in which our situation differs from that of the Christians of Rome in the first few centuries of the Church is that we have the capacity to apply *historical* analysis to the Johannine text, the process of dialogical engagement with the biblical meaning and our own situation is fundamentally similar. In the remaining chapter of this volume, to which we now proceed, we will follow in the footsteps of the early Christians of Rome by exploring how John's presentation of death and resurrection can impact on our own Christian experience and identity.

7

A Theological Conclusion: The Raising of Lazarus and Christian Identity

The Lazarus Narrative: History and Theology

We have now mounted an argument for John's having presented the raising of Lazarus from the dead as prototypical of the ultimate destiny of the Christ-followers for whom he wrote his Gospel – their resurrection (Chapter 5). We have also argued that the depictions of Lazarus in catacomb frescoes and in other early Christian art from Rome constitute evidence that the Christians of that time and place viewed the Lazarus story in the same light (Chapter 6). In the current and concluding chapter of this volume we wish to raise a theological 'So what?' over these results. What relevance does John's message for his addressees that the raising of Lazarus was prototypical of the resurrection in which they hoped have for Christians today? What impact can it have on our experience and identity, on our beliefs and values? In addressing these questions we will need to bear in mind the context within which the evangelist situates his message on death and resurrection, namely, the family of Lazarus, Martha and Mary tied to one another by the intimacy of family and reciprocally tied to Jesus by the intimacy of friendship and love, as we have explained in Chapter 4.

Since we began this volume with a brief résumé of the long history of the Christian afterlife and appropriation of the story of Lazarus in theology, in popular belief and in art, it would be rather surprising if there was nothing we could make of it theologically. If among the early Christians of Rome – in the face of the death of relatives and friends – this narrative had such a compelling hold on their imaginations that it became the most popular motif in catacomb frescoes after depictions of the Good Shepherd, can it fail to move us? Could we have become so estranged from the long lines of our ancestors in faith who have found Lazarus highly pertinent to their experience of life and, even more, of death, that his raising from the dead has now lost its significance for the big questions that we confront with regard to death and ultimate salvation? We think not.

We see this as a theological issue in the broad sense that it deals with fundamental questions relating to our relationship with God and with one another. At the same time, in seeking to bring the results of our exegetical and art-historical enquiries to bear upon the character of Christian life and hope today, we are adopting the broad approach that we have set out and applied in earlier chapters of this work. This means that we have departed from the long dominant model of New Testament theology that involves using historical analysis of the biblical texts to unearth 'timeless' truths that can then be fed into a treatise in systematic theology (here probably under the rubric of 'eschatology').[1] Rather, we are applying the different approach developed by one of us recently that sees the *theological significance* of *historical investigation* of a New Testament passage or work to lie precisely in bringing *the specific meaning it carried in its original setting* into creative and critical confrontation with our modern experience in an overarching framework of intercultural communication and communion.[2]

When one is assessing the message Paul is delivering to his addressees in Rome to settle the ethnic divisions between Judean and Greek Christ-followers existing in the congregations by reminding them of their new common ingroup identity in Christ, the most promising area of modern experience with which to bring this message (in all its particularity) into critical contact is that of inter-ethnic conflict and genocide.[3] The issue with the narrative of the raising of Lazarus in the Fourth Gospel is very different. The pivotal topics around which our dialogue with John's message in relation to Lazarus must turn are the reality of death and the prospect of resurrection. We must insist that

1 For a critical assessment of the use of the concept 'eschatology' in New Testament exegesis, see Esler 2003, pp. 250–2.

2 For this approach see Esler 2005a.

3 See Esler 2005a, pp. 273–82.

both elements are foundational, especially as for some Christians today there is a sense that the resurrection and the eternal life associated with it soften the harshness of death. We are led by the Johannine picture and by our own instincts and experience to insist that an interest in what lies beyond death must be inextricably connected with an appreciation of the fundamental horror and alienation of death.

Lazarus and the Reality of Death

For some critics, John's account of Lazarus takes away death's sting. Thus we find S. Schulz asserting that for believing Christians in the here and now there is no death in its earthly sense, since bodily death has lost any meaning.[4] Similarly, W. Stenger claims that although the believer might die in his or her earthly life, he or she has a life in a higher and ultimate sense; for believers such as these, Stenger suggests, there is no death in the ultimate sense and dying has become insubstantial.[5] We have already argued to the contrary of these views, that in telling the story of Lazarus John most certainly does not render death meaningless or insubstantial. The death of Lazarus is all too real. The resulting outpouring of grief from Martha, Mary and Jesus and the blunt recognition that after four days his corpse will have begun to produce the appalling smell of human decomposition leave no room for any doubt that John (and his audience) fully recognized the physical realities and bitterness of death.

This aspect of the Johannine meaning represents a powerful and salutary challenge to modern Christian consciousness. For we are the recipients of remarkably contradictory messages about death.[6] On the one hand, at least in Western cultures, we have lost much of our direct experience of death, since the bodies of our relatives are generally taken straight off to mortuaries and later to the church and cemetery or crematorium. The older custom of keeping the body of the deceased family member at

4 Schulz 1983, p. 158.

5 Stenger 1974, p. 31.

6 On this subject the remarks of Ratzinger (1988, pp. 60–71) and Jeanrond (1995, pp. 47–50) are particularly valuable. Also see Esler 2005a, pp. 229–31.

home for a few days prior to burial and thereby observing the gradual change in the appearance of the deceased as the processes of decomposition begin has now largely disappeared. But those who are familiar with this practice will be well aware of the awesome sense of the reality of death that it produces. On the other hand, films, television and computer games so routinely expose us to media representations of death that we have become curiously desensitized to the phenomenon. Because of its portrayal in these arenas, death has become trivialized.

So even if we have faith in life beyond the grave, through resurrection for example, we must acknowledge the limitations to such belief:

> Such reflection in no way shelters us from the reality of death. We still face the fact that death is inevitable but will come we know not when. Extremes of pain, discomfort and indignity may still precede it. What it entails is still beyond our experience. We must still die alone. In death we must still be separated from friends and loved ones. Death will still extinguish our hopes and aims for the future on this earth. Perhaps, finally, there is that niggling doubt that death does mean our utter annihilation.[7]

Factors such as these serve two functions. First, they encapsulate the immensity of death whatever our vision of ultimate vindication, but, second, they are the necessary presuppositions for reflecting upon a new relationship in Christ that may open up in death. Both aspects are visible in John's account of Lazarus. To minimize the reality of death is to enfeeble the meaning of resurrection. But let us move on to consider how the Johannine vision of the raising of Lazarus as prototypical of the resurrection of Christ-followers may enrich our contemporary Christian identity and sense of hope. We will begin with the context of the intimacy of familial ties and friendship in which it is set.

7 Esler 2005a, pp. 230–1, drawing on Davis 1989, p. viii.

Domesticity and Friendship: The Context for the Death of Lazarus

One of the prominent features of the Johannine depiction of the death and raising of Lazarus is the setting of domesticity and friendship within which events occur. There is a family of siblings; there is the context of a family tragedy; there is the friendship and love of Jesus for Lazarus; and, after Lazarus' raising, there is a household meal with Martha serving and Mary anointing Jesus. We have suggested that these details serve to provide a picture of a community of Christ-followers in which the life of the household and friendship provide the model for relationships. Soon after, the disciples of Jesus will be promised a place in another 'house', that of the Father (John 14.3), and eventually they will be encouraged to look upon one another as 'brothers' (cf. John 20.17). Already at the outset of the Gospel, John has signalled the theological basis for such a relationship by the statement that those who respond to Jesus, the Word, will be 'children of God' (John 1.12–13). God looks after 'his children'; in effect, the children are 'brothers and sisters' of one another.

Such a model is not unique to the Fourth Gospel. It can be found in the Synoptic Gospels (cf. Mark 3.31–35), for example. But prior to John 11—12, it is not much emphasized in the Fourth Gospel. The importance attaching to the recognition of Jesus and his role has been uppermost. Defections have occurred as some disciples fall away, and the defection of Judas has been strongly signalled as an event of significance yet to come (John 6.66ff.). In sharp contrast to these concerns, the family of Lazarus expresses a highly positive example of love and concern towards one another and (despite their initial disappointment) towards Jesus.

Subsequent followers of Christ have often seized upon the model of calling one another 'brothers and sisters', but rarely has this image been so richly filled out as in the poignant display of the family of Bethany in John 11—12. The call to 'fictive kinship' is here portrayed in terms of 'real kinship'. What it means to treat others as though they were one's kin is shown in a situation of life-and-death 'real' family concerns. The Johannine presentation reveals both the pain of death when it occurs to a family member, but also a framework of love and mutual concern within which the death and its aftermath can be accommodated and dealt with. This pattern will be replicated later in the Gospel when, in that unique Johannine scene, Jesus' mother, and her sister and the Beloved Disciple also face the death of a loved one as they stand at the foot of the cross. Here a dying Jesus consigns his mother and the Beloved Disciple into one another's care in the setting of the latter's home (John 19.25–27), thus creating a second household in the Gospel exposed to the tragedy of death while being the recipients of Jesus' love.

The 'badge' of these households has been a bond of love and John uses this 'badge' more widely with respect to Christian relationships in general. Unlike the disciples later in the Gospel, however, the Lazarus family does not need to be commanded to love one another. Their every action displays such love. And the quality of such love is based on the natural concern for family. It is as though John is saying to his readers, 'If you want to know what love towards one another and to Jesus means, look at the sisters of Lazarus.' Shortly hereafter, Jesus will give the disciples the *command* to love one another as he has loved them (John 13.34). Jesus affirms that this will mark them off from the world (13.35). But for the meaning of the love commandment, one has to look elsewhere. For a Gospel that is often said to be full of abstract symbols, it is worth noting that the description of an experience becomes the template by which the evangelist conveys the nature of the relationship of love that is commanded.

What happens when we take such a message, originating in and speaking to a particular group in a very specific time, place and context, and seek to bring it into creative yet critical dialogue with the experience and identity of Christians today – in line with the theological approach we are applying in this volume? At one level, we will be struck by the familiarity of some aspects of John's communication. Christians, like the members of virtually all other religious communities, find in their families the first line of support when faced with the deaths of those they love. The tragedy of the death of a parent or a child, a husband or a wife, a brother or sister, or of any other relative, falls most heavily on the family members who survive. Primarily within the family will they grieve and then seek to come to terms with their grief. This was the case with Martha and Mary, and it is with us. Here we encounter a powerful dimension of our shared humanity.

Yet there are differences that have the potential to challenge (and hence enrich) our contemporary Christian ways of thinking, feeling and acting. The first of these is the close proximity of

Martha and Mary to the death of their brother and his interment (especially in their anointing his body for burial, which we believe John's audience would have understood them to have attended to personally). As we have noted above, the bodies of our deceased relatives are normally removed very soon after death into the hands of the professionals. The second difference is that the close integration between family intimacy and belief in Jesus that forms the context for the events among this family of Bethany is not a feature of modern Christian belief and practice. We may pay lip-service to the idea that our fellow parishioners are our brothers and sisters in Christ. Yet with requiem services occurring in the local church and not in the home of the deceased and where his or her family is one of many families who may know one another (and in various degrees) or not as the case may be, we encounter a set of understandings and behaviours very different indeed from what John has presented in relation to Lazarus, Martha and Mary, and, indeed, in relation to Jesus' mother and the Beloved Disciple in the scene that takes place at the foot of the cross.

But death, although its bitterness is fully stressed, is not the end of the story. What of the resurrection of believers for which, as we have argued, the raising of Lazarus forms a protoytype? To this issue we now turn, noting in advance that we will soon see how the household even figures in the Johannine vision of the future life.

Lazarus and Resurrection

The initial challenge for the writers of this volume (when invited to speak at the conference in July 2003 where we first outlined our thesis)[8] was to use a social-scientific analysis of the Lazarus narrative to say something about its theology. There are clearly implications for Johannine theology, not least being the way in which a strongly realized understanding of the 'eternal life' still left important unresolved questions that moved those responsible for this Gospel (at some stage) to offer hopes of resolution in terms of the future destiny of believers. These two visions of ultimate vindication for Christ-followers are integrally related, stimulated by the experience of 'death in the community of eternal life'.

---

8 See the Preface for details.

Once one accepts this, then the precise nature of future belief becomes increasingly of interest. The story of Lazarus is a very straightforward revivification story. There seems no interest in some sort of disembodied soul in heaven/purgatory/ hell, despite the opportunity offered by four days of death and even though there are signs of an interest in a pre-resurrection intermediate state after death elsewhere in the biblical and apocryphal traditions.[9] In this respect it is quite unlike the parable about the 'Lazarus' in Luke 16. Only the Johannine reference to Lazarus 'sleeping' (11.11) offers some glimpse of a post-mortem, pre-resurrection state, and interestingly this depiction is of a reassuringly peaceful state. Nor do we seem to find here a scheme of 'vindication', because Lazarus is never presented as a martyr, in contrast to the death of Jesus where his raising is a victory over opponents. This seems further to underline the distinction between the two raisings, those of Lazarus and Jesus. For believers, the raising of Lazarus is less a victory over death than a sign of divine love. Even though hostile authorities surround the story, and he becomes a target for them later, Lazarus' raising is an act of grace rather than vindication. The ultimate fate of Lazarus is left unrecorded. It is to other places that one must go to find a fuller scenario of the Johannine understanding of the future destiny of Christ-followers. The function of the Lazarus story seems primarily to offer a reassurance of care, alluding to (rather than realizing) the resurrection to life indicated in John 5.28. The challenge thereby presented to present-day Christians is to interact with the Johannine picture of this future destiny.

It is a noteworthy feature of the Fourth Gospel that the story of the Bethany family also serves to lay the foundation for a later Johannine glimpse of the afterlife. The strongly domestic setting that is presented in connection with Lazarus, Martha and Mary, to which we have drawn attention earlier and which is recaptured in the anointing meal in John 12 after the raising of Lazarus, is not merely an image of Christian existence in the present. We suggest that it is also projected into the future in John's vision of Christian existence, of Christian 'possible selves', after resurrection.

While John 5.25–29 declares that John envisages a future

9 See Cooper 2000, and also Esler 2005a, pp. 199–208 for post-mortem existence in Hebrews.

resurrection, and while John 6 returns to the theme of believers being raised on the last day (cf. vv. 39, 40, 44, 54), none of this material suggests a picture of what the resurrected life will be like for Jesus' followers. In the Synoptic Gospels, the picture of the future is frequently tied closely to the preaching of God's coming *kingdom*. The presumption is the believers will have some exalted place in this kingly rule (cf. Matt. 25.31–34; 16.19). Even the image of an end-time meal is in the context of a kingdom celebration in Matthew 8.11–12/Luke 13.28–29. The establishment of this kingdom will be accompanied by signs involving both nations and the cosmos at large (cf. Mark 13). We do not find in the Fourth Gospel such a prominent or dramatic image of a future kingdom. References to a kingdom are not entirely absent, as John 3.3 and 5 show. Jesus' own 'kingship' is a theme in his trial before Pilate, although there it is decisively indicated that any kingship of Jesus is 'not of this world' (John 18.36). There is little to suggest that John thought in terms of a new heaven and new earth, or even a new Jerusalem (cf. Revelation 21). So any kingship of Jesus is left without much actual description. With respect to kingdom terminology, John is more interested in defining the nature of Jesus' kingship than in describing the position of believers in some kind of kingdom. And in that description the household receives emphasis.

For we find a singularly striking image for the afterlife in the Farewell Discourse in John 14.2–3:

> In my Father's house (*oikia*) are many rooms (*monai*); if it were not so, would I have told you that I go to prepare a place for you? And when I go and prepare a place for you, I will come again and will take you to myself, that where I am you may be also. (RSV)

The imagery here is of a 'house'. This 'house' is the Father's house to which Jesus is to go when he departs from his followers and in which he will prepare a (future) place for them. So first and foremost, the Johannine believers were encouraged to hold onto the image of joining Jesus and the Father in the Father's *house*. Such a household communion between Jesus and his close followers is precisely what is prefigured in John 12.1–3 (and, indeed, in 19.26–27).

There is therefore evidence of a pattern in the Fourth Gospel in which the household serves as a present and future model for relationships between followers (and with Jesus and the Father). The recognition of this correspondence between John 11—12 and John 14.2–3, and the relative lack of emphasis on kingly or imperial structures for the future, encourages one to dwell upon the significance of such a feature. Does it reflect the reality of early Christian worship being located in households? Does it reflect a conscious preference for the kinds of relationships that exist in households as the model of community over the kinds of relationships associated with imperial entities? We consider that both of these questions should be answered in the affirmative.

The significance of John 14.2–3 cannot just lie in a limitation of ambition with respect to this world, whereby political powers are not engaged. Greater powers such as 'the ruler of this world' (cf. John 12.31) have been engaged by Jesus. A kingship *in heaven* was still an option. Yet it is an option that does not appear to have been taken, at least with respect to a way of understanding the future life of believers. The imagined future instead stresses care and support (and in a domestic context) more than victory. This model has much to say to modern-day Christians, especially those in countries where secularization has now terminated, or at least seriously incapacitated, the dominant role that the Church had played in civic affairs and politics since Constantine's Edict of Milan in 313 CE. The old patterns of house churches, or of congregations meeting in small and largely private buildings, that disappeared with Constantine and his building of huge basilicas for Christian worship,[10] may be due for a recovery.

Our work also provides a challenge to Johannine studies to reassess the function of Christology in the Gospel in order to understand better how some statements that seem on the surface to be central confessional claims of belief *about Jesus* may in fact serve to add authority to assurances or demands of quite different kinds, that reach more into the realms of everyday Christian experience and identity, the life of the family especially, than have relevance for treatises of systematic theology.

10 For a discussion of Christian churches before Constantine and the transition to basilicas that he introduced, see Lowrie 1969, pp. 87–110 and White 1996–7.

The Role of the Lazarus Story in Christian Imagination and Identity

Much of our examination has so far been directed to the historical question of how the message of the evangelist in this passage would have been understood by his original audience, which we consider was a distinctive local one. Nevertheless, we have already demonstrated that by applying a model of prototypicality and social identity to the text we have discerned meanings that rather effortlessly escape their initial social context and are capable of achieving a much wider impact and currency. The frescoes of the raising of Lazarus in the Roman catacombs are very early evidence of this, from a culture perhaps not radically different from that in which the Fourth Gospel first appeared. Yet the avalanche of later pictorial representations of this Johannine narrative, for which G. Schiller provides a helpful survey as far as the Baroque period,[11] testifies to its enduring popularity in times and places increasingly remote from its original context. The theological model of intercultural communication and communion that we have utilized in this volume provides one way to comprehend how this Johannine narrative can have this function.

This popularity is proof of the continuing appeal of the Lazarus story to Christian imagination and thought. Why should this be the case? It seems likely that part of the answer must lie in the way in which the prospect of death, and the experience of beloved Christians dying (especially if it is untimely), present a continuing point of natural anxiety. The need for reassurance transcends the original context – in pastoral situations at least. The reassurance lies not simply in the promise of future bliss. The story of Lazarus also addresses the reality of death. Could not God have prevented bad things (such as premature death) happening to those whom he loves? One gets no general explanation for such tragedies, but one is faced with the fact that a divine deliberation is involved. The mystery is not lessened, but a kind of reaffirmation is offered.

For Christian adherents, there are other attractive features of the Lazarus story that have undoubtedly contributed to its continuing popularity. Through the figures of Lazarus and his sisters, we have suggested that an understanding of Christian existence

---

11 Schiller 1971, pp. 181–6.

in the world was set out. Here is a Christianity that is not so much dogmatically based as relationally based. Above all, Christians are characterized by friendship, love and examples of devotion. The kinship group provides the 'natural' context for depicting such an ethos. Within such a context Lazarus is the exemplar as a recipient of divine mercy. He depicts an alternative metaphor to being 'born anew'. He 'lives anew'. Mary in turn becomes an exemplar for devotion to Jesus, while Martha is exemplary in her confession of faith in Jesus and in her service to him and other members of the group. Even though understandings of kinship groups and friendship have undoubtedly changed from the original first-century Mediterranean context, and even though we cannot claim that popular appreciation of the Lazarus story in later times was able fully to recover the original sense of the story, concepts such as love and friendship still provide a picture of Christian identity in the world in which relationships have a prominent place.

Thus the difficulty does not lie so much in understanding how in popular Christian circles the Lazarus episode has been able to transcend in some measure the context to which it was originally written. We have argued against the idea that a biblical message needs to be stripped of its original context and historical significance in order to convey meaning in the present. The difficulty lies in how one turns this into an enduring theology capable of the same vitality. We have suggested that one answer lies in a framework of intercultural dialogue between us and John, our ancestor in faith. In this perspective, it is not at all surprising that the vitality may lie above all in the story, understood with the greatest possible fidelity to its historical context so that the raw difference of its meaning may work its identity-shaping ways with us.

A dominant characteristic of contemporary Christianity, at least in industrial or post-industrial societies, is a disinterest in the fate of the dead. Notions of the immortality of the soul or of final resurrection, if not actively disbelieved, are rarely the subject of intense interest and are quite often simply ignored.[12] Christians mouth a belief in the communion of saints at many eucharistic

12 For an important exception, see Hick 1976. The topic is also frequently covered in articles in the journal *Faith and Philosophy*.

liturgies, for example, yet there may be no real conviction behind such affirmations. Karl Rahner captured the situation fairly accurately when he wrote:

> Most contemporary Christians have already ceased to have any sense of being actively in communication with their own dead, the members of their families and the relations whom they have lost. Though there are exceptions to this the general attitude is that they have departed and vanished from this life . . . It is not that we contest the fact that they are, in principle, living on in the presence of the God of the living, but so far as we are concerned they are not alive. They have been, so to say, completely and totally removed from our sphere of existence.[13]

While this situation may represent an inevitable concomitant of modernity and post-modernity, the account of the raising of Lazarus in John 11 prompts us to recall that the future fate of the believer was of intense interest to the early Christ-movement, to its experience and identity, and remained so until quite recently. Perhaps, in the end, this brilliant Johannine narrative throws down the challenge that failure to confront the ultimate questions of death and its aftermath risks driving a wedge between Christians today and the long line of people before us whom we collectively remember and, even more, call our own.

---

13 Rahner 1971, pp. 6–7.

Appendix 1

Translating *Ioudaioi* as 'Judeans' in the Fourth Gospel

On many occasions in the Fourth Gospel, including the sections dealing with Lazarus, Martha and Mary, the Greek text refers to *Ioudaioi*. Virtually all translators and most interpreters translate this word as 'Jews'. We consider this translation is unacceptable for many reasons, which we will outline – only briefly here, since one of us has written extensively on this subject in recent years.[1]

Around the Mediterranean world of the first century CE there were many groups that are usefully classified as ethnic. In broad terms, we follow Fredrik Barth's self-ascriptive and processual approach to ethnicity, where the fundamental feature is the group's sense that it is a group (so that cultural indicia are the result and reflection of group identity, not its driving force).[2] At the same time, we find useful as a diagnostic (and not prescriptive) set of characteristics in play with most groups that can sensibly be described as ethnic those set out by John Hutchinson and Anthony Smith: (1) a common proper name to identify the group; (2) a myth of common ancestry; (3) a shared history or shared memories of a common past, including heroes, events and their commemoration; (4) a common culture, embracing such things as customs, language and religion; (5) a link with a homeland, either through actual occupation or by symbolic attachment to the ancestral land, as with diaspora peoples; and (6) a

1 See Esler 2003, pp. 40–76 for a general discussion of ethnicity and ancient Judean ethnicity, Esler 2006a for a discussion of Judean ethnic identity in Josephus' *Contra Apionem* and Esler 2006b for a specific application to this approach to John's Gospel.

2 See Barth 1969.

sense of communal solidarity.[3] We note that in this approach to ethnicity, religion is one of many indicative factors; probably this element was more important for Judeans than for other ethnic groups in the region, but it still only forms one part of a much larger complex.

'Ethnicity' may not be a perfect designation for Judean identity (no group designation is), but it is the best available. These groups were universally known by the territory in which they arose, whether they still lived there or were settled in diaspora communities: there were, for example, *Romaioi* from Rome, *Hellēnes* from Hellas, *Aigyptioi* from Egypt, *Parthians* from Parthia and, in the same way, *Ioudaioi* from Judea. To translate *Ioudaioi* as 'Jews' is to strip this group of the territorial connection characterizing them and all other ethnic groups in their environment. This is also an illicitly exceptionalist argument, since it attributes to the 'Jews' what is plainly regarded as an identity (religious in nature) different in kind from these other groups.

The circumstance that the *Ioudaioi* – referred to under that name both by themselves and others – were present in Palestine and in numerous other places (often in great numbers) around the Mediterranean means that John and his community could have been located anywhere in the region where a significant population of *Ioudaioi* were to be found. That John often shows detailed knowledge of Palestinian conditions does not militate against this result, since he could have acquired this knowledge by reason of having been raised or spent a reasonable time there. One needs only to think of the numbers of Judeans who were expelled from Judea following the victory of Titus in 70 CE to appreciate the reality of such a possibility.

In addition, the subsequent history and vicious oppression of the 'Jews' in the medieval and modern periods anachronistically colours how we understand the *Ioudaioi* of the first century CE. None of this is to suggest that some modern-day Jews may not be biological descendants of ancient *Ioudaioi*, or that all of them may not look back on these people from the past as their spiritual ancestors, just as Christians can.[4] Our point is that such considerations should not impede our designating the *Ioudaioi* in a

3 Hutchinson and Smith 1996, pp. 6–7.

4 See Esler 2005a.

way that most accurately reflects their ethnic identity in the first century CE.

Finally, the fact that some *Ioudaioi* in the Fourth Gospel favour Jesus and some are homicidally opposed to him is no reason for claiming (although one sometimes hears the claim) that only the latter should be regarded as ethnic 'Jews'. They are all *Ioudaioi*, all Judeans, with the context in the Gospel indicating whether they are opposed to Jesus or not. Although Jesus himself was a Judean (John 4.22), it is an essential feature of the meaning of the Fourth Gospel to announce the inception of a new type of group identity, socio-religious rather than ethnic in character, an identity described as early as John 1.12–13.[5]

The specific presentation of 'the Jews' (*hoi Ioudaioi*) in the Fourth Gospel has given rise to a very considerable body of scholarly discussion. While the use of the term *hoi Ioudaioi* has a meaning derived in part from its broad usage in the world of the ancient Mediterranean, John builds upon this usage in order to create one or more roles for *hoi Ioudaioi* in the drama of his Gospel. Although *hoi Ioudaioi* are often presented in a negative light, John's usage can seem at times to be 'torn between love and hatred'.[6] A somewhat similar observation can be made regarding Johannine use of 'the world' (*kosmos*).

Discussion usually begins with the question of who *hoi Ioudaioi* are. U. C. von Wahlde has provided extensive reviews of the range of possible interpretations in two articles.[7] Most scholars (ourselves included), with the exception of some narrative critics who require a consistent portrayal of characters in John's Gospel, accept that *hoi Ioudaioi* can bear more than one nuance or meaning, depending upon context. There are occasionally favourable ethnic uses, as when Jesus declares to the Samaritan woman that 'salvation is from the *Ioudaioi*' (4.22). There are neutral ethnic-religious references to the feasts of the *Ioudaioi* (for example, 2.13; 11.55). There is (rarely) a limited geographical sense when the region of Judea (as opposed to Galilee) is associated with

5 See Esler 2006b.

6 Ashton 1991, p. 131.

7 See Wahlde 2000, and his earlier essay (1982). See also a collection of articles on this topic by H. J. de Jonge, M. C. de Boer, R. F. Collins, P. J. Tomson and A. Reinhartz in Bieringer, Pollefeyt and Vandecasteele-Vanneuville 2001.

the *Ioudaioi* (cf. 7.1). There are references to a political constituency, when Pilate puts the title over the cross to declare that Jesus is 'king of the *Ioudaioi*' (19.19). In some of these cases, moreover, the reference is not so much to any particular group of characters playing a role in the Johannine narrative, but rather to *hoi Ioudaioi* in a very general sense. The references to the feasts of the *Ioudaioi*, for example, almost have the quality of 'background information'.[8] But even here we note that their feasts (the Passover, for example) served vital purposes in the maintenance of Judean ethnic identity and to consider that they are simply 'religious' phenomena would be unacceptably reductionist. Judean ethnicity did have a strong religious dimension, but it covered much more than what we have in mind by the word 'religious'.

Despite these varied nuances, however, the overwhelming portrayal of *hoi Ioudaioi* in the Fourth Gospel is negative. Even though John will occasionally note how some *Ioudaioi* did believe in Jesus, this is not the dominant trait associated with the *Ioudaioi* in John's Gospel. The dominant trait is to represent those who reject belief in Jesus, God's Son and exclusive agent. This culminates in the Passion Narrative, where the trial of Jesus occurs, as one of us has argued,[9] but John signals the theme of rejection much earlier. It is striking how the description of (apparently) some *Ioudaioi* believing in Jesus in John 8.30 is followed immediately (without clear differentiation of audience)[10] by a condemnation of the *Ioudaioi* as being 'of your father the devil' in 8.44, one of the strongest condemnations in the Gospel. As von Wahlde recognizes,[11] this designation is part of the insider/outsider language of the Gospel. It is 'anti-language' as described by social-scientific scholars such as Malina and Rohrbaugh, but in a sense that confirms the basic perceptions also of other scholars such as J. L. Martyn.

Much of the debate regarding the Fourth Gospel's negative use of the vocabulary, however, has been focused upon whether *hoi Ioudaioi* refers to the Judean (in the ethnic sense described above)

---

8 See Tolmie 2005, pp. 378–380.

9 See Piper 2006 forthcoming.

10 There is, however, something of a differentiation of audience if Judeans who 'believed him' (8.31) have a lesser degree of attachment than those who 'believed in him' (8.30).

11 Wahlde 2000, p. 38.

people as a whole or whether it refers to the Judean religious authorities in particular.[12] Although Wahlde prefers the modern translation 'Jewish' to 'Judean' for this group, he is among those who have argued persuasively for the religious authorities being the main opponents of Jesus in the Fourth Gospel, at times becoming blurred with references to the Pharisees. More carefully he affirms:

(a) the use of the term *hoi Ioudaioi* in the Fourth Gospel as outsider language, distancing John and audience from the group;
(b) the use of the term commonly to designate an 'official' position of the opponents of Jesus, and probably the synagogue opponents of the author;
(c) the identification of Judea as the prime geographical location for this hostility.[13]

We largely agree with this description of the Johannine understanding of the Judeans in the Fourth Gospel. Indeed, despite von Wahlde's hesitations, it serves to reinforce our translation of *hoi Ioudaioi* as 'the Judeans'. We acknowledge that such a designation is capable of being misunderstood in modern usage, and no translation can claim to be definitive or perfect. Nonetheless, to translate *Ioudaios* as 'Judean' is certainly the best option. This translation preserves not only a terminology that owes much to comparative usage in the ancient world,[14] including the way in which all ethnic groups were identified by reference to the territory from which they originated (whether they were living

12 De Jonge (2001) has argued the *Ioudaioi* represent in the world of the author 'non-Johannine Christians', not 'non-Christian Jews'. They are believers of inadequate faith. Our analysis of John 10 (see Chapter 1 of this volume), however, argues for a distinction between those who are not sheep of Jesus at all (Judeans), and sheep (Christians) who are outside the Johannine fold. The prediction about being cast out of the synagogue in John 16.1–4, which clearly is meant by the author to apply to the time after Jesus has departed (the time of the subsequent Christ-movement), seems to depict a genuine continuing concern with (non-Christian) Judeans of the synagogues.

13 Wahlde 2000, p. 54.

14 See Tomson 2001.

in their homeland or in diaspora settlements), as we have noted above, but it also has strong justification in terms of Johannine usage.

However much believers may be found among *hoi Ioudaioi*, the traits depicted by the Judeans in the Fourth Gospel are overwhelmingly those of the official opposition to Jesus, an opposition located primarily in Jerusalem in the narrative and closely associated with those who are the leaders of this people and purport to be acting on its behalf. Thus, in response to Jesus' raising of Lazarus, we find Caiaphas the High Priest warning the Sanhedrin (which here includes the chief priests and the Pharisees): 'If we let him go on thus, every one will believe in him, and the Romans will come and destroy both our holy place and the nation (*to ethnos*)' (John 11.48; RSV). Caiaphas is here making a plea for the preservation of Judean ethnic identity. It is important to note that precisely this sentiment is referred to later in the narrative, when the representatives from the chief priests and the Pharisees (John 18.3) take Jesus from the garden in the Kidron valley to Annas, the father-in-law of Caiaphas, the High Priest: 'It was Caiaphas who had given counsel to the Judeans that it was expedient that one man should die for the people (*huper tou laou*)' (18.14; RSV, except 'Judeans' for 'Jews'). Furthermore, at the Johannine trial of Jesus by Pilate, there is no reference to the crowds (in contrast with the Synoptic Gospels). It is the same leadership or their representatives who take Jesus from the house of Caiaphas to the praetorium (18.28). The opposition to Jesus at the trial is 'official', as shown in Pilate's statement to Jesus in its context in the Passion Narrative: 'Your own nation (*to ethnos*) and chief priests have handed you over to me; what have you done?' (18.35; RSV). Sometimes described just as 'the Judeans' (as at 19.7, 12, 14), those who cry out for his crucifixion are in fact not the populace but 'the chief priests and officers' (19.6). The chief priests have the last words in the trial (19.15), by which they 'officially' declare that they have no king but Caesar.[15] The *dominant* traits of the Judeans in the Fourth Gospel are therefore not those of a vacillating populace, but those of an official opposition to Jesus.

---

15 Piper 2006 forthcoming.

Appendix 2

The Spice Used by Mary in Anointing Jesus (John 12.3)

Critical to our discussion in Chapter 3 was a particular position we have taken on a text-critical issue in John 12.3. The received text is: *Ἡ οὖν Μαριὰμ λαβοῦσα λίτραν μύρου νάρδου πιστικῆς πολυτίμου ἤλειψεν τοὺς πόδας τοῦ Ἰησοῦ καὶ ἐξέμαξεν ταῖς θριξὶν αὐτῆς τοὺς πόδας αὐτοῦ· ἡ δὲ οἰκία ἐπληρώθη ἐκ τῆς ὀσμῆς τοῦ μύρου,* which is translated by the RSV as: 'Mary took a pound of costly ointment of pure nard and anointed the feet of Jesus and wiped his feet with her hair; and the house was filled with the fragrance of the ointment.' On our view, however, the correct reading for 12.3a is: *Ἡ οὖν Μαριὰμ λαβοῦσα λίτραν πιστικῆς μύρου πολυτίμου ἤλειψεν τοὺς πόδας τοῦ Ἰησοῦ*; in other words, the word *νάρδου* (nard) was not in the version the evangelist dictated to his scribe and has been added later, and *πιστικῆς* preceded *μύρου*. Furthermore, we translate like this: 'Mary, when she had taken a pound of best quality, a precious lotion, anointed the feet of Jesus' – where 'best quality', translating *πιστικῆς*, refers to myrrh of the best available type. We now offer our argument in support of this interpretation. The two issues requiring attention are, first, whether *νάρδου* appeared in the Gospel as dictated by the evangelist and, second, what meaning to give to *πιστικῆς* if it did not. We will deal with these in turn. We will argue that the evangelist did not include *νάρδου* in his text at this point and that by *πιστικῆς* he meant *myrrh* of the best quality.

The Non-presence of *ΝΑΡΔΟΥ* in the Original Form of John 12.3

The currently accepted reading appears in the vast majority of textual witnesses, but there are three important exceptions that lack *νάρδου* and which we consider reflect the original text: P66, Codex Bezae and the Old Latin.

The Bodmer biblical papyri were found in 1952 in Egypt not far from Nag Hammadi. One of them, Number II, was a codex of 78 leaves (or 156 pages) containing much of John's Gospel, of which the *editio princeps* was published by Victor Martin and J. W. B. Barns in 1956, 1958 and 1962. Although Martin dated the papyrus to around 200 CE, Philip Comfort has recently made a strong case for a date in the middle of the second century CE. Even if P66 is to be dated to around 200 rather than 150 CE, it represents the oldest extant witness to this part of John's Gospel.

A critically important feature of P66 is that it shows signs of work by three scribes. First, there was the original scribe who copied the text from an earlier exemplar of the Gospel, doing so in large print, presumably so it could be read aloud to a Christian congregation.[1] James Royse has made a strong case for this first scribe having been a Christian;[2] for example, he used the standard *nomina sacra*, and special *nomina sacra* for 'cross' (*σταυρός*) and 'crucify' (*σταυρόω*) and he harmonized John 6.69 to Matthew 16.16 and John 21.6 to Luke 5.5.[3] Colwell saw in the first scribe someone who made numerous errors, especially of dropping a letter, a syllable, a word or even a phrase, a practice that would not be particularly amenable to the argument we are advancing here.[4] But more recently Comfort has reviewed the evidence and reached the view that although the first scribe was quite free in his interpretation of the text and produced several independent readings, many of them were additions.[5] Longer omissions are not common in P66 except in the section comprising John 17—19.[6]

In fact, in P66 additions are almost as numerous as omissions. Royse analysed six papyri and produced the following statistics, to which we will add a line formed by dividing omissions by additions:

1 Comfort 1999, p. 371.
2 Royse 1981, pp. 407–9.
3 Comfort 1999, p. 372
4 Colwell 1969, p. 118.
5 Comfort 1999, p. 372.
6 Comfort 1999, pp. 371–4.

	P45	P46	P47	P66	P72	P74
Additions	28	55	5	14	16	12
Omissions	63	167	18	19	29	41
Omissions /Additions	2.25	3.04	3.6	1.36	1.81	3.42

This chart shows that when Royse states 'these figures suggest strongly that the general tendency during the early period of textual transmission was to omit',[7] he is clearly in error as far as P66 is concerned. With P66 we find nearly as many additions as omissions. In addition, when Royse goes on to deduce from these figures as a principle of textual evaluation of these papyri that 'other things being equal, one should prefer the longer reading',[8] it is precisely in respect of P66 that no such principle can be inferred.

The second scribe paginated pages 1–99 (covering John 1—12) and made a number of corrections to the manuscript, many of them bringing the text into line with an Alexandrian text type, and probably using a different exemplar from the first scribe to do so. A third scribe paginated the remaining pages and made a few corrections to John 13.[9] The importance of this understanding of the production of the codex will emerge shortly.

In P66 John 12.3 reads as follows (set out in the lines as they appear in the codex):

η ου
μαρια λαβουσα λειτραν μυ
ναρδου
ρου πιστικης πολουτιμου ηλει
ψεν τους ποδας του ιυ και ε
ξεμαξεν ταις θριξιν αυτης
τους ποδας αυτου· η δε οικια
επληρωθη εκ της οσμης του
μυρου.

7 Royse 1995, p. 246.

8 Royse 1995, p. 246.

9 See Comfort 1999, pp. 374–8. Comfort is not so ready as Martin (1956, p. 30) and Fee (1968, p. 58) to see in the first scribe a careless workman who made numerous errors, including omission.

Apart from *οὐ* for *οὖν* at the beginning of the verse and some inconsequential changes in orthography, this appears to be the same as the received text. Yet the point of critical importance is that *νάρδου* has been added to the text, as a superlinear correction, by the second scribe.[10] This means either that the exemplar used by the first scribe lacked *νάρδου*, or that it occurred in his text but he omitted it (either by accident or by design). The former option is far more probable. First of all, as we have just seen, P66 is not marked by a presence of omissions (in contrast to the other papyri analysed by Royse). Thus, there can be no bias in favour of a longer reading in P66. Deliberate deletion is rendered virtually impossible by virtue of the very similar words in Mark 14.3: *μύρου νάρδου πιστικῆς πολυτελοῦς* (to which we will return below). Could it have been an accidental omission? Although it is possible that the alpha and rho in *μαρία* in the text preceding this have triggered omission of *νάρδου*, with its alpha and rho, this would be a surprisingly small provocation for so striking an omission (especially when this Christian scribe probably knew Mark 14.3) and does not seem in any way probable. In addition, strong support for the view that the exemplar used by the first scribe lacked *νάρδου* can be found in the fact that two other early forms of the text: Codex Bezae and the Old Latin also lack mention of nard. In our view, it is far more likely that the first scribe's exemplar lacked *νάρδου* and that it was then added by the second scribe on the basis of the Alexandrian text type exemplar he was using to make his corrections than that the first scribe's exemplar had the word and he accidentally (or still less likely, intentionally) omitted it.

In Codex Bezae the relevant section of the text is: *λαμβανι λειτραν πιστικης μυρου πολουτειμου.*[11] Once again, although *πιστικῆς* now precedes *μύρου* (and we will return to this later), there are orthographic variations and a verb (*λαμβάνι* for *λαμβάνει*) in the place

10 See the text in Martin 1956, p. 117 and Comfort and Barrett 1999, p. 425.

11 For the text, see Dujardin 1899, Folio 150b. It should be noted that although the Latin translation provided with Codex Bezae runs 'Maria accipiens libram pistici unguenti pretiosi et unxit pedes . . .', older views that this represents a text form independent of the Greek have now largely been abandoned in favour of the view that the Latin is a translation of the Greek (Aland and Aland 1987, p. 185).

of the aorist participle *λαβοῦσα*, this version is the same as P66 (= *λαβουσα λειτραν μυρου πιστικης πολουτιμου*). The lack of *νάρδου* in Codex Bezae is highly significant, since this is a manuscript that reveals a pronounced scribal tendency to add to the text, not to omit.[12] The agreement of P66 and Codex Bezae in this respect is a highly significant phenomenon which has hitherto been given insufficient weight by scholars working on John 12.3. (It should be noted that *νάρδου* is also absent from the Codex Bezae text of Mark 14.3.)

The Old Latin has the following text at this point: *Maria ergo accepit libram unguenti pistici et unxit pedes Iesu et extersit capillis suis eius et domus impleta est ex odore unguenti.*[13] Again, the omission of nard from this form of the text is striking. To many scholars it seems likely that a Latin translation of the New Testament may have appeared in Rome by the second part of the second century or the early part of the third, and there may have been such a translation in North Africa even earlier.[14] The earliest manuscripts of the Old Latin New Testament (that is, the Latin versions which preceded Jerome's translation that ultimately prevailed) are from the fourth century.[15] John 12.3, for example, appears in Old Latin manuscripts 'a' (from the fourth century) and in 'b', 'd' and 'e' (from the fifth century), to name only the earliest.[16] It is unclear whether the Old Latin represents the work of numerous translators, [17] or, as a majority of textual critics now believe, the whole known Old Latin tradition goes back to a single translation of the Greek.[18] Metzger notes that the 'textual affinities of the Old Latin versions are unmistakably with the Western version of the text. Not infrequently noteworthy Old Latin readings agree with the Greek text of Codex Bezae and the Old Syriac.'[19] Accordingly, it is impossible to know in the present case whether the Old Latin omission of nard in John 12.3 merely

---

12 For a detailed study of Codex Bezae, see Parker 1992.

13 See Aland and Matzkow 1963, p. 134 (note the description of this edition in Petzer 1995, p. 116).

14 Metzger 1977, pp. 287–9.

15 Aland and Aland 1987, p. 183. More generally, see Elliott 1992.

16 See the list and details in Nestle-Aland 1993, p. 715.

17 So Metzger 1977, p. 286.

18 So Petzer 1995, p. 123.

19 Metzger 1977, p. 325.

reflects the P66 and Codex Bezae readings we have noted above or whether it stems from a different Greek *Vorlage*. Nevertheless, here we have a tradition, based on a translation of early Greek manuscripts, which persisted in retaining a version of John 12.3 that lacked nard in spite of its presence in Mark 14.3. This is even more significant in view of the fact that most Old Latin manuscripts show signs of contamination by Vulgate readings.[20]

In our view, by far the most likely conclusion to draw from this textual discussion is that the form of John 12.3 composed by the evangelist did not contain *νάρδου*. Are we able to explain why this word appears in the other textual witnesses? We suggest that there are two persuasive reasons for the addition. The first is by virtue of harmonization with Mark 14.3 and the second is the difficulty that attaches to the feminine form *πιστικῆς* and to the meaning of this word.

As to harmonization, it is well known that scribes added details from one Gospel when copying another, or more generally harmonized differing accounts of similar topics. There is no doubt that harmonization was extremely common.[21] Colwell has noted that harmonization may occur in two ways. First there is harmonization to remote parallels (as when at John 6.69 P66 adds 'the Christ' from Matt. 16.16). This is the less common type. The second type, to which the scribes were much more addicted, is 'harmonization to the immediate context'. Here 'the influence of a neighboring word, of a balancing clause in the same sentence, of the familiar phraseology' of the other Gospel with which they were familiar 'was evidently inescapable'.[22] This scribal tendency means that 'when one reading agrees with a parallel account and a second reading does not, one may think of the second as the more original'.[23] Or, as Metzger puts it, the 'reading which involves verbal dissidence is usually to be preferred to one which is verbally concordant'.[24] In relation to this phenomenon, we find a statement extremely close to that of John 12.3 in virtually all

20 Petzer 1995, pp. 119–20.

21 Holmes (1990, p. 651) points out that in Metzger 1971, harmonization (or the influence of parallel passages) is mentioned in the discussion of 13 of the first 20 variants in the Gospel of John.

22 Colwell 1965, p. 377.

23 Royse 1995, p. 240.

24 Metzger 1971, p. xxvi.

versions of Mark 14.3 (except for the Codex Bezae): *ἦλθεν γυνὴ ἔχουσα ἀλάβαστρον μύρου νάρδου πιστικῆς πολυτελοῦς, συντρίψασα τὴν ἀλάβαστρον κατέχεεν αὐτοῦ τῆς κεφαλῆς*. The scribal tendency to harmonize just described indicates that the textual witnesses containing *νάρδου* in John 12.3 represent a later form of the text than the three surviving witnesses that lack this word. Indeed, in the supralinear addition of *νάρδου* in P66, which we have discussed above, we actually catch a scribe in the very act of such harmonization. For since we have already discounted the possibility that *νάρδου* had been accidentally or deliberately omitted by the first scribe of P66, the overwhelmingly probable explanation is that the second scribe of this codex is in the process of harmonizing John 12.3 with what Colwell has called 'the immediate context' of Mark 14.3.

The Meaning of *πιστικῆς*

This brings us to our second broad reason for proposing that *νάρδου* was not in the form of the Gospel composed by the evangelist and also to our preferred solution as to what spice Mary used for anointing Jesus in John 12.3, the issues surrounding word *πιστικῆς*. These issues also require determining what this word meant. We are dealing with an adjective, *πιστικός*, in the feminine. Leaving aside the difficulty concerning what the word means for the moment, the critical point is that it is in the feminine.

In Mark 14.3 we find *ἀλάβαστρον μύρου νάρδου πιστικῆς πολυτελοῦς*. Mark is describing an alabaster container of lotion (*μύρον* being, as we will further explain below, the generic word for lotion) to which he adds an appositive genitive expression: *νάρδου πιστικῆς πολυτελοῦς*, meaning: 'namely, valuable *πιστική* nard'. The two adjectives are feminine because here nard is feminine (= *ἡ νάρδος*). In Liddle and Scott's *Greek–English Lexicon* *νάρδος* is only listed as a feminine noun (an unfortunate error, as we will soon see).

This immediately raises a question in relation to P66 (*λειτραν μυρου πιστικης πολουτιμου*) and Codex Bezae (*λειτραν πιστικῆς μυρου πολουτειμου*): since *μύρου* is definitely neuter (= *τὸ μύρον*, as indeed at John 12.5), how can one have *πιστικῆς* in the text without a feminine noun for it to qualify? In Codex Bezae we also have the extra awkwardness of a feminine adjective appearing before a neuter noun and with another epithet appearing after it. The problem does not arise in the Old Latin, since πιστικός (now become a Greek loanword in Latin) simply appears as a neuter adjective agreeing with *unguentum* (= *libram unguenti pistici*).

But how do we interpret the presence of πιστικῆς, a feminine epithet in the genitive singular without a feminine noun to qualify, in P66 and Codex Bezae? This seems rather anomalous and may have encouraged the second scribe of P66 to add νάρδου from Mark 14.3, in that Gospel a feminine noun. Without such a noun, there is only one explanation for πιστικῆς, namely, that it is an example of the common phenomenon in Greek of an adjective used as a noun, as in, for example, ὁ δίκαιος, 'the just man', or φίλος, 'a friend.'[25] This usage appears not infrequently in the New Testament. Sometimes a noun is implied, as in ἡ ὀρεινή (γῆ) in Luke 1.39, and sometimes not.[26] These 'substantivized adjectives' can be used either with the article or anarthrously.[27] In John 12.3 in P66 and Codex Bezae πιστικῆς can only be an anarthrous substantivized adjective of this type. But what does it mean?

A major problem is that πιστικός is unattested before its appearance in Mark 14.3 and John 12.3 and, indeed, appears only in these passages and in writers dependent on them.[28] The most likely explanation is that it derives from πιστός (a word which literally means 'faithful') and in this context conveys the meaning 'genuine'. There is also the possibility, which would indicate a similar meaning, raised by Köbert in 1948 and noted by Brown,[29] that πιστική is a translation of the common Aramaic *qushta*, meaning 'faith', which Köbert surmises (although without citing a single example) could occur with nard.[30] We need to note, however, that we are pursuing an argument on the basis that nard did not appear in the original text.

25 See Goodwin 1894, p. 204.

26 See Moule 1959, pp. 96–8.

27 See Blass and Debrunner 1961, pp. 138–9. An anarthrous example is σοφοῖς τε καὶ ἀνοήτοις at Rom. 1.14.

28 Barrett 1978, p. 411.

29 Brown 1966, p. 448.

30 Köbert 1948, p. 281. Note that Brown misinterprets Köbert to say that *qushta* is often found with nard (1966, p. 448); as noted, Köbert offers not a single example of the two words together.

Barrett, following J. Lightfoot, also suggests it could derive from Mark's transliteration of the Aramaic *pistaqa*, or pistachio nut, the oil of which was used to make a perfume.[31] If this latter suggestion be correct, Mark must have intended nard mixed with pistachio oil.[32] But this sounds a very unlikely mixture which should not be proposed without firm ancient evidence that it existed. Liddle and Scott derive the word from πίνειν, 'to drink', and thus render 'liquid'. But this seems far-fetched.

Yet our arguments that νάρδου did not occur in the original form of John 12.3 and that πιστική is a substantivized adjective in that verse carry a significant consequence for how we interpret the word: *we should not rush to assume that the word refers to nard.* One little noticed fact of great importance underlines the need for caution here. Although in Mark 14.3 νάρδου is feminine, in the LXX the word has masculine gender. There are only three instances of νάρδου in the LXX, all in the Song of Songs (1.12; 4.13, 14), and its masculine gender emerges in the very first of these (νάρδος μου ἔδωκεν ὀσμὴν αὐτοῦ), with the word also being masculine in the Masoretic Text of this verse. So if we take the reasonable step of giving priority to John's knowledge of the Old Testament (where nard is masculine) over his knowledge of Mark 14 (where it is feminine), the feminine gender of πιστική suggests that we need to look for some other spice. But which one, on the basis that πιστική means something like 'genuine'?

Such a descriptor indicates that the perfume or spice in question can vary in quality and that the product in question is of the top quality. Moreover, we need a spice that was well enough known to be able to be so designated by the epithet alone. It is not hard to find modern analogies to such a phenomenon. In the United Kingdom many brewing companies produce beer that they describe as 'Best Bitter'. Someone ordering such a beer in a hotel served by one of these companies can ask for a pint of 'best' without any chance he or she will be misunderstood. Similarly, enthusiasts for traditional styles of beer know of one by the name 'Old Peculier' (*sic*). This is a beer produced by the Theakston company that is dark-coloured with a tight, fairly long-lasting head. This modern comparison shows how products can come

31 Barrett 1978, p. 412.
32 Brown 1966, p. 448.

to be designated in relation to epithets reflecting their character. Accordingly, it is surprising to find the following remark by C. K. Barrett: 'To suppose that *πιστικός* is a local or trade name (so that we should transliterate, 'pistic nard') is a counsel of despair, but not necessarily wrong.'[33] It is very probable indeed that *πιστική* was a local or trade name, but not, as we have seen, necessarily referring to nard. If a first-century Judean ordered a jar of 'pistic', what perfume or lotion did he or she have in mind? We have been able to answer this question to a satisfactory level of probability by a consideration of perfumes and ointments in the Bible and the ancient world.[34]

In the LXX the word *μύρον* is used generically of any perfume or lotion, meaning a free-flowing liquid containing a substance or substances that produced a pleasant smell. In Exodus 30.25 it emerges that olive oil could be a base for such a perfume or lotion. On the other hand, the word *ἀρώματα*, 'spices' (which could be in solid or liquid form) referred to the odiferous substances that could be used for various purposes on their own (as when they were burnt (in which case they were *θυμιάματα*, 'incenses') or used for embalming) or could be mixed with a base like olive oil to produce a perfume or lotion (= a *μύρον*). Mention is made both of *μύρον* or *μύρα and ἀρώματα/θυμιάματα* at 1 Chronicles 9.30, 2 Chronicles 16.14, Proverbs 27.9 and Song of Songs 1.3. Often *μύρον* or *μύρα* are mentioned without any specific information as to the spices used to produce the desired olfactory result (for example, Judith 10.3; Psalm 132.2; Wisd. 2.7; Isa. 25.7 and 39.2; Jer. 25.10 and Ezek. 27.17).

One aspect of the generic nature of *μύρον* is that some forms were regarded as more precious than others. Thus, mention is made of the 'the first lotions' (*πρῶτα μύρα*) at Amos 2.7. The Song of Songs is an important source of information. In chapters 1 and 2 there are a number of statements about *μύρα*: 'The smell of your lotions (*μύρα*) is better than all spices, your name is a lotion (*μύρον*) poured forth' (1.3); and 'With lotions (*μύρα*) strengthen me' (2.5). 'We will run after you for the smell of your lotions (*μύρα*)' (1.4). Then we come to a much more detailed description at Song of Songs 4.13–14:

33 Barrett 1978, p. 412.
34 See Harrison 1966.

Ἀποστολαί σου παράδεισος ῥοῶν μετά καρποῦ ἀκροδρύων,
κύπροι μετὰ νάρδων,
νάρδος καὶ κρόκος,
κάλαμος καὶ κιννάμωμον
μετὰ πάντων ξύλων τοῦ Λιβάνου,
σμύρνα αλωθ μετὰ πάντων πρώτων μύρων.

(Your shoots are a garden of pomegranates, with the fruit of choice berries; camphor with nards, nard and saffron, calamus and cinnamon, with all woods of Lebanon, myrrh, aloes, with all first lotions.)

In this passage, there seems little doubt that myrrh (*σμύρνα*) and aloes (*αλωθ*) are included among the first rank, with myrrh having priority, but it is also possible that the author is affording nard, saffron, calamus and cinnamon the same status. Myrrh and aloes are the spices used to anoint Jesus in John 19.39.

Myrrh (*σμύρνα*) is a resin produced from a low, thorny shrub, balsamodendron.[35] Pliny (*Natural History* 12.35) notes that the best type of myrrh comes from the juice exuded by the tree before it has been tapped. From early times it was held in high regard in the ancient Near East as a domestic perfume and as an aromatic deodorant, especially for use in embalming.[36] Pliny also notes that myrrh can be adulterated with various substances (*Natural History* 12.35). This suggests that *σμύρνα πιστική* would refer to myrrh of the purest and highest quality. Myrrh appears ten times across four books in the LXX: in Exodus 30.23, in Psalm 44.8, seven times in the Song of Songs (3.6; 4.6, 14; 5.1, 5 (*bis*), 13) and in Sirach 24.15. It is thus far more common and widespread than nard. In addition, on four occasions it is accompanied by an epithet that designates a superior kind of myrrh. Mention is made of *σμύρνα ἐκλεκτή* at Exodus 30.23 and Sirach 24.15 and of *σμύρνα πλήρης* in Song of Songs 5.5 and 5.13, both expressions essentially meaning 'choice myrrh'. Sirach 24.15 is particularly interesting because here the speaker says 'I gave a sweet odour like choice myrrh' (*σμύρνα ἐκλεκτή*) and like five other named spices, none of which is qualified by an epithet. Indeed when one

35 Harrison 1966, p. 46.
36 Harrison 1966, p. 45.

surveys the main spices mentioned in the LXX the only other one that is accompanied by an epithet is frankincense (*λίβανον*) which is described as 'pure' (*καθαρόν*) in Leviticus 24.7 and 'transparent' (*διαφανής*) in Exodus 30.34. Neither of these epithets, however, directly serves to distinguish a superior quality of herb from others of lesser quality. This data strongly suggest that anyone familiar with the LXX would have been aware of one spice, and one alone, that was referred to by an epithet designating genuineness and that was myrrh. Although we must grant that *πιστική* is not exactly the same as *ἐκλεκτή* or *πλήρης*, nevertheless it has much the same function. It is not much of a step to propose that myrrh was so important a spice and the need to single out the high quality samples of it so prominent that there was, at least in John's regional context, the practice of referring to it as *πιστική* rather than as *σμύρνα πιστική*. Elsewhere, this particular meaning may not have been understood.

This view still leaves open the question of the differing word order as between P66 (*λειτραν μυρου πιστικης πολουτιμου*) and Codex Bezae (*λειτραν πιστικης μυρου πολουτειμου*). In our view Codex Bezae is more likely to represent the original text. This is because of its difference from Mark 14.3 in this respect, since it is possible that in the exemplar used by the first scribe of P66, although his text had not been accommodated to Mark 14.3 in relation to the introduction of nard, it may have been modified to correct what might have seemed an awkward word order. We translate the Codex Bezae expression as: 'a pound of "pistic" (meaning best quality myrrh), a precious lotion'.

Conclusion

In our view the original text was: *Μαριὰμ λαβοῦσα λίτραν πιστικῆς μύρου πολυτίμου ἤλειψεν τοὺς πόδας τοῦ Ἰησοῦ* . . . This meant: 'When Mary had taken a pound of best quality [myrrh], a precious lotion, she anointed the feet of Jesus . . .' Here *πιστική* was a known expression for myrrh of the highest quality. The existence of Mark 14.3, however, began to impact upon this text. The first step was probably the placement of *πιστική* after rather than before *μύρου*, thus removing the apparently awkward original position of the word present in Codex Bezae. The next step was the insertion of *νάρδου*, highly visible in the supralinear addition in P66. In the Old Latin (*Maria ergo accepit libram unguenti pistici*), the translator preserves a text without nard but, hardly surprising, has not understood the meaning of πιστική and has transformed it into an epithet, neuter in gender and genitive in case, in agreement with *unguenti*. Its status as a Greek loanword in Latin indicates his incomprehension as to its precise meaning. As the scribe apparently found πιστική difficult to distinguish in meaning from πολυτελοῦς, he omitted the latter as redundant.

References

Achtemeier, Paul J. (1990) '*Omne Verbum Sonat*: The New Testament and the Oral Environment of Late Western Antiquity', *JBL* 109: 3–27.

Adam, Barbara (1990) *Time & Social Theory*. Cambridge: Polity Press.

——(1994) 'Perceptions of Time', in Ingold, Tim (1994) ed. *Companion Encyclopedia of Anthropology*. London and New York: Routledge, 503–26.

Aland, Kurt and Aland, Barbara (1987) *The Text of the New Testament: An Introduction to the Critical Editions and to the Theory and Practice of Modern Textual Criticism*. ET of 1981 German original by Erroll F. Rhodes. Grand Rapids and Leiden: William B. Eerdmans and E. J. Brill.

Aland, Barbara and Kurt, Karavidopoulos, Johannes, Martini, Carlo M. and Metzger, Bruce M. (eds) (1993) *Nestle-Aland: Novum Testamentum Graece*. 27th edition. Regensburg: Deutsche Bibelgesellschaft.

Aland, Kurt and Walter Matzkow, eds. (1963) *Itala: Das Neue Testament in altlateinischer Überlieferung. Nach den Handschriften herausegeben von Adolf Jülicher; im Auftrage der Kirchenväterkommission der Preussischen Akademie der Wissenschaften zum Druck besorgt von Walter Matzkow*. Volume 4. Berlin: Walter de Gruyter.

Albertson, Fred A., (1995) 'An Isiac Model for the Raising of Lazarus in Early Christian Art', *Jahrbuch für Antike und Christentum* 38: 123–32.

Ashton, John (1991) *Understanding the Fourth Gospel*. Oxford: The Clarendon Press.

Assmann, Jan (2000) *Religion und kulturelles Gedächtnis: Zehn Studien*. München: Verlag C. H. Beck.

——(2002 [1992]) *Das kulturelle Gedächtnis: Schrift, Erinnerung und politische Identität in frühen Hochkulturen*. Fourth edition. München: Verlag C. H. Beck.

Baltz, Frederick W., (1996) *Lazarus and the Fourth Gospel Community*. Mellen Biblical Press Series 37. Lewiston *et alibi*: Mellen Biblical Press.

Bardenhewer, O., Weyman, K. and Zellinger, J., ed. (1927) *Des Heiligen Bischofs Gregor von Nyssa Schriften*. Bibliothek der Kirchenväter. Munich: Verlag Josef Kösel & Friedrich Pustet KG.

Barrett, Charles Kingsley (1978) *The Gospel According to St John: An Introduction with Commentary and Notes on the Greek Text*. Second edition. London: SPCK.

Bar-Tal, Daniel, (1998) 'Group Beliefs as an Expression of Group Identity', in Worchel, Stephen, Morales, J. Francisco, Páez, Darío and Deschamps, Jean-Claude, eds. (1998) *Social Identity: International Perspectives*. London, Thousand Oaks and New Delhi: Sage Publications, 93–113.

Barth, Fredrik, (1969a) *Ethnic Groups and Boundaries: The Social Organization of Culture Difference*. London: George Allen and Unwin.

——(1969b) 'Introduction', in Barth 1969a: 9–38.

Barton, Stephen C. (1998) 'Can We Identify the Gospel Audiences?', in Bauckham 1998a: 173–94.

Bassler, J. (1989) 'Mixed Signals: Nicodemus in the Fourth Gospel', *JBL* 108: 635–46.

Bauckham, Richard J., (1993) 'The Beloved Disciple as Ideal Author', *JSNT* 49: 21–44.

——(1996) 'Lazarus', in Wood, D.R.W., Marshall, I. H. and Millard, A. R. *et al.*, *New Bible Dictionary*. 3rd edition, Leicester & Downers Grove: Intervarsity Press, 678–79.

——ed. (1998a) *The Gospels for All Christians: Rethinking the Gospel Audiences*. Edinburgh: T & T Clark.

——(1998b), 'For Whom Were the Gospels Written?', in Bauckham 1998a: 9–48.

——(1998c) 'John for Readers of Mark', in Bauckham 1998a: 147–71.

Beattie, Tina (1997) 'A Discipleship of Love: Mary of Bethany and the Ministry of Women', *The Month* 30: 171–5.

Becker, Jürgen, (1969–70) 'Wunder und Christologie. Zum literarkritischen und christologischen Problem der Wunder im Johannesevangelium', *NTS* 16: 130–48.

Belle, Gilbert Van (1994) *The Signs Source in the Fourth Gospel: Historical Survey and Critical Evaluation of the Semeia Hypothesis*. BETL 116. Leuven: Leuven University Press.

Bieringer, Reimund, Pollefeyt, Didier and Vandecasteele-Vanneuville, Frederique, eds. (2001) *Anti-Judaism and the Fourth Gospel*. Louisville, London & Leiden: Westminster John Knox.

Billig, Michael, (1990) 'Collective Memory, Ideology and the British Royal Family', in David Middleton and Derek Edwards, eds., (1990) *Collective Remembering*. London *et alibi*: Sage Publications, 60–80.

Blass, F. and Debrunner, A. (1961), *A Greek Grammar of the New Testament and Other Early Christian Literature*. A translation and revision of the ninth-tenth German edition incorporating supplementary notes of A. Debrunner by Robert W. Funk. Chicago and London: The University of Chicago Press.

Bond, Helen K. (2004) *Caiaphas: Friend of Rome and Judge of Jesus?* Louisville, KY: Westminster John Knox Press.

Bourguet, Pierre du, S. J. (1965) *Early Christian Painting*. The Contact History of Art. London: Weidenfeld and Nicolson.

Boyd, Jane and Esler, Philip F. (2004) *Visuality and Biblical Text: Interpreting Velázquez'* Christ with Martha and Mary *as a Test Case*. Arte e Archeologia, Studi e Documenti 26. Florence: Leo S. Olschki Editore.

Brown, Raymond E. (1966) *The Gospel according to John (i–xii). Introduction, Translation and Notes*. The Anchor Bible 29a. New York: Doubleday.

——(1971) *The Gospel According to John (xiii–xxi). Translated, with an Introduction and Notes*. The Anchor Bible. London: Geoffrey Chapman.

——(1974) 'The Relationship of "The Secret Gospel of Mark" to the Fourth Gospel', *CBQ* 36: 466–85.

——(1978) '"Other Sheep Not of this Fold": The Johannine Perspective on Christian Diversity in the Late First Century', *JBL* 97: 5–22.

——(1979) *The Community of the Beloved Disciple. The Life, Loves and Hates of an Individual Church in New Testament Times*. London: Geoffrey Chapman.

Brown, Rupert (2000) *Group Processes: Dynamics Within and Between Groups*. Second edition. Oxford: Blackwell Publishers.

Bultmann, Rudolf (1971) *The Gospel of John. A Commentary*. Translated by G. R. Beasley-Murray. Oxford: Basil Blackwell.

Burkett, Delbert (1994) 'Two Accounts of Lazarus' Resurrection in John 11', *Novum Testamentum* 36: 209–32.

Burridge, Richard (1998) 'About People, By People, For People: Gospel Genres and Audiences', in Bauckham 1998a: 113–45.

Busse, Ulrich (1992) 'Johannes und Lukas: Die Lazarusperikope. Frucht eines Kommunikationsprozesses', in Denaux, A., ed. (1992) *John and the Synoptics*. BETL 101. Leuven: Leuven University Press 281–306.

Byrne, Brendan (1991) *Lazarus: A Contemporary Reading of John 11:1–46*. Homebush, New South Wales: St Paul Publications.

Carlson, Stephen C. (2005) *The Gospel Hoax: Morton Smith's Invention of* Secret Mark. Waco, Texas: Baylor University Press.

Carr, D. (1991) *Time, Narrative, History*. Bloomington: Indiana University Press.

Charlesworth, James H. (1995) *The Beloved Disciple: Whose Witness Validates the Gospel of John?* Valley Forge: Trinity Press International.

Cinnirella, Marco (1998) 'Exploring Temporal Aspects of Social Identity:

The Concept of Possible Social Identities', *European Journal of Social Psychology* 28: 227–48.

Clarke, John R. (2003) *Art in the Lives of Ordinary Romans: Visual Representation and Non-Elite Viewers in Italy, 100 B.C.–A.D. 315*. Berkeley: University of California Press.

Coakley, J. F. (1988) 'The Anointing at Bethany and the Priority of John', *JBL* 107: 241–86.

Cohen, David William (1994) *The Combing of History*. Chicago: Chicago University Press.

Colwell, E. C. (1965) 'Scribal Habits in Early Papyri: A Study in the Corruption of the Text', in Hyatt 1965: 370–89 (this is the same as Colwell 1969b).

——(1969a) *Studies in Methodology in Textual Criticism of the New Testament*. New Testament Tools and Studies 9. Leiden: Brill.

——(1969b) 'Method in Evaluating Scribal Habits: A Study of P45, P66, P75', in Colwell 1969a: 106–24.

Comfort, Philip W. (1999) 'P66: Introduction', in Comfort and Barrett 1999: 367–78.

Comfort, Philip W. and Barrett, David P., eds. (1999), *The Complete Text of the Earliest New Testament Manuscripts*. Grand Rapids, MI: Baker Books.

Condor, Susan (1996) 'Social Identity and Time', in Peter Robinson, ed. (1996) *Social Groups and Identities: Developing the Legacy of Henri Tajfel*. Oxford: Butterworth Heinnemann, 285–315, 289–91.

Cooper, John W. (2000) *Body, Soul, and Life Everlasting: Biblical Anthropology and the Monism-Dualism Debate*. Reprinting of 1989 edition with a new Preface (reviewing recent developments). Grand Rapids, MI and Cambridge: William B. Eerdmans Publishing Company and Leicester: Apollos.

Culpepper, R. A. (1983) *Anatomy of the Fourth Gospel: A Study in Literary Design*. Philadelphia: Fortress Press.

Darmstaedter, Robert (1955) *Die Auferweckung des Lazarus in der altchristlichen und byzantinischen Kunst*. Inaugural dissertation in the Faculty of Bern. Bern: Arnaud Druck.

Davis, Stephen T., ed. (1989a) *Death and Afterlife*. London: Macmillan.

——(1989b) "Introduction", in Davis 1989a: viii–xi.

de Boer, Martinus C. (1996) *Johannine Perspectives on the Death of Jesus*. Contributions to Biblical Exegesis and Theology 17. Kampen: Kok Pharos.

de Jonge, Henk J. (2001) '"The Jews" in the Gospel of John', in Bieringer, Pollefeyt and Vandecasteele-Vanneuville 2001: 121–140.

Dodd, C. H. (1953) *The Interpretation of the Fourth Gospel*. Cambridge: Cambridge University Press.

——(1963) *Historical Tradition in the Fourth Gospel*. Cambridge: Cambridge University Press.

Dujardin, Paul, photographic reproducer (1899), *Codex Bezae cantabrigiensis quattuor Evangelia et Actus apostolorvm complectens graece et latine: sumptibvs Academiae phototypice repraesentatus.* Volume 1 (of 2). London: J. Clay and Sons.

Duke, Paul D. (1985), *Irony in the Fourth Gospel.* Atlanta, GA: John Knox Press.

Ehrman, Bart D. and Holmes, Michael W., eds. (1995) *The Text of the New Testament in Contemporary Research: Essays on the Status Quaestionis. A Volume in Honor of Bruce M. Metzger.* Grand Rapids, MI: William B. Eerdmans Publishing Company.

Ellemers, Naomi, Spears, Russell and Doosje, Bertjan, eds. (1999) *Social Identity: Context, Commitment, Content.* Oxford and New York: Blackwell Publishers.

Elliott, John H. (2000) *1 Peter. A New Translation with Introduction and Commentary.* The Anchor Bible. New York *et alibi:* Doubleday.

Elliott, J. Keith (1992) 'The Translation of the New Testament into Latin: The Old Latin and the Vulgate', *ANRW* 2.26.1, edited by H. Temporini and W. Haase. Berlin and New York: de Gruyter, 198–245.

Esler, Philip F. (1987) *Community and Gospel in Luke-Acts: The Social and Political Motivations of Lucan Theology.* SNTS Monograph Series 57. Cambridge: Cambridge University Press.

——(1994) *The First Christians in Their Social Worlds: Social-Scientific Approaches to New Testament Interpretation.* London and New York: Routledge.

——(1998a) 'Community and Gospel in Early Christianity: A Response to Richard Bauckham's *Gospels for All Christians*', *Scottish Journal of Theology* 51: 235–248

——(1998b) *Galatians.* London and New York: Routledge.

——(2002) 'Ludic History in the Book of Judith: The Reinvention of Israelite Identity', *Biblical Interpretation* 10: 107–43.

——(2003) *Conflict and Identity in Romans: The Social Setting of Paul's Letter.* Minneapolis: Fortress.

——(2005a) *New Testament Theology: Communion and Community.* Minneapolis: Fortress.

——(2005b) 'The Incident of the Withered Fig Tree in Mark 11: A New Source and Redactional Explanation', *JSNT* 28: 41–67.

——ed. (2005c) *Ancient Israel: The Old Testament in Its Social Context.* Minneapolis: Fortress.

——(2005d) 'Social-Scientific Models in Biblical Interpretation', in Esler 2005c: 3–14.

——(2006a) 'Judean Ethnic Identity in Josephus's *Contra Apionem*', to appear in a forthcoming *Festschrift.*

——(2006b) 'From *Ioudaioi* to Children of God: The Development of a Non-Ethnic Group Identity in the Gospel of John', paper delivered at meeting of the Context Group in March 2006 and to appear in a forthcoming *Festschrift*.

——(2006c) 'Paul's Contestation of Israel's (Ethnic) Memory of Abraham in Galatians 3', *Biblical Theology Bulletin* 36: 23–34.

——(2006d) '"Remember My Fetters": A Social- and Cognitive-Science Approach to the Memorialisation of Paul's Imprisonment in the Pseudo-Pauline Letters', paper delivered in Helsinki in September 2005; submitted to publisher in conference volume.

Fee, Gordon D. (1968) *Papyrus Bodmer II (P66): Its Textual Relationships and Scribal Characteristics*. Studies and Documents, 34. Salt Lake City: University of Utah Press.

Fitzgerald, John T., ed. (1997) *Greco-Roman Perspectives on Friendship*. Atlanta, GA: Scholars Press.

Forestell, J. Terence (1987) Book Review of Kremer, Jacob, *Lazarus: Die Geschichte einer Auferstehung: Text, Wirkungsgeschichte und Botschaft von Joh 11:1–46*, *CBQ* 49: 506–7.

Fortna, Robert Tomson (1970) *The Gospel of Signs: A Reconstruction of the Narrative Source Underlying the Fourth Gospel*. SNTS Monograph Series 11. Cambridge: Cambridge University Press.

——(1988) *The Fourth Gospel and Its Predecessor*. Philadelphia: Fortress.

Goodwin, William W. (1894) *A Greek Grammar*. London: Macmillan, St Martin's Press.

Hakola, Raimo (1999) 'A Character Resurrected: Lazarus in the Fourth Gospel and Afterwards', in Rhoads, David and Syreeni, Kari, eds. (1999) *Characterization in the Gospels: Reconceiving Narrative Criticism*. JSNT Supplement Series, 184. Sheffield: Sheffield Academic Press, 223–63.

Halbwachs, Maurice (1980) *The Collective Memory*. ET of the 1950 French original *La Mémoire collective* by Francis J. Ditter Jr. and Vida Yazdi Ditter, with an introduction by Mary Douglas. New York *et alibi*: Harper Colophon Books.

Harrison, R. H. (1966) *Healing Herbs of the Bible*. Leiden: E. J. Brill.

Haslam, S. Alexander (2001) *Psychology in Organizations: The Social Identity Approach*. London, Thousand Oaks, New Delhi: Sage Publications.

Hedrick, Charles W. and Olympiou Nicolaus (2000) 'Secret Mark: New Photographs, New Witnesses', *The Fourth R: An Advocate for Religious Literacy* 13: 3–16.

Hick, John (1976) *Death and Eternal Life*. London: Collins.

Hinkle, Steve and Brown, Rupert, (1990) 'Intergroup Comparisons and Social Identity: Some Links and Lacunae', in Dominic Abrams and Michael A. Hogg, eds. (1990) *Social Identity Theory: Constructive and Critical Approaches*. New York *et alibi*: Harvester Wheatsheaf, 48–70.

Hogg, Michael A. and Abrams, Dominic (1988) *Social Identifications:*

A Social Psychology of Intergroup Relations and Group Processes. London and New York: Routledge.

Holmes, Michael W. (1990) 'The Text of the Matthean Divorce Passages: A Comment on the Appeal to Harmonization in Textual Decisions', *JBL* 109: 651–64.

Hunter, David (2002) 'Marginalising the Majority? Theology of the Poor in the Gospel of John', in *Prophecy and Passion: Essays in Honour of Athol Gill*, edited by David Neville. Australian Theological Forum Series 5. Adelaide: Australian Theological Forum, 247–69.

Hutchinson, John and Smith, Anthony D., eds. (1996a) *Ethnicity*. Oxford: Oxford University Press.

——(1996b) 'Introduction', in Hutchinson and Smith 1996a: 3–14.

Hyatt, J. Philip, ed. (1965) *The Bible in Modern Scholarship: Papers Read at the 100th Meeting of the Society of Biblical Literature*. Nashville: Abingdon.

Jeanrond, Werner (1995) *Call and Response: The Challenge of Christian Life*. New York: Continuum.

Jensen, Robin Margaret (1995) 'The Raising of Lazarus', *Bible Review* 11: 20–28, 45.

——(2000) *Understanding Early Christian Art*. London and New York: Routledge.

Kelber, Werner H. (1983) *The Oral and the Written Gospel: The Hermeneutics of Speaking and Writing in the Synoptic Tradition, Mark, Paul and Q*. Philadelphia: Fortress Press.

Klink, Edward W. III (2005) ' The Sheep of the Fold: A Critical Assessment of the Audience and Origin of the Gospel of John.' A dissertation successfully presented in the University of St Andrews for the award of a Doctor of Philosophy.

Köbert, R. (1948) 'Nardos Pistike –Kostnarde', *Biblica* 29: 279–81.

Koester, Craig R. (2003) *Symbolism in the Fourth Gospel. Meaning, Mystery, Community*. Second edition. Minneapolis: Fortress Press.

Kremer, Jacob (1985) *Lazarus: Die Geschichte einer Auferstehung. Text, Wirkungsgeschichte und Botschaft von Joh 11,1–46*. Stuttgart: Verlag Katholisches Bibelwerk.

Kysar, R. (1975) *The Fourth Evangelist and His Gospel: An Examination of Contemporary Scholarship*. Minneapolis: Augsburg.

Labahn, Michael (1999) *Jesus als Lebensspender. Untersuchungen zu einer Geschichte der johanneischen Tradition anhand ihrer Wundergeschichten*. BZNW 98. Berlin and New York: W. de Gruyter.

Lee, Dorothy A. (1994) *The Symbolic Narratives of the Fourth Gospel: The Interplay of Form and Meaning*. JSNT Supplement Series 95. Sheffield: JSOT Press.

Legault, A. (1954) 'An Application of the Form-Critical Method to the Anointings in Galilee and Bethany', *CBQ* 16: 131–41.

Lincoln, Andrew T. (2000) *Truth on Trial. The Lawsuit Motif in the Fourth Gospel*. Peabody, MA: Hendrickson.

Lindars, Barnabas (1992) 'Rebuking the Spirit: A New Analysis of the Lazarus Story of John 11', *NTS* 38: 89–104.

Lowrie, Walter (1969 [1947]) *Art in the Early Church: A Detailed Survey of Painting, Sculpture, Mosaics, and Textiles, from Apostolic Times to Byzantine and Romanesque*. New York: W. W. Norton and Co Inc.

Malina, Bruce J. (1985) *The Gospel of John in Sociolinguistic Perspective*. Berkeley, CA: Center for Hermeneutical Studies in Hellenistic and Modern Culture.

——(1989a) 'Christ and Time: Swiss or Mediterranean', *CBQ* 51:1–31; reprinted in Malina 1996: 179–214.

——(1989b) 'Dealing with Biblical (Mediterranean) Characters: A Guide for U.S. Consumers', *BTB* 19: 127–41.

——(1992) 'Is There a Circum-Mediterranean Person? Looking for Stereotypes', *BTB* 22: 66–87.

——(1996) *The Social World of Jesus and the Gospels*. London and New York: Routledge.

——(2001) *The New Testament World: Insights from Cultural Anthropology*. Third edition. Louisville, KY: Westminster John Knox Press.

Malina, Bruce J. and Rohrbaugh, Richard L. (1998) *Social-Science Commentary on the Gospel of John*. Minneapolis: Fortress Press.

Markus, Hazel and Nurius, Paula (1986) 'Possible Selves', *American Anthropologist* 41: 954–69.

——(1987) 'Possible Selves: The Interface between Motivation and Self Concept', in K. Yardley and T. Honess, eds. (1987) *Self and Identity: Psychosocial Perspectives*. Chichester: John Wiley & Sons, 157–72.

Martin, James P. (1964) 'History and Eschatology in the Lazarus Narrative: John 11.1–44', *SJT* 17: 332–43.

Martin, Victor (1956) *Papyrus Bodmer II: Evangile de Jean chap. 1–14*. Cologny-Geneva: Bibliotheca Bodmeriana.

——(1958) Supplément: *Evangile de Jean chap. 14–21*. Cologny-Geneva: Bibliotheca Bodmeriana.

Martin, Victor and Barns, J. W. B. (1962) *Papyrus Bodmer II:* Supplément: *Evangile de Jean chap. 14–21*. Second edition. Cologny-Geneva: Bibliotheca Bodmeriana.

Martyn, J. Louis (1979) *History and Theology in the Fourth Gospel*. Second revised edition. Nashville: Abingdon.

——(2003) 'Glimpses into the History of the Johannine Community', in Marinus de Jonge, ed., *L'Evangile de Jean: Sources, redaction, théologie*. Bibliotheca Ephemeridum Theologicarum Lovaniensium 44. Gembloux: Duculot, 259–99, reprinted in *History and Theology in the Fourth Gospel*. Third edition. Louisville: Wesminster John Knox Press, 145–67.

Meeks, Wayne A. (1972) 'The Man from Heaven in Johannine Sectarianism', *JBL* 91: 144–58.

Metzger, Bruce M., ed. (1971) *A Textual Commentary on the Greek New Testament*. London and New York: United Bible Societies.

——(1977) *The Early Versions of the New Testament: Their Origin, Transmission, and Limitations*. Oxford: The Clarendon Press.

Middleton, David and Edwards, Derek, eds. (1990a) *Collective Remembering*. London *et alibi*: Sage Publications.

——(1990b) 'Introduction', in Middleton and Edwards 1999a: 1–22.

Mitchell, Alan C. (1992) 'The Social Function of Friendship in Acts 2:44–47 and 4:32–37', *JBL* 111: 255–72.

Mitchell, Margaret M. (2005) 'Patristic Counter-Evidence to the Claim that "The Gospels Were Written for All Christians"', *NTS* 51: 36–79.

Moule, C. F. D. (1959) *An Idiom Book of New Testament Greek*. Second edition. Cambridge: Cambridge University Press.

——(1975) 'The Meaning of "Life" in the Gospel and Epistles of St John: A Study in the Story of Lazarus, John 11:1–44', *Theology* 78: 114–25.

Moxnes, Halvor, ed. (1997) *Constructing Early Christian Families: Families as Social Reality and Metaphor*. London and New York: Routledge.

Muddiman, John (2001) *A Commentary on the Epistle to the Ephesians*. Black New Testament Commentaries. London and New York: Continuum.

Munn, Nancy D. (1992) 'The Cultural Anthropology of Time: A Critical Essay', *Annual Review of Anthropology* 21: 93–123.

Murray, Sister Charles (1981) *Rebirth and Afterlife: A Study of the Transmutation of Some Pagan Imagery in Early Christian Funerary Art*. BAR International Series 100. Oxford: British Archaeological Reports.

Nestle, Eberhard and Erwin, with Aland, Barbara and Kurt *et al.*, eds. (1993) *Novum Testamentum Graece*. 27th revised edition. Stuttgart: Deutsche Bibelgesellshaft. (Cited here as Nestle-Aland 1993).

Nestori, Aldo (1993) *Repertorio Topografico delle Pitture delle Catabombe Romane*. Revised edition. Città del Vaticano: Pontificio Istituto di Archeologia Cristiana.

Neyrey, Jerome H. (1988) *An Ideology of Revolt: John's Christology in Social-Science Perspective*. Philadelphia: Fortress.

——(1998) 'The Sociology of Secrecy and the Fourth Gospel', in Segovia, Fernando F., ed. (1998) *What is John? Vol. 2: Literary and Social Readings of the Fourth Gospel*. SBL Symposium Series 7. Atlanta: Scholars Press, 79–109.

Oakes, Penelope J., Haslam, S. Alexander and Turner, John C. (1994) *Stereotyping and Social Reality*. Oxford and Cambridge, MA: Blackwell.

O'Grady, John F. (1999) *The Witness of the Beloved Disciple*. Mahwah, NJ: Paulist Press.

Olick, Jeffrey K., ed. (2003a) *States of Memory: Continuities, Conflicts, and Transformations in National Retrospection*. Durham and London: Duke University Press.

——(2003b) 'Introduction', in Olick 2003a: 1–16.

Osiek, Carolyn, and Balch, David L. (1997) *Families in the New Testament World: Households and House Churches*. Louisville: Westminster John Knox Press.

Osiek, Carolyn, and Balch, David L., eds. (2003) *Early Christian Families in Context: An Interdisciplinary Dialogue*. Grand Rapids, MI: W.B. Eerdmans Publishing Co.

Painter, John (1993) *The Quest for the Messiah: The History, Literature and Theology of the Johannine Community*. Second edition. Nashville: Abingdon.

Parker, David C. (1992) *Codex Bezae: An Early Christian Manuscript and Its Text*. Cambridge: Cambridge University Press.

Petzer, Jacobus H. (1995) 'The Latin Version of the New Testament', in Ehrman and Holmes 1995: 113–30.

Piper, Ronald A. (2000) 'Satan, Demons and the Absence of Exorcisms in the Fourth Gospel', in Horrell, David G. and Tuckett, Christopher M. (eds.) (2000) *Christology, Controversy and Community: New Testament Essays in Honour of David R. Catchpole*. Leiden, Boston, Köln: E. J. Brill, 253–78.

——(2005) 'The One, the Four and the Many', in Bockmuehl, Markus, and Hagner, Donald, eds. (2005) *The Written Gospel*. Cambridge: Cambridge University Press, 254–73.

——(2006 forthcoming) 'The Characterisation of Pilate and the Death of Jesus in the Fourth Gospel', in Van Belle, Gilbert, ed. (2006 forthcoming), *The Death of Jesus in the Fourth Gospel*. BETL. Leuven: Leuven University Press/ Peeters.

——(2007 forthcoming) *The Dark Side of John: The Portrayal of Evil in the Fourth Gospel* (forthcoming monograph)

Pollard, T. E. (1973) 'The Raising of Lazarus (John xi)', in Livingstone, E. A., ed. (1973) *Studia Evangelica, VI*. Texte und Untersuchungen zur Geschichte der altchristlichen Literatur 112. Berlin: Akademie-Verlag, 434–43.

Polletta, Francesca (2003) 'Legacies and Liabilities of an Insurgent Past: Martin Luther King Jr. on the House and Senate Floor', in Olick 2003a: 193–226.

Puchner, Walter (1991) *Studien zum Kulturkontext der liturgischen Szene: Lazarus und Judas als religiöse Volksfiguren in Bild und Brauch, Lied und Legende Südosteuropas*. Two volumes. Österreichische Akademie der Wissenschaften, Philosophisch-historische Klasse, Denkschriften 216. Wien: Verlag der Österreichischen Akademie der Wissenschaften.

Quast, Kevin (1989) *Peter and the Beloved Disciple: Figures for a*

Community in Crisis. JSNT Supplement Series 32. Sheffield: JSOT Press.

Rahner, Karl (1971) 'Why and How Can We Venerate the Saints?', in his *Theological Investigations: Volume VIII. Further Theology of the Spiritual Life 2*. Translated by David Bourke. London and New York: Darton, Longman and Todd and Herder and Herder, 3–23.

Ratzinger, Joseph (1988) *Eschatology: Death and Eternal Life*. ET by M. Waldstein and edited by A. Nichols. Washington, DC: Catholic University Press of America.

Reicher, Stephen and Hopkins, Nicolas (1996) 'Self-Category Constructions in Political Rhetoric: An Analysis of Thatcher's and Kinnock's Speeches Concerning the British Miners' Strike (1984–5)', *European Journal of Social Psychology* 26: 353–71.

Reinhartz, Adele (1992) *The Word in the World: The Cosmological Tale in the Fourth Gospel*. SBL Monograph Series 45. Atlanta: Scholars Press.

——(1998) 'The Johannine Community and Its Jewish Neighbors: A Reappraisal', in *What is John? Vol. 2: Literary and Social Readings of the Fourth Gospel*, edited by Fernando F. Segovia. SBL Symposium Series 7. Atlanta: Scholars Press, 111–38.

Reiser, William E. (1973) 'The Case of the Tidy Tomb: The Place of the Napkins of John 11:44 and 20:7', *Heythrop Journal* 14: 47–57.

Rochais, Gérard (1981) *Les récits de résurrection des morts dans le Nouveau Testament*. SNTS Monograph Series 40. Cambridge: Cambridge University Press.

Rowe, C. Kavinn (2005) 'History, Hermeneutics and the Unity of Luke-Acts', *JSNT* 28: 131–57.

Royse, James Ronald (1981) 'Scribal Habits in Early Greek New Testament Papyri', PhD Dissertation, Graduate Theological Union.

——(1995) 'Scribal Tendencies in the Transmission of the Text of the New Testament', in Ehrman and Holmes 1995: 239–52.

Sanders, J. N. (1954–55) '"Those Whom Jesus Loved" (John xi.5)', *NTS* 1: 29–41.

Sandys-Wunsch, John and Eldredge, Laurence (1980) 'J. P. Gabler and the Distinction between Biblical and Dogmatic Theology: Translation, Commentary, and Discussion of His Originality', *SJT* 33: 133–58.

Sauser, Ekkart (1981) 'Das Bild von der Auferweckung des Lazarus in der fruehchristlichen und in der oestlichen Kunst', *Trierer Theologische Zeitschrift* 90: 276–88.

Schiller, Gertrud (1971) *Iconography of Early Christian Art. Volume 1. Christ's Incarnation, Childhood, Baptism, Temptation, Transfiguration, Works and Miracles*. English translation by Janet Seligman from the second (1969) edition of *Ikonographie der christlichen Kunst*. London: Lund Humphries.

Schnackenburg, Rudolf (1980) *The Gospel According to St John, Vol II:*

Commentary on Chapters 5–12. ET by Cecily Hastings *et al.* London: Burn & Oates.

Schneiders, Sandra M. (1987) 'Death in the Community of Eternal Life: History, Theology and Spirituality in John 11', *Interpretation* 41: 44–56.

Schulz, Siegfried (1983) *Das Evangelium nach Johannes*. Das Neue Testament Deutsch. Göttingen: Vandenhoeck & Ruprecht.

Scott, Bernard Brandon (1989) *Hear Then the Parable: A Commentary on the Parables of Jesus*. Minneapolis: Fortress.

Shellard, Barbara (2002) *New Light on Luke: Its Purpose, Sources and Literary Context*. JSNT Supp Series 215. Sheffield: Sheffield Academic Press.

Shils, Edward (1981) *Tradition*. London and Boston: Faber and Faber.

Sim, David C. (2001) 'The Gospels for All Christians? A Response to Richard Bauckham', *JSNT* 84: 3–27.

Smith, D. Moody Jr. (1999) *John*. Abingdon New Testament Commentaries. Nashville: Abingdon Press.

Smith, Eliot R. and Zarate, Michael A. (1990) 'Exemplar and Prototype Use in Social Categorization', *Social Cognition* 8: 243–62.

Smith, Morton (1973) *Clement of Alexandria and a Secret Gospel of Mark*. Cambridge: Harvard University Press.

——(1985) *Jesus the Magician*. Wellingborough: Aquarian.

Snyder, Graydon (2003) *Ante Pacem: Archaeological Evidence of Church Life Before Constantine* . Revised edition. Macon, GA: Mercer University Press.

Sproston North, Wendy E. (2001) *The Lazarus Story within the Johannine Tradition*. JSNT Supplement Series 212; Sheffield: Sheffield Academic Press.

Stenger, Werner (1974) 'Die Auferweckung des Lazarus (Joh 11, 1–45): Vorlage und johanneische Redaktion', *Trierer Theologische Zeitschrift* 83: 17–37.

Stibbe, Mark W. G. (1992) *John as Storyteller. Narrative Criticism and the Fourth Gospel*. SNTS Monograph Series 73. Cambridge: Cambridge University Press.

——(1994) 'A Tomb with a View: John 11.1–44 in Narrative-Critical Perspective', *NTS* 40: 38–54.

Story, Cullen I. K. (1991) 'The Mental Attitude of Jesus at Bethany: John 11.33, 38', *NTS* 37: 51–66.

Tajfel, Henri (1972) 'La Catégorisation sociale', in S. Moscovici, ed., *Introduction à la Psychologie Sociale*. Vol. 1. Paris: Larousse, 272–302.

——(1978) *Differentiation between Social Groups: Studies in the Social Psychology of Intergroup Relations*. London *et alibi*: Academic Press.

Thompson, L. M. (1978) 'The Multiple Uses of the Lazarus Motif in Modern Literature', *Christian Scholars' Review* 7: 306–29.

Tolmie (2005) 'The *Ioudaioi* in the Fourth Gospel: A Narratological Perspective,' in Van Belle, G., van der Watt, J.G. and Maritz, P.(2005) *Theology and Christology in the Fourth Gospel: Essays by Members of the SNTS Johannine Writings Seminar*. BETL 184. Leuven: Leuven University Press / Peeters, 377–98.

Tomson, Peter J. (2001) '"Jews" in the Gospel of John as Compared with the Palestinian Talmud, the Synoptics, and Some New Testament Apocrypha', in Bieringer, Pollefeyt and Vandecasteele-Vanneuville 2001: 176–212.

Toynbee, Jocelyn Mary Catherine (1971) *Death and Burial in the Roman World*. London: Thames and Hudson.

Turner, John C. (1999) 'Some Current Issues in Research on Social Identity and Self-categorization Theories', in Ellemers, Spears and Doosje, 1999: 6–34.

Turner, John C., with Hogg, Michael A., Oakes, Penelope J., Reicher, Stephen S., and Wetherell, Margaret S. (1987) *Rediscovering the Social Group: A Self-Categorization Theory.* Oxford: Basil Blackwell.

Van Belle, Gilbert (1994) *The Signs Source in the Fourth Gospel: Historical Survey and Critical Evaluation of the Semeia Hypothesis*. BETL 116. Leuven: Leuven University Press.

Van Seters, John (1975) *Abraham in History and Tradition*. New Haven and London: Yale University Press.

Waele, Ferdinand Jozef Maria de (1927) *The Magic Staff or Rod in Graeco-Italian Antiquity*. Gent: Drukkerij Erasmus.

Wagner, J. (1988) *Auferstehung und Leben: Joh 11,1–12,19 als Spiegel johanneischer Redaktions- und Theologiegeschichte*. Biblische Untersuchungen 19. Regensburg: Verlag Friedrich Pustet.

Wahlde, U. C. von (1982) 'The Johannine Jews: A Critical Survey', *NTS* 28: 33–60.

——(2000) '"The Jews" in the Gospel of John: Fifteen Years of Research (1983–1998)', *ETL* 76: 30–55.

Webb, Matilda (2001) *The Churches and Catacombs of Early Christian Rome: A Comprehensive Guide*. Brighton: Sussex Academic Press.

White, L. Michael (1996–97) *The Social Origins of Christian Architecture. Vol. I: Building God's House in the Roman World: Architectural Adaptation among Pagans, Jews, and Christians. Vol. II: Texts and Monuments of the Christian Domus Ecclesiae in its Environment.* Harvard Theological Studies 42. Valley Forge, Pa: Trinity Press International.

Wilckens, Ulrich (1959) 'Die Erweckung des Lazarus', *Theologische Zeitschrift* 15: 22–39.

Wilpert, Giuseppe (1903) *Roma Soterranea: Le Pitture delle Catacombe Romane*. Rome: Desclée, Lefebvre.

Wright, N. T. (2003) *The Resurrection of the Son of God.* London: SPCK.

Wuellner, Wilhelm (1991) 'Putting Life back into the Lazarus Story and its Reading: The Narrative Rhetoric of John 11 as the Narration of Faith', in Culpepper, R. Alan and Segovia, Fernando F., eds. (1991) *The Fourth Gospel from a Literary Perspective*. Semeia 53. Atlanta: Scholars Press, 113–32.

Zangenberg, Juergen (2006 forthcoming) '"Buried According to the Customs of the Jews": John 19,40 in its Material and Literary Context', in Van Belle, Gilbert, ed. (2006 forthcoming), *The Death of Jesus in the Fourth Gospel*. BETL. Leuven: Leuven University Press/Peeters.

Index of Secondary Authors

Index of Subjects